Messengers of Love

Pastor and Mrs. Robert E. Ward
with their children
Kristine and Daniel

Missionaries to
TANGANYIKA TERRITORY
EAST FRICA

August 22, 1954
'BRETHREN, PRAY FOR US.' I THES. 5:25

DEDICATION

This book is dedicated to my uniquely
wonderful family:
Jeanne my wife,
Kris, Dan, Kathy, Joel
and Heidi
who fill my life with the joy
only a family can experience
who have shared
in serving The Lord of The
Harvest overseas.

First Printing 1000
April 1999

ISBN: 0-7392-0291-X

Library of Congress Catalog Card Number: 99-94971

For additional copies write or contact:

Rev. Robert Ward
38650 N. W. Harrison Rd.
Banks, OR   97106
Tele: 503-324-8123
Fax: 503-324-9018
Email: Rward15@Compuserve.com

Printed in the USA by

MORRIS PUBLISHING

3212 East Highway 30 • Kearney, NE 68847 • 1-800-650-7888

TABLE OF CONTENTS

LIST OF ILLUSTRATIONS

ACKNOWLEDGMENTS

It would be great error if I failed to acknowledge the help and suggestions which I have received in writing this book. Dr. J. Birney Dibble gave invaluable advice about its style and format.

Jeanne, my wife, Mrs. Barbara Guenthner, and my daughter Heidi spent many hours reading and correcting the manuscript.

Mr. & Mrs. Dean Buchanan pointed out other clarifications necessary concerning the maps included. They also concurred with me that I should revise the original copy of the completed MSS.

To Mrs. Myrtice Haney who did the excellent calligraphic work on the chapter titles.

My sincere and heartfelt thanks to them all.

*   *   *

All Scripture verses which are not identified in the text are taken from the 1901 American Revision Committee's Standard Edition of the King James Bible. Thomas Nelson & Sons
Other sources are identified as follows:

N.I.V.   -   New International Version Study Bible, Zondervan Corp. 1985

Phillips -   J. B. Phillips - Macmillan, 1958

N.E.B.   -   New English Bible - Cambridge U. Press

K.J.V.   -   King James Bible

Prologue

St. John of the Cross, a medieval mystic and poet, 1542-1591, gave this description of Mission, "Mission is putting love where love is not." In our time when meanings must be spelled out, the words, "the love of Jesus Christ," need to be added to this definition to avoid any misunderstanding. Christians have the great privilege to be called by our Lord to be Messengers of His Love everywhere. This should be the experience of every believer. I believe there are some unusual blessings for those who agree to answer His call to serve as messengers abroad.

Even so, accusations are leveled against overseas missionary/messengers from many sources. They have been called exploiters of the lands to which they have been sent. They have been alleged to be devastators of the cultures where they minister. They also are spoken against because they are thought to bring with them the values held in their countries of origin. Some critics speaking within the church claim that missionaries, now going out to serve, rob the national churches of their opportunities to engage in outreach. Jawaharlal Nehru, a former Prime Minister of India, pointed out that Christian medical missions should be done without any reference to the missionary's Christian faith or convictions. Otherwise these acts are tainted and have the flavor of being done for the purpose of proselyting. To him, this was unacceptable.

The subject and theme of this book is to point out that

the prime activity and objective of the Christian Church is
to carry the Good News of the love and salvation of Christ
Jesus to every place on earth. This must be done in order
that people -- men, women and children -- may learn of it
and accept our Lord's invitation to them to be redeemed.
Christian missionaries have only one motivation -- they are
messengers of God's love made known in Christ. That love is
given to each one of them like a glowing torch by their Lord
and Master, Jesus Christ. They measure the success of their
work by how well Christ has succeeded in communicating His
love to others through their work and witness. At the time
of Tanganyika's independence ceremony in 1961, a torch was
lighted and carried by Government messengers to the highest
point on Mt. Kilimanjaro. This act symbolized the reality of
a momentous happening. Christ, as well, has lighted a real
flame in the heart of each missionary He has called. This
flame and call are completely trustworthy. They sustain an
overseas missionary through difficulties, separations from
loved ones -- even from their own children, and the other
hardships which they will experience. This select band are
the individual witnesses of what Christ has done in their lives
in a drama and relationship that is forever new and on-going.
It is as intensely personal to them as it is to every other
follower of Christ who experiences His hand in their destiny.
This call, which an overseas worker has, is a very personal
call and leading from the Lord by His Spirit. It is a direct
command to become a messenger of Christ's love in another part

of the World. Many times a call places a missionary in a location where the message of Christ's Love and Salvation has never before been heard.

In the record of the history of Missions, each era has its own agenda under which a missionary works. In earlier times, disease and intrigues cut off many messengers' physical lives and witness after a very short period of work. Satan, the adversary, used all the methods he could to halt the spread of the Gospel. But there continued to come forward those who knew, without doubt, that they had been called to become Messengers. Their testimony is the Apostle Paul's who said: "For if I preach the Gospel, I have nothing to glory of, for necessity is laid upon me; for woe is unto me, if I preach not the Gospel." I Cor. 9:16 Therefore, those who are called to be overseas messengers refuse to take "no" for an answer even when their route to messenger service is put on <u>hold</u>. Sometimes the delay for them involves waiting a period of years to go abroad through no fault of their own.

There are still so many places that, in the Lord's will, await the coming of His messengers. So it remains the responsibility of those of us who are faithful Christians, to either "go," or to "send" those able to "go" into Christ's Greatest Commission. He enlists us all to "pray the Lord of the harvest, that He send forth laborers into His harvest" Lk. 10:2.

It is my hope and prayer in sharing some of the many experiences of God's faithfulness to my family and me over the last 38 years, that someone like you who reads this book will be encouraged to either "send" or "go" as one of God's "Messengers of Love".

> "God's man in God's place,
>
> will never lack God's resource."
>
> J.Hudson Taylor

The Call

CHAPTER 1

"You have not chosen me, but
I have chosen you, and ordained
you, that you should go and bring
forth fruit...."Jn. 15:16a N.I.V.

Our Lord of Mission and outreach calls a man, a woman, or a child personally to enter His service. I had just returned from serving in the Second World War in the Pacific area and on occupational duty in Japan. I was impatient to get on with my life. Upon being discharged from the Navy in San Francisco in mid-August, 1946 my plan was to visit my parents who lived in Indianapolis, Indiana. Then I wanted to return to the Pacific Northwest, where I had an Aunt and Uncle living in Portland, Oregon. I found that to get a space to travel by train back to the mid-west from the west coast was next to impossible; passages were booked solidly for days in advance. It took over a week of daily visits to the train depot before I succeeded in getting the space of someone else who had canceled their reservation.

I was in a hurry to visit my parents, and then be off to set out upon the journey of building my future. There were homestead possibilities in Alaska's Matanuska Valley that the Government was making available to Veterans. There was the possibility of a newspaper reporter's job. I had a little taste of this kind of work in Japan while I was in the Navy, and it looked promising. I visited Indianapolis, then Portland in quick succession. My Uncle got me an interim job - - a month's assignment on the La Grande Observer, in La Grande, Oregon as Sports Editor. The man who held this position was away having surgery.   After that I returned to Portland and got a job repairing radios - - a high school hobby I had enjoyed.   Uncle Roy, also upon learning that I was a Lutheran, introduced me to First Immanuel Lutheran Church, located very close to where he had his home in northwest Portland.   I immediately joined in the activities there: the choir, the young adults group, and joined the congregation as a member. As it happened, the young adults group in the church were all planning to journey by train to Los Angeles for a Youth Convention to be held **February 11th - 14th, 1947.**   They told me I should go along with them.   I chuckled to myself.   I was barely out of uniform - - which meant I had practically nothing in the way of a wardrobe.   I was just taking in enough money to meet monthly expenses.   I was very new on my current job. I would hardly dare to ask my employer for time off so soon after being hired.   I just couldn't go.   Even though I wanted so much to say yes, it was simply impossible at that time for me to schedule anything because of my financial state. However, a close friend in the church group said: "Bob, just ask your boss for the time off and see what he says."   I went very apologetically to the manager of the store where I worked and presented my request for some time off, and why I wanted it.

His reply: "Why yes, I don't see any reason why you can't go to the convention."

I was in one way overjoyed, but in another way very concerned about how I would finance the trip. Even so, expense money as well as train fare seemed to appear, so it was "on to L. A.," together with a very enthusiastic group of youth from First Immanuel.

I enjoyed all the convention's sessions by Pastor Wilton Bergstand, Pastor Samuel Miller, and many others. The Conference theme was **"Christ Is Able."**

One session I didn't attend, however, was the one made up of those interested in entering the pastoral ministry. I knew from my educational background at Omaha Tech High, primarily a vocational high school, that the courses I had taken would not allow me a chance to pursue a college education. So I didn't even attempt attendance at the sessions on vocational guidance that the counselor, Dr. H. Conrad Hoyer, held all week. But close to the end of the conference I got a chance to talk with Pastor Hoyer. I said, "I know I could never hope to qualify to become a pastor, but would you give me a little information about what you discussed during this past week's sessions?" He looked at me for a long moment. "Which College would you like to attend?"

"Look here, I'm not qualified to go to college. I just wanted to ask..."

He interrupted me. "Bob, which College do you want to attend?"

I remembered our very revered Pastor in Omaha, Rev. Nels Lundgren. He had been my idol when I was a small boy and had always talked about Augustana College. So I said, "I suppose Augustana."

"Come to my room #__ at 10 A.M. tomorrow morning."

I didn't give very much weight to the outcome of this

meeting, but at 10 A.M. the next morning I went to his room. He opened his door in answer to my timid knock, and spoke quickly in an almost curt way: "You have been accepted and pre-registered at Augustana College in Rock Island, Illinois. Your classes will begin in a month's time, the first week in March, you be there!" Then he dismissed me because he said he had another appointment.

I left his room utterly stunned by his message.

"Where could I, how could I -- no it wasn't possible;....but...I was pre-registered and admitted!"

During the course of the week at the convention I had squeezed out enough money from my tight budget to buy the **new RSV** New Testament of the Bible. I had been thrilled with it, and had used it as a reference for Dr. Miller's wonderful Bible studies on the book of Titus. When I got back to my room, my mind and thoughts were in a state of chaos and confusion. As I reached my room, I had already started to give up the new hope and dream that Pastor Hoyer had given to me. College educations cost money. I was practically destitute right now.

"Come on now Bob--be realistic--this is an unobtainable dream," I told myself. I got into my room, and sat down and opened my new Bible. There it was, right there in front of my eyes:

"Therefore I tell you, do not be anxious about you   life, what you shall eat or what you shall drink, nor about your body, what you shall put on. Is not life more than food, and the body more than clothing?
Look at the birds of the air: they neither sow nor reap, nor gather into barns, and yet your heavenly father feed them. Are you not of more value than they? And which of you by being anxious

can add one cubit to his span of life.

And why are you anxious about clothing? Consider the lilies of the field, how they grow, they neither toil nor spin yet I tell you, even Solomon in all his glory was not arrayed like one of these. But if God so clothes the grass of the field, which today is alive and tomorrow is thrown into the oven, will he not much more clothe you, O men of little faith? Therefore do not be anxious, saying, "What shall we eat?" or "What shall we drink?" or "What shall we wear?' For the Gentiles seek all these things; and your heavenly Father knows that you need them all.

But seek first his kingdom and his righteousness, and all these things shall be yours as well.

Therefore do not be anxious about tomorrow, for tomorrow will be anxious for itself. Let the day's own trouble be sufficient for the day." Mt. 6:25-34

I read it, and then I re-read it again and again. It was God's Word and His promise to me. I could hardly believe the personal way He had made His call to me become so real. Even now, a half century later, reading this portion of Scripture brings a thrill to my spirit, a lump to my throat and tears to my eyes. The New Testament I purchased at the L.A. Youth Convention is long gone now - - worn out. But the promises which the Lord gave me through its passages continue to be redeemed by Him anew with each passing day.

Tanganyika

PART 1

1954 - - 1975

Our First Journey

CHAPTER 2

"Go ye, therefore, and teach all
nations, baptizing them in the
name of the Father, and of the
Son, and of the Holy Spirit..."
                    Matt. 28:19

September was a blustery month on the North Atlantic. In spite of the great size and stability of the Queen Elizabeth and its boasted huge gyros, which caused it to have the last word in stability, many people making the voyage from New York to London became very seasick. I marveled one evening as we waited to board one of the elevators to go down to our cabin's deck level from that of the dining lounge. A very nicely dressed lady standing beside us suddenly and without any warning up-chucked her dinner. We were very glad to escape to the elevator whose doors had just opened invitingly.

Our party was made up of: Rev. Vernon Swenson, his wife Doris and their small sons David and Daniel, my wife Jeanne, our daughter Kristine, (2 years) and our son Daniel (9 Months), and me. Arriving in England, we went to London, and to a house used by our Board as a transit stop, called "The House of Rest." It was conveniently located a short walk from a subway station. The weather was already quite cold in England, and we learned to use our new acquaintance with the 'bob' (shilling), to good advantage. There was a small fireplace in our room which was located on the fourth floor. The gas heater in the fireplace, with the application of a shilling, would provide a fire to warm us up very nicely - - well almost! We next learned that there was a dock strike in progress, and that the ship we were scheduled to take from the U. K. to Africa would not be sailing as planned. The following bit of news we were to hear was that a ship was just returning from the Africa "run," and that to avoid the strike, it would call in at Liverpool - - not to dock - - but just to take on passengers and freight from "lighters," and set off for Africa again. By this time we were extremely anxious to be on our way. So within the week we were on board a ship called the Warwick Castle, (pronounced Warick), and sailing south. We found the Warwick Castle's crew to be disgruntled and tired. They had been looking forward to some leave time and rest in the United Kingdom. This became apparent to us as soon as we embarked. The cabins on board the ship were very untidy, so much so that Jeanne did quite a bit of 'scrubbing up' in our cabin as soon as we came on board. Even so, we were pleased to finally be off on the last leg of what would be a six week's journey to reach Tanganyika, East Africa.

Our cabin was small but adequate for our needs. Toilets and showers were centrally located a few steps from our door. We were soon to learn that the cabin stewards were really below par. One morning the steward who cleaned our cabin had put a lot of very caustic cleaning disinfectant in our waste basket and left it there. Our son Dan, who was just nine months old, was allowed to play on the cabin floor. He over-turned the basket on himself, and the fluid covered his head and shoulders, getting all over him. He was screaming with pain as Jeanne ran with him into the public shower room and held him under a cascading water supply. He didn't suffer more serious injury because of her speed in getting the fluid off his body.

The kids had a lot of fun in their bunk during the voyage. Something resembling a small-mesh volley ball net was tied over the open side of their berth, and they would stand, leaning out against the net, swaying with the roll of the ship. There were other interesting things to become accustomed to on board a British ship. The first was the service of morning tea at 6 A.M. to one's cabin each day. Another difference was that our children were fed separately and earlier than the times when all the adults had their meals. Rev. Vernon Swenson and his wife Doris and family were also shipping out to the field in Africa with us on this same ship. Their infant son, David, became seriously ill at the beginning of this voyage, and for a while we stood a very real danger of losing him. The Lord in His mercy returned him to health in answer to our urgent prayers.

We had been underway for just a short time when Jeanne also came down with a high fever. She wasn't able to eat and just lay in her berth. I took her to the ship's physician, called the "Quack" by the crew. He wasn't able to diagnose her disease, which caused me even more concern. He gave her some medicine, and by the time we reached our first port of call Genoa, Italy, she had regained her health.

The ship was scheduled to spend only a day and a half in Genoa, so we eagerly took this opportunity, our first since beginning our voyage, to walk on dry land again. We went ashore to visit what, to me, will always be remembered as an incredible sight. In Genoa there is a very large grave yard. The townspeople visit it daily. They wash and caress and often kiss the tombs and the mausoleums as if these were their deceased relatives themselves. We were told a story by our guide about a presumed penniless widow. She had worked and slaved all her life and lived in abject poverty. In living her life, she had one goal. It was to have a well appointed grave in the Genoa cemetery paid for when she died. She succeeded in attaining her goal. In doing this she became the envy of the whole community.

The day our ship left, hawkers were on the docks with real bargains. One man had beautiful inexpensive wrist watches for sale. I bought one for a dollar. It was a real bargain. When I got back to our cabin, I attempted to set the time on the watch, and found that it had no 'works' inside. Kristy had been asking for a **real** wrist watch to play with. The **empty** watch from her very clever daddy satisfied her.

Setting off from Genoa, our next stop was Port Said, located at the entrance of the Suez Canal. Our trip through the Canal took place shortly after the take-over of the Canal by Egypt from the British. The Arab shop-keepers at Port Suez were jubilant about this happening. They weren't even interested in bargaining over prices for their goods. One merchant told me, "You're American, you will pay the full price from now on!"

Traveling through the Canal, one got the impression that on-coming ships were literally floating on a sea of sand. What a marvel of engineering this project was. From the Canal we entered the Red Sea. One man called it, "The Red Hot Sea." It can be brutally hot at certain times of the year, we were told. We also learned that the "Red" designation may come from a number of sources: the color and reflection from the surrounding hill country, or the microscopic sea animals which cause the water to have a reddish cast at certain seasons of the year. Or this color can be caused by desert sands blown into the sea causing great reddish streaks.

This is the sea area which spawns tales of sailors frying eggs on the decks of their ships. It is better to stay below deck for most of the daylight portion of one's travel through this Sea. I remember our joy as we finally reached Aden and the promise of cooler sailing from there on into the Indian Ocean. One of the crew-members told me, however, that we had not really experienced a 'hot' voyage this time.

We called in at Port Sudan on our way south. A very sainted Scottish Missionary, Doctor MacDonald and his party, left the ship there. He told us of spending years working with the pygmies in the Belgium Congo. He had many fascinating stories to tell about his life and work in the Congo. It was so very hot when his party left the ship that it seemed as though they were walking into an open furnace. At that time, in 1954, there were few harbor facilities at the Port. Some local shore hands appeared on board to handle freight. They were very tall black folks with heads of hair that got for them the name: Fuzzie-Wuzzies. I marveled that they could stand the heat carrying their incredible loads of hair. However they didn't seem to notice the heat at all as they worked.

When we left the Gulf of Aden and entered the Indian Ocean, we had been on our way for something like four weeks since our departure from Liverpool. We were beginning to look forward with eagerness to our arrival in Dar Es Salaam (Haven of Peace), in Tanganyika. But there were several very interesting ports we would visit before our ship would bring us to Dar. The first was at the Port of Tanga. It is located on the northern most tip of Tanganyika. At last we had reached Tanganyika, although not our final port of arrival.

We were welcomed here by missionaries we knew from the States, Pastor Carl Johannson and his wife Alice, who themselves were recent arrivals and first term missionaries. They were stationed in Tanga, and took us on a quick visit to their home.

We boarded our vessel again and sailed to the spice island of Zanzibar, an island in the Indian ocean just opposite the mainland port of Dar Es Salaam. We spent a very interesting day touring the Island. Zanzibar has had a long history, during

PLATE I

QUEEN ELIZABETH DINING LOUNGE
Jeanne, Kris and I

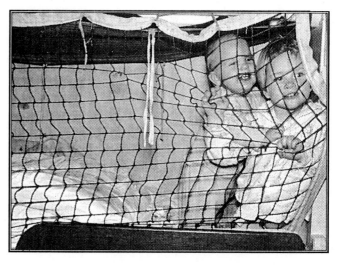

BIRTH SWINGING ABOARD SHIP
KRIS AND DAN

RICKSHA RIDE AT ZANZIBAR
by JEANNE

DAR ES SALAAM HARBOR's
NARROW CHANNEL TO THE SEA

which Zanzibar's ruler, the Sultan, had a tremendous influence on mainland Tanganyika. It was pre-independence Zanzibar at the time of our visit. We took a ride in a rickshaw, a mode of travel which was outlawed with the coming of independence. We also visited a few of the wood shops that created the very famous Zanzibar chests. Zanzibar is the world's supplier of cloves and is known as the "Spice Island".

We then went back on board our ship to spend our last night aboard. The following day we sailed south across the channel to the mainland, and into Dar Es Salaam harbor. The harbor did not have docking facilities, so the ship anchored in the off-shore area, but within the sheltered harbor very close to the beach. We, and all our baggage, were carried to the docks on board small boats and lighters. Standing on the dock to welcome us was our very close friend, Rev. Carl Danielson, who had been my internship supervisor a year and a half before in Minneapolis. He had joined the Mission and now was the Pastor of the Azania Front Lutheran Church in Dar. This historic old Lutheran Church had been built by the Germans many years before, while this was still Deutsch Ost Afrika. We had now reached our destination. With gratitude to our Lord in our hearts for safety over the many miles we had just sailed, we sent off a cable to our Board office in far away Minneapolis: "The lines are fallen unto me in pleasant places; yea, I have a goodly heritage." Ps 16:6

Tanganyika

CHAPTER 3

"Ask of me, and I will
give the the nations for
thine inheritance and the
uttermost parts of the
earth for thy possession."
Ps. 2:8

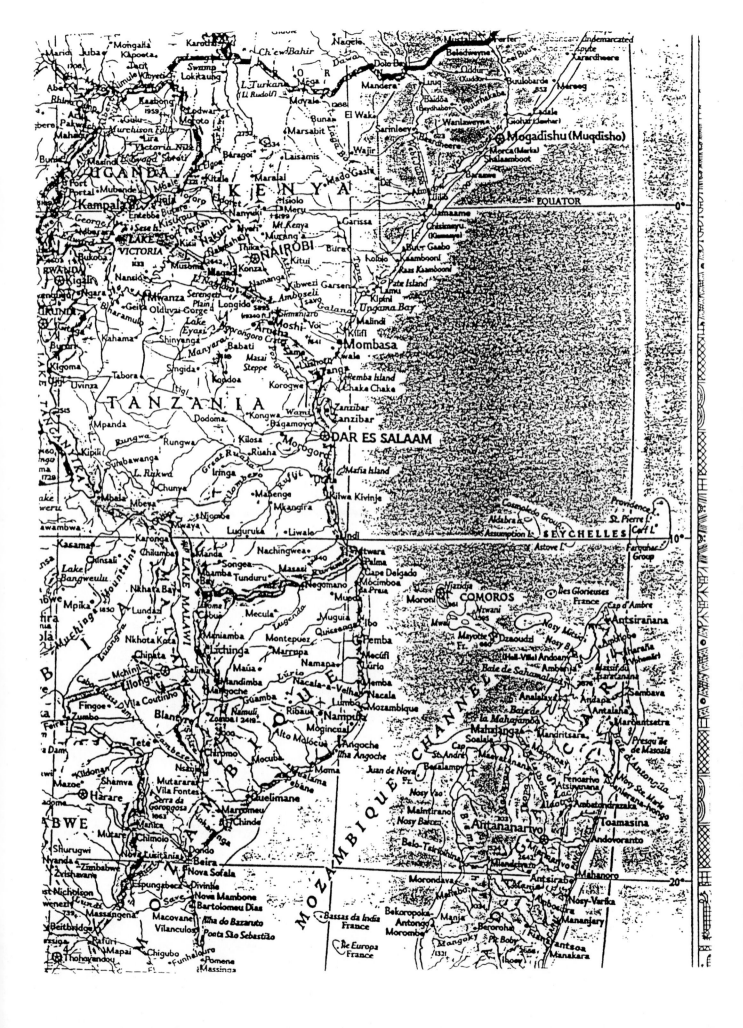

TANGANYIKA - - - - TANZANIA

Located on the coast of East Africa, Tanganyika borders on the Indian Ocean, with a coastline of five hundred miles. At its northern point on the Indian Ocean, the border turns inland in a north-westerly direction and shares a common border with its northern neighbor, Kenya. It then continues west, cutting across Lake Victoria, giving half of the Lake to Tanganyika, half to Kenya. On the western side of the Lake the border touches Uganda, where it turns south passing east of the States of Rwanda and Burundi. Then it bisects lengthwise Lake Tanganyika giving half to the Congo while running south for a distance of 450 miles. It is the longest and deepest fresh-water lake in the world. The border then continues south, and leaving the lake's shore, it divides Tanganyika from Zambia for about 200 miles. Extending farther south, it borders on Lake Malawi for 175 miles, and then it turns east demarcating the boundary between Mozambique and Tanganyika and continues east until it reaches out to the Indian Ocean again.

Tanganyika was granted its full independence from Great Britain in 1961, and took the name of Tanzania later in April of 1964 to show that the important island of Zanzibar joined with Tanganyika at this time to form one sovereign state.

A very interesting facet of Tanganyika-Kenya history took place over a century ago, when Queen Victoria gave a birthday present to her nephew, Kaiser Wilhelm. Instead of Mt. Kilimanjaro remaining as part of Kenya, as the border had originally been drawn, this border was modified to make a jog north - west - and south again, in order to include this mountain as a part of Deutsch Ost Afrika - Tanganyika. Indeed, one of history's interesting quirks.

Tanzania has a land mass of 363 thousand square miles, roughly comparable to the area in the United States covered by the states of Oregon, Washington, Montana and Idaho. Most of the country has a very marginal rainfall, which makes the yearly harvest very unpredictable. A large portion of Tanzania is used for cattle grazing, which can harm the ecology severely if overgrazing takes place, and given the opportunity as cattle numbers increase, it does. This over-stocking is resolved by the onset of a famine which seems to come regularly in the seven to nine year weather cycle. A famine imposes involuntary destocking.

In the northern and southern regions of the country are areas of highlands: such as the Usambara Mountains, the Southern Highlands, the Northwest Bukoba area, and probably the most famous of all, the Mount Kilimanjaro area, which as I have already stated is right on the KenyaTanzania border. Kilimanjaro rises to a height of 19,340 feet, and has a permanent snowcap and glacier which is remarkable for its beauty.

Beginning at the sea port town of Dar Es Salaam, as one travels west and "up-country", the central part of the country rises in something like one thousand foot increments, each to a successively higher plateau, peaking at 7000 feet. Continuing on to the west, the elevation then declines in steps the farther one travels, until the shore of Lake Tanganyika is reached. The elevation on the Lake is two thousand five hundred feet above sea-level. The plateaus referred to are made up of broad sweeping grasslands, called Savannah, and these are interspersed with Acacia Thorn and Miombo tree forests, where in the past, and still in some locations even today, wild game live in abundance.

The African population is made up of one hundred and thirteen distinct tribes. These tribes fit into three categories. The first are the cattle groups: Maasai, Sukuma, Barabaig, and Wataturu all of Nilo-Hamitic origin. The second group is made up of sedentary farmers who are of Bantu origin. The third classification of people are those of the Khoisan (Bushman) group who are hunters and collectors. Usually populations living near large bodies of water depend heavily upon fishing to satisfy their food needs, no matter what their original tribal customs were. Present day Tanzania also includes people of Asian, Indian, Arabic and European origin.

As in any part of the world, climate plays a key role in the life and development of a country. The rains in East Africa are a life and death issue for the people each year. In Tanzania, they follow a two season (bi-modal) pattern.

The _early_ rains of October and November, and the _latter_ rains which fall beginning in the month of December until a mid January break. Rainfall then resumes the middle of February, and falls through April or into May. In October the smell of the first rain drops falling and mixing with the dust ending the long dry season is something everyone should have an opportunity to experience. It is the smell of a new creation, literally a yearly rebirth of life out of the dust. December rains often begin with a heavy lightning and electrical display and violent thunderstorms with rain falling in torrents. Rainfall continues for a month until the middle of January. Then a halt takes place called: "The January break in the rains". Mid February again brings heavy rainfall. It falls for several hours in the afternoon period most days, and you must set your travel and work schedule accordingly. In the month of April the pattern changes. In swahili, this rainfall period is called: "Mwezi wa Tisa," _the ninth month rains._ This season corresponds to the summer season in North America and is the one that brings the crops into harvest. Rain routinely begins falling shortly after darkness sets in each day, and falls very softly throughout most of the night.

In a few areas of the country the rainfall is so limited that farmers need to anticipate its coming before it actually arrives. They cultivate their shambas (gardens) even to the point of putting seed into the dry ground, then when the rain comes, they don't lose a day of its utilization. In this harsh and risky environment, crops grown vary in kind from: maize, millet, beans, peanuts (called groundnuts from British times in Tanzania), to the important famine standby: cassava, from which we get tapioca. This plant has a tuber like that of a sweet potato. It is able to mature with practically no rainfall, and survive extended famine conditions also. The skin of this tuber is removed, (it has a poison located immediately under its skin which must be peeled away). The vegetable is then either boiled whole, or it may be ground raw into meal and cooked in the same way that ground corn flour is prepared. Cassava has very little food value. Even so, it is the staple food of many places in Africa.

Some areas of Tanzania are habitations of <u>risk</u> because of a concentration of the Tsetse Fly. These flies spread Sleeping Sickness (Trypanosomiasis). Their bites are fatal for domestic animals. However they are not all infected with the trypanosomes that cause human illness. It is alleged that infection comes from every seventh bite, but I have been bitten countless times without becoming infected. There was a great increase of this illness among the nationals living in the Yaida Swamp area in the '70s. The Government insisted that it build one of its Ujamaa Villages at a place called Munguli where there was a high concentration of Tsetse.

A large scale attempt during the time of British Colonial rule to control and eradicate the fly achieved only a measure of success. Large areas of forests and shrubs were cut. They had provided the shade required by the flies in which to breed. It was then found that the fly successfully mutated in its requirement of habitat from forest to grass cover. In this development the fly has been victorious in its bid for survival.

Testse flies love to follow vehicles in motion and they hitch a free ride for many, many miles. During earlier attempts at controlling their movement, drive-through sheds were put up on major roads exiting fly areas. One drove into these sheds, all the doors were closed, and an attendant with a net went over your vehicle to capture any tiny hitch-hikers that might be there.

Malaria is also endemic throughout every region of the country. It seems to have its seasons which follow the onset of the rains, the exceptions being on the coast and in the Lake regions where it is continually a health hazard.

In the Highland areas the amount of rainfall is much greater than in other parts of the country and cash crops such as coffee, tea, bananas, tobacco, sugar cane, and cardamom can be grown. Sisal planting and production, which produces fiber to make rope, is carried on in some very low rainfall areas near to or at the coast. At one period in the recent past, Tanzania led the world in sisal production. Then synthetic rope came into vogue, until the petrol crisis made its production unprofitable. Presently, a redeveloped sisal industry is on its way to becoming one of Tanzania's biggest money makers in foreign exchange. There is also a mining industry producing gold, diamonds, rubies, and Tanzanite stones.

Since independence, there has been a concerted effort by the Government to insist upon the use of Swahili as the

common language. This was formerly the language of trade and
not understood by most upcountry women and children, and many
men as well. There is little desire by the authorities to
continue to use tribal vernacular languages. This reaction
has arisen out of an attempt to overcome tribalism which has
a very divisive affect on the building of a homogeneous society.
The authorities hope that traditions will one day melt into
a workable pattern allowing national intermarriage, and an
individual's loyalty to develop toward the Government of the
whole   country,   instead   of   toward   his   local   group.

Swahili is a language that is a mixture of Arabic and Bantu
words and is spoken in its purest form in Tanzania and Zanzibar.
This is a matter of national pride.

The **Pre**-**History** of Tanganyika is largely a matter of
speculation. Some anthropologists wonder what might have been
the result in that part of the world if the Imperialistic
nations had not come on the scene in the 19th century. For
example, when the Germans arrived in Tanganyika in 1844, it
had long been exploited by Arab and Portuguese slave and ivory
traders.

One thing was certain at that time. It was that the Maasai
tribe was in full control of all of East Africa wherever they
chose to live and rule, the Arabs and the Portuguese not
withstanding. As the Maasai migrated down from the north they
were their own worst enemy because of their very destructive
internecine warfare. They actually caused the demise of one
whole clan in their group by their in-fighting. They parted

company with the Samburu, a part of this migrating group, leaving the Samburu, by their own choice, in the area that is now northern Kenya. The Samburu had had enough of the Maasais' viciousness and elected to separate from them.

Another human migration was on the move out of southern Africa at this same time - -the Zulu who were cattle herders like the Maasai. Shaka, the Zulu Chief, was their phenomenal leader who crafted new methods and techniques of combat for them. He also modified their traditional weapons and they then became almost invincible against their spear carrying enemies. Because of the occupation of the area between these tribes by the colonial powers in the last half of the 1800's, what might have happened had the Maasai and the Zulu warriors confronted each other in battle will forever be a subject of speculation.

The Tanganyika mainland was then under the nominal control of the Sultan of Zanzibar. Any expedition that entered the mainland was always made up and cleared in Zanzibar. Then it proceeded across the bay to the mainland where travel was by foot safari using many porters, sometimes with ox carts.

Dr. Carl Peters entered the East African scene in 1844. He entered the mainland without passing through Zanzibar. He was the head of a private group called "The Society for German Colonization." At this time, Peters had as his purpose secretly to contact mainland Chiefs and badger them into becoming his vassals. He succeeded in producing documents, resulting from three months of inland safari, in which the

Chiefs acknowledged him and his Company as their protector. They asked for and acknowledged the Society as being their guardian. This meant that Peters acquired the "rights" to something like sixty thousand square miles of East African mainland.

In the negotiations that followed in Germany, Chancellor Bismarck succeeded in getting Kaiser Wilhelm to grant a charter to Peter's Society, and it was then called: <u>The German East Africa Company</u>. In the book, "Battle For The Bundu," written by Charles Miller in 1974, Miller makes these comments about Tanganyika under German rule. "Between 1884 and the First World War, German rule in East Africa passed through three separate and distinct stages.

The first stage was the Company's stewardship which lasted until 1891. In that year due to a number of past significant problems and an all-out rebellion led by the coastal Arabs, the German East Africa Company appealed to Germany for relief from its mandate. At that time, Chancellor Bismarck selected Captain Herman von Wissman, a well qualified German soldier-explorer, to go to East Africa (Deutsch Ost Afrika). Wissman became Tanganyika's first governor. Thus began the second stage of Tanganyika's relationship with Germany. This was characterized as the subjugation-development of the whole country and its very diverse population.

Communications across this vast area was a great problem, but I have been told that the Germans solved this by setting a mirror-semaphore-flashing light system that could relay a message across the whole country in a day. In that day and age, this was incredible.

The Germans also built a number of forts on hilltop vantage points. These were the administrative centers from which to issue orders and the bases to enforce them and to retaliate against any who would dare question the Germans' total authority.

We lived nine miles from Fort Mkalama, the site of one of these forts in north-central Tanganyika. The local people in that area still have stories to tell, no doubt related to them by their elders, of how the huge baobab tree located in the Fort's compound often had many bodies hanging from its boughs - - to show the countryside what happened to those who gave any sign of not recognizing their total subjugation to German Imperial authority. Fort Mkalama was replete with its own Ghost, the spirit of one of the German soldiers who committed suicide there. One of the requirements for the indoctrination of new British administrators was to spend a night sleeping at the Fort. The loose iron roofing scraping in the wind was a very realistic imitation of the moans and shrieks of the suicide victim. Under German administration, a network of roads was set up, some of which survive to this day. The construction of some of these roads utilized borders of Manyara, a green tubular plant with branches growing to twenty or thirty feet in height. This border plant provides ideal protection against wind and rain erosion. The plant is unique in its ability to flourish in completely dry and desolate places. The Germans planted miles of this border. They also brought out master builders from Germany who were capable of building stone structures from local rock without the use mortar. Some examples of this work still survive the ravages of wind and weather.

In 1905, natives in the southern half of the territory commenced a full scale revolt no doubt largely in response to a very heavy-handed German Imperial rule. This revolt gained a large native following. The people believed in a magical protection offered them by their medicine men using 'blessed water.' Later, interestingly enough, in the Belgium Congo the 'Simba' warriors in 1965 were guaranteed invincibility through the use of 'blessed water' when they revolted against Belgium rule. Drinking this water would prevent a warrior from being killed by bullets fired at him, because the bullets would be magically turned into water. The rebellion in Tanganyika was known as the "Maji - Maji" rebellion. Maji is the swahili word for water. Miller relates that the German reprisal against this rebellion was immediate and thorough. By 1907 the leaders of the rebellion had all been hanged, and the southern half of Tanganyika, the size of Germany itself, had undergone a scorched-earth campaign which together with famine and pestilence would make this area a wasteland for more than twenty years.

The year 1907 brought the third stage of development in German-Tanganyika history. It was due to many factors: the resolute character of the Germans, the change of Colonial policy to a more benign rule, and to the development and facility of the Schutztruppe (the home defense army), which utilized nationals of Tanganyika as the "keepers of the peace" in the territory. Under excellent German Army officer supervision and command, and in typical army fashion, local people were indoctrinated into an **elan** of organization and discipline that to this day they carry in their memory with pride and recognition. The story of the organization and facility of the Schutztruppe is a well documented story told by Miller. It culminates with the campaign of the First World War, and Tanganyika's role in it. It was led by an officer of the highest caliber: Colonel Paul Emil von Lettow Vorbeck. At the beginning of World War I, British and French troops fought some token engagements with the Germans in Tanganyika. In 1916, British and Belgian troops began a larger thrust into Deutsch Ost Afrika, but they realized no military victory over the colony. It must be acknowledged that Colonel von Lettow Vorbeck's leadership was responsible for their lack of effectiveness.

At the conclusion of World War I, the League of Nations parceled out Tanganyika. The largest part of it was given to Great Britain. Rwanda and Burundi were given over to Belgium control. A section known as the Kionga triangle in the far south of Tanganyika was given to what then was Portuguese East Africa and is now Mozambique. Following the creation of the United Nations, the remainder of Tanganyika became a U. N. Trust Territory administered by the British, who on December

9, 1961, handed over the Government and its administration to Mr. Julius Nyerere, Tanganyika's first Prime Minister. On December 9th, 1962, Tanganyika became a Republic, and Mr. Nyerere became its first elected President.

First Impressions

CHAPTER 4

"The lines are fallen unto me
in pleasant places; yea I
have a goodly heritage."
                    Ps. 16:6

The picture which presented itself to our eyes as we stepped off the dock at Dar Es Salaam was one of great beauty. No doubt this was enhanced by the knowledge that we had finally arrived at our destination. Lining the shore were many causarina trees that had luxuriant green and red leaves. The omnipresent crows squawked and scolded interminably. The warm ocean smell had none of the aroma of decay that had greeted us in ports like Port Said and Aden.

Dar in 1954 gave the appearance of a very beautiful, well kept city. Its avenues were tree-lined with eucalyptus and jacaranda and palms. Frangipani shrubs, with their beautiful white-yellow flowers, graced many locations in the city. The jacaranda tree, whose blooms always herald the advent of the coming rainy season with its delicate fern like leaves and lavender blossoms, seemed to be everywhere in the city. As the season advances, its blossoms fall and cover the ground making a beautiful carpet under each tree. There is a saying in East Africa that "the new rain will always beat off the last of this year's blossoms from the jacaranda tree."

The buildings, in 1954 mostly frame government structures, were well maintained and painted white or green. Throughout the country many of the unique former German Bomas (administrative centers), built of sun dried mud brick, remained in use.

Benches lined the harbor, and one could spend hours sitting on them. It was a grandstand seat to observe the arrival of a ship or the departure of another, but this was not an everyday occurrence. Most of the traffic in the city was by foot or by cyclists who passed you frequently on the black-topped streets.   A small ferry in the harbor periodically crossed the channel entrance which accesses the ocean. The ferry usually carried people, but had the capacity to transport several cars on a trip as well.

The rusting wreck of a German ship was on the opposite side of this narrow channel, which made it necessary for ships to come very close to the shore on the city side of the channel as they came in or departed from the inner harbor.   Standing on the shore it seemed possible to reach out and touch a passing vessel.   The appearance was deceiving because the channel was far wider than it appeared to be.   One of our first thrills was to swim in the channel and see a ship looming over us as it passed. When we first arrived, we were allowed to stay in one of the large houses which had been built on the Azania Front Lutheran Church compound. This was located just a stone's throw away from the waterfront.

At high tide, the Arab dhows were anchored close in to the beach. At low tide they were left "high and dry" on the sand of the beach. This made it possible for the crew to scrape barnacles off the dhow's hulls and to apply waterproof caulking to seams that needed it.   Also, it was a time to carry out other maintenance jobs.

The Danielsons hosted us for the next several days. This time was spent getting train tickets for one of its bi-weekly trips up-country. We also shopped for a few things in Asian shops. We didn't purchase many things. The bulk of our freight was to come by another ship that would soon arrive. Our shipment would be stored in a bonded warehouse until we could have it cleared by our Clearing and Forwarding agents.

At this time in Kenya -- the next country to the north -- the Mau Mau emergency was in effect. The only hint to me that it even existed came when I brought my guns and ammo into customs. I had brought these items with us on the Warwick Castle. The customs official, a young British police officer, gave me an understanding nod and said that I had been wise to come out prepared. His statement shocked me when I understood the meaning of his words. I replied that I had not come to Africa to use my weapons on anything but game. I remember his look of condescension.

We enjoyed the fellowship with the Danielsons very much. Dorothy prepared excellent meals using fish that were brought to her door almost every day by local fishermen. She also introduced us to a dessert-salad standby which was served almost everywhere we went and was always enjoyed very much. It was made up of three fruits: cut up bananas, golden pineapple bits, and diced papaya, the latter a yellowish or sometimes crimson colored fruit which has a unique taste that blends in very well with the other two fruits.

The day soon came for our departure. The train was scheduled to leave in the afternoon. We occupied our second class coach and were seen off by the Danielsons.

We now faced a trip of about five hundred miles to reach the station of Itigi. It couldn't be called a town by our standards. It had a railroad hostel, some maintenance buildings, and an Arab shop or two. From this station a railroad bus would take us the remaining distance of about ninety miles to Singida, the town located in the center of our Iramba-Turu Mission area.

The maximum speed of operation on the Tanganyika railroad was just over 20 miles an hour(32 Km.), so your food wasn't in danger of being thrown off the table in the dining car. The trip up to Itigi took about 24 hours to complete -- with many extended stops. The rail line itself was a single track system, making it necessary for our train to pull off onto a siding often in order that other trains going the opposite direction could pass us and continue on their way. This procedure, together with stopping at stations, took a lot of time. On this trip the last mail car on the train was discovered to have a "hot-box"(a wheel bearing that was heating up). I was astounded when the train crew simply uncoupled the car and left it standing by itself on the main track!

You were warned about 'Dar Tummy' before you embarked on the train to begin your safari up-country. This condition probably was caused from the water you were served to drink on the train. No one really knew more than that: "it was sure to come." I was on a real "high of excitement," on this first journey inland. The train traveled slowly enough so that the local people we passed had time to return my waved greeting

-- and I waved to every one of them. There were also herds of game to be seen along the way. "Look at that giraffe!"

As the hours passed by my excitement grew. With each one of the train's many stops, I was out of our coach and up talking with the Welshman, who was the engineer, (called the "Driver" in British parlance). I made the suggestion, after several visits forward, that he allow me to stay in the engine's cab with him for the next part of the trip. He willingly showed me the operation of the brakes, the throttle, and the all powerful whistle rope. Its shriek cleared the tracks ahead of people, but much more often of wandering game animals.

The final pinnacle of joy for me came when he actually gave me operating control of the engine and train. Under his guidance I learned how to apply steam to the engine's pistons -- slowly -- so that I wouldn't cause a shattering "jerk" to the train of coaches being pulled. I also learned how to apply air to the brakes to avoid a shock that might have provoked a surly visit by the conductor-train master.

Time was the thief that ended my wonderful experience. Dusk began to set in, and I had Jeanne and our two kids wondering: "what ever happened to their husband-dad? Had the lions gotten him?"

We all slept fitfully through the night, the train awakening us with each stop it made. Mosquitoes were also a problem in our compartment. We were up at daylight and enjoyed a full breakfast in the dining car. Now we began to weary of the safari and the train's starts and stops, so that when we finally reached Itigi, we were more than ready to let the train proceed on without us.

We found a large rather antique bus waiting at the station, and very soon after our arrival, we set off again, this time by road, for Singida.

Along the gravel road we now saw a "first" for us, a Tanganyika road grader. At first sighting, it simply appeared to be a great column of dust on the road traveling ahead of our bus, making it impossible to see anything coming down the road from the opposite direction. As we approached and passed it holding our breath and penetrated the dust blindly, we saw that it was made up of a very large acacia thorn tree being pulled along the roadbed on a chain connected to a tractor. The branches of the tree smoothed and graded the sandy roadbed. But the tree did leave an occasional thorn to wait for an unfortunate vehicle tire to give it a final greeting. As we travailed along, we also noticed that the licenses on just about all of the few cars we met had similar plates: "G T", followed by some numerals. We learned that "G T" meant: Government of Tanganyika owned vehicles.

At the outset of the safari on the bus, several nationals riding the bus introduced us to "Culture, Tanganyika style". They carried on, to us, a monotonous communication quite slowly:
First Speaker: inflection of his voice up. "Ehh---"
Second Speaker: inflection of his voice going down. "Ehh---."

"Ehh---."   (up)

"Ehh---."   (down) - Back and forth it went.

This exchange continued on and on as the safari miles and hours passed. Once in a while the word, which can be translated: "Very Much", was spoken like a punctuation made to the conversation. "Sana."

This was followed by a short sentence, and the proceedings started all over again. It was the East African way of "keeping a friend company." I noted, with satisfaction, that I didn't feel strange or out of place in this new East African setting. I was not in some weird unusual place, but "at home" and very comfortable in being where I felt the Lord had placed my family and me.

The dirt road from Itigi to Singida was bordered on each side by heavy forests of acacia thorn trees. Once in a while we passed a track leading off from the main road without a sign to guide the unknowing traveler as to its destination. When we finally approached Singida, the forest bordering the road gave way to grassy planes. On them we saw small herds of cattle, sheep and goats being tended by little children.

We had expected someone to meet us when we arrived in Singida, to take us on to our language study location, Mgori. But the news hadn't gotten through so we were puzzled about what our next move should be. It was getting rather late into mid-afternoon. We were told that the "only" hotel in Singida was not a very satisfactory place to spend the night. Then we learned about Mossum's Garage in the city where we had just arrived. All the mission's vehicles were repaired here. Mossum Dewji, who's most famous phrase we later learned was:

"Boy, leta nyundo" -- "Worker, bring me the hammer."

Mossum received us cordially. He told us there was a brand new jeep in the garage awaiting collection by one of our missionaries. I got his O K, and commandeered the pick-up, loaded my family into it, and got the directions to reach Mgori, arriving in good time before darkness (which comes on at 6:45 P.M. the year round) set in. The distance to Mgori was 14 miles. The road out of the city went east up to a plateau. Then leaving that road, a minor road led down into the valley in which the station was located. On the Mgori side of the hill, the countryside was heavily forested with thorn trees. Rev. Les Peterson, our host, told me when we arrived that it was well we hadn't tried to travel after dark. Up the hill, not far from his station a rhino was lying in wait for travelers of any description, and it had charged and even injured some traveling by foot.

We were introduced to kerosene "storm" lanterns, water in very short supply which had to be boiled and filtered, scorpions who love to travel after dark, but most encouraging of all, to a very warm welcome by the Peterson family: Rev. Les, his wife Ruth, and their four daughters, Rachael, Luella, Marilyn and Bobbie Lou.

Mgori was a very new station located in the Turu tribal area of our Iramba-Turu field. It had two houses on its site, a primary school, and housing for the teachers. Because it was still so new, there had not been time to build a church. The congregation worshiped outside under the trees at a location demarcated by tree branches on the ground. Pews were movable wood seats, 12 feet in length.

The worship services were carried on under the watchful eyes of several church elders. People came from the surrounding community and the emphasis was on attendance by the whole family. Dogs belonging to a number of the households also came to church. They didn't get along well together at all. At least once during the service growls and snarls escalated into pitch battles which were carried on anywhere "in church".

I vividly recall our first attendance at worship. One of our elders held a long stick. His face was void of emotion as he calmly stepped into the middle of a savage battle between several dogs. He beat them without stopping until they ran off. They decided it would be far less painful for them to carry on their fight elsewhere. The whole affair didn't seem to disturb the service all that much.

We were just getting settled into a routine of language study, when Les brought me word from Singida that two matters had come up. The first was the report that our freight had arrived. It was waiting to be cleared at Leslie & Anderson's bonded warehouse in Dar. This company was our clearing and forwarding agent. Often it was given the responsibility to do the job of clearing alone. Added to this information was the additional bit of news that a new car had also arrived for use at one of our other stations. "Would I be willing to go to Dar and drive it back to the field?" Since this tied in very well with the desire I had to be on hand when our things passed through customs, I agreed at once. I left Jeanne,

Kris and Dan in the good care of Les & Ruth, and returned to

Dar by the next available train.

My First Assignment

CHAPTER 5

"And such trust have we through
Christ toward God. Not that we
are sufficient of ourselves to
claim anything as coming from us;
our sufficiency is from God.."
                    2 Cor. 3:4-5

When I returned to the capital city, Rev. Carl and his wife Dorothy made it possible again for me to stay in church housing at Azania Front Lutheran Church. Leslie & Anderson, our clearing agent, was located just a few blocks away, so I was able to walk to their "go-down" (warehouse) and office the day after my arrival. I sat down with a very competent Asian man whose name was Mr. Reed. He guided me through the preparation of documents listing all the things that we were importing to meet the needs of our life on the field, making certain that I indicated all the articles which had already been in use. This allowed these items to be imported duty free. Reed's humor knew no bounds when he described one missionary who had imported a barrel of "used" toilet tissue.

The customs officials were very courteous, and gave me no argument on the rather large number of sheets, towels, shoes, etc., we were importing. Hopefully we had enough of everything to last the family four years, for our first term of service.

I was able to carry very little back with me on my return "up-country", because of the small size of the vehicle I was driving. But I took what I could, and managed to pack in quite a load on the half ton pick-up I was going to use to make my first safari by road in Africa!

It seemed that I had just arrived in Dar when all my tasks were completed. Even so I had already been gone from Mgori and the family almost two weeks. So as I now set off from Dar by road, I urgently wanted to be reunited with my family again. This made me forget the caution I should have exercised on making this trip. I thought I could drive "straight through" the five hundred plus miles I would need to cover to reach Singida and then Mgori.

I did well indeed the first half of the trip. I reached Dodoma, covering a major part of the distance of my safari by late afternoon. Someone had suggested that I should sleep at Dodoma and safari on the following day. I would have none of that -- I wanted to "get home" to Jeanne and the kids. So after a snack at Dodoma, I proceeded up the road, entering an area called the Bahi Swamp.

As I drove into the oncoming darkness of night, I could see flashes of lightning ahead in the distance. A light rain began to fall. This was the beginning of the October-November early rainy season. I was not forewarned that there was a new bridge being put in on the road at the Bahi village location.

When I came around a curve on the road, I saw a new embankment of earth making up the roadbed. It was sharply graded at a sloping angle to accommodate vehicles rounding the curve with speed. The new rain that was falling on the fresh earthen embankment without a sand surface made it slippery as ice. I started sliding toward the low side of the road. I wasn't going very fast or I would have been in real trouble. As it was, I stopped before I completely left the track of the road, and tried to back up out of my position. I wasn't able to get any traction at all. It was completely dark now, a blackness that you can only experience in a place when black clouds totally cover the sky at night. I had a flashlight (called a torch in East Africa), so I got out of the truck and crawled underneath it to assess the situation. I found that the back differential housing was mired down in the mud and anchored the truck from making any movement, forward or backward. I lay on my stomach and worked very hard digging a channel so that the vehicle could reverse. This operation took a long time because I didn't have a shovel with which to dig. All this happened while the rain continued to fall with increasing intensity.

Finally, cold, wet and covered with mud, I got back into the cab of the truck and tried to back out. It was all to no avail. The angle of the roadbed, the mud, and my tires which were now coated with mud and therefore were smooth, all these things added up to one result. I was stuck for the night, or until help might appear. One further introduction to Africa was given me that I hadn't anticipated. The soil in the Bahi swamp is very heavily alkaline, so I spent a very miserable night; wet, cold, and itching all over my body from a coating of the alkaline mud which I had no way of washing off. The mosquitoes were there in the truck, too, and took their toll.

Several times during the night, I heard sinister sounds being made near the truck. I turned on the truck's lights hoping to catch a glimpse of what was making the noise. The

windshield was almost opaque from the rain and mud so I could
see nothing, but switching on the headlights seemed to frighten
off whatever was outside.

With the coming of day when it turned half light at dawn,
I was out of the truck and on the road walking in search of
help. As I rounded the curve ahead on the road, I saw a
wonderful sight - off to the right side of the road was a small
mission church compound. It had a church, a parish house and
other buildings. All were neatly fenced in. I went to the
gate. As I entered it, I wondered what I must look like -
covered with mud from head to toe.

I went toward the church because I could hear someone
chanting and singing a liturgy. Then as I approached the door
of the church, I thought better of going in. I was afraid that
I might disturb the service which was obviously in progress.
I walked by on one side of the church, and as I did, the voice
chanting the liturgy turned in my direction. The chanting
followed me as I walked past the church toward the parish house.

Reaching the parish house, I climbed the steps of the
veranda and knocked on the front door. No answer -- no
response.

I knocked again, this time much harder. Again no response,
but I heard the hardly audible sound of a woman's voice whisper:
"Don't breathe a word."

I didn't hesitate a moment when I heard this. I was just
too miserable, dirty, wet, cold, tired and hungry. I turned
and walked out of the compound, closing the gate behind me

and left it as I found it. Returning to the road, I walked
on in the direction away from the truck. It was then that
I saw a column of smoke some distance ahead on the left.
It was coming from the temporary site of a "PWD" (Public Works
Dept) road camp. I walked into the camp and a young Italian
man who spoke English with difficulty, warmly welcomed me into
his small mobile house on wheels. He gave me some water to
wash the mud from my face and hands, and out of my hair where
it was caked in chunks. He also offered me refreshment: "Have
a beer".

This seemed to be all the food he had on hand. I didn't
take him up on that offer, but I did on the next one he made.
He had a very large Forsberg tractor and in just a very few
minute's time I was riding behind him as he piloted it down
the road to where my truck was stuck.

With the tractor's power and traction, we had no trouble
at all in getting my vehicle out of the mud. My new found
friend warned me in his broken English that the road ahead
to Manyoni was now impassable because of the rains. Now I had
no choice but to return to Dodoma. I thanked him, truly with
all my heart, for the help and kindness he had shown me. Then
with careful driving and with the help of daylight I got back
to Dodoma and booked in at the Railroad Hotel. I enjoyed a
hot bath, and then a good breakfast although by this time it
was almost midday. I was informed then, that the only way
to get to Singida now was to put my truck on a railroad flat
car and bypass the impassable stretches of road. That could

be done by paying a small fee to EAH&R (East African Harbours and Railways). When tomorrow's train arrived my truck and I would be booked to travel west with it. Fee paid, booking made!

As the afternoon passed I had a lot of time to express my thanks to a gracious God who had been with me throughout the long night I had just endured. In His goodness He had brought me safely back to Dodoma. My clothes had been stored in the back of the pick-up which had no cover, so everything clean I had was now very damp and wet. After sunset the hotel whose lobby was open to the night air became cold. Then in my damp clothes I began to shiver. A young lady, sitting in the lobby writing letters noticed my predicament and came over and asked if I was suffering from an attack of malaria.

I replied: "No, I have damp clothes from being stuck in the rain"

She immediately went to her room and came back with a large woolen sweater which I gratefully accepted and put on.

I learned from the conversation that followed that the lady's name was Greta Ekstrand. She was a Lutheran missionary nurse from Canada. As it turned out, she was on a short leave from Isanzu, the very station to which Jeanne and I were assigned to serve following our language study. I thought of trying to get word to Jeanne at Mgori about my enforced delay. This was impossible because even to communicate with Singida would not have gotten the message to Mgori. They also informed me that with the coming of the rains, telephone communication often went out of operation for several days at a time or until the lines dried out.

Early the following morning I had a very adequate breakfast and then drove to the train station. I waited several hours before I succeeded in getting my truck on a flat car. However, very soon after that, the Goods Train coming up from Dar arrived at the station. My flat car was attached to the rear of the train. I now was on my way sitting in the cab of my truck on the flat car. My destination, Manyoni, was a number of stations away to the west, a distance of about 75 miles.

Getting to Manyoni was no problem, but getting help to place the flat car next to an off-loading dock was more difficult. The Goods Train had continued on its way at once after we arrived at Manyoni and my car was uncoupled from it. Now there was no motive power to push the flat car parallel to the dock so that I could drive off. Finally, after what seemed like hours of waiting, several strong station workers, using a sort of pry-bar, inched the flat car along the rails to the dock where I could off-load the truck. I didn't stop even for a farewell greeting to the railroad workers as I left. Down the ramp, and off I sped on my way. I later regretted not stopping to thank the railroad workers who had helped me reach the dock.

I now encountered a good all weather road, and although it had some large standing pools of water to drive through, there was no danger of becoming stuck. I reached Singida by late afternoon. I left the information of my arrival with Mossum at his Singida garage, where I promised also to return the following day with the new truck.

It was a happy moment when I reached Mgori. I embraced Jeanne and kissed her again and again. Then the kids got their share of my love and happiness. Jeanne listened well into the night as I recounted all that had happened since we'd last been together. We began the habit then which has carried on to this day of saying "Praise the Lord for a safe and successful safari." In looking over the mud covered truck and assessing the state it was in, I wondered at how the new owner would view my efforts to drive it to Singida. With a good cleanup at Mossom's garage the next day it must have passed the test.

Language Study

CHAPTER 6

"For we cannot but speak the things
which we have seen and heard."
Acts 4:20   K.J.V.

Jeanne and I had begun studying Swahili long before we left home in the U. S. We had the book, **Swahili Exercises**, written by Edward Steer. We also had a hymnal: **Nyimbo Za Kikristo**, which had been printed on the field in Africa. From the hymnal, which had the Swahili words set to hymns familiar to us, we were able to sing these hymns and translate the words with a dictionary.

Using the vocabulary listed in the **Exercises**, we had made up flash cards with nouns and verbs on them. We drilled each other with these cards and had mastered a lot of vocabulary before we reached Tanganyika. But one has a lot to learn before you can put nouns and verbs into meaningful sentences.

The Petersons had anticipated a good three months language study for us when they'd invited us to come to Mgori. The head teacher of the primary school would be our instructor and the key man in our instruction. Unfortunately, there was an acute shortage of teachers at Mgori. The head teacher had the responsibility of teaching many extra hours of class to make up for this shortfall. After eight class sessions he told us he was sorry, but it was impossible for him to continue teaching us. He didn't have the time because of his primary school responsibilities. So we were then compelled to work with only a book as our teacher.

Pastor Les volunteered an elder from the Mgori church to help us in our study. The Elder came daily to the house varanda where we were staying. He was accompanied by his huge Swahili Bible. I don't believe he knew one word of English, and I was very unsure of anything I said in Swahili. We began each session with a big smile that we gave each other. Then we opened our Bibles, his in Swahili, mine in English. From this mode of a comparison of verses, he slowly worked to enable me to speak this new language. It didn't work. Jeanne gave up after a session or two. It is very frustrating to have what seems to be a black bag over one's head. You can hear the sounds of language being spoken, but they don't seem to relate to anything, even though the speaker is trying so hard to communicate.

As time went on, after several hours of trying each morning with the old man, I would call a halt. Then dismissing my teacher, I took my gun and a guide or two into the surrounding countryside. Les and Ruth and my guides as well, appreciated a regular supply of meat which came from the impala we hunted. It wasn't long before I developed a very fluent vocabulary related to hunting and hiking. I even began to have some fluency in conversational Swahili. We were at Mgori several weeks when the announcement was made that a general meeting of the pastors of the L.C.C.T. (Lutheran Church of Central Tanganyika) was to be held. These meetings lasted a day or two at Mission stations able to host them. It was the opportunity for executive action and guidance to take place among the pastors of the church.

The meetings usually took place in the churches located on the compound of the host's station. All 'first termers' were required to sit in the front row at these meetings. They were also required to have with them a pencil and paper and a Swahili dictionary. New missionaries paid close attention to the flow of words coming from the older delegates. Every new and unfamiliar word which the student heard was recorded and then looked up in the dictionary. I derived a lot of benefit from these sessions. My vocabulary increased and my conversational fluency also improved.

Unfortunately Jeanne suffered a great handicap in her language learning by not being able to attend these sessions. It took a very long time for her to make up for this loss.

Jeanne was kept more than busy at Mgori. Ruth was ill with malaria during a portion of our stay there, so Jeanne helped with meal preparation and doing the laundry. These activities together with taking care of our children gave her very full days.

We soon understood the difficulties faced by a station that didn't have a well for supplying water. Stations without wells had to depend on annual rainfall. This rain was collected on roofs of station houses and then channeled to cement cisterns for careful use for the balance of the year. Les had just gotten a bore hole dug for the water supply at Mgori. He was making the installation of the pipes, pump and its rods himself. This can be a very hazardous work if one doesn't have all the necessary installation equipment. Les suffered the loss of a finger before he completed the work on his well.

The rains were late in arriving at Mgori in 1954 and the cistern went dry. All the water we used therefore had to be trucked from the local area water hole shared by all, including the local livestock. No matter how early we arrived to fill our barrels (44 gallon drums), we found the cows had gotten there first. They had churned up the water and the mud in the hole so that the water was about 25% a solid.

Les had a lot of territory to cover to administer his parish. He often invited me to travel with him by Jeep to carry on his work. A number of times we weren't able to get back to Mgori until very late in the evening. These trips he called new missionary indoctrination, but it also pointed up something else that was a reality in the '50s on our field. Most wives rarely traveled away from their stations of residence except to attend the annual missionary conference or to go on their yearly month's vacation with their families. The roads were very poor, and because of this traveling with children was rarely done except to get medical treatment.

During the rains a family or a station could be isolated because of muddy roads or impassable rivers. My kids often commented that we really had not been on safari during the rainy season unless we got stuck -- at least once. This loneliness was no doubt one of the great reasons why some families couldn't adjust to life on the field and did not return for a second term. Ten years after we arrived on the field

I installed a 13-station two-way radio communication system.
This was very beneficial for our work, particularly for keeping
in touch with our two hospitals. This system also made it
possible for wives to chat during off hours. That was a
blessing to many in their need to escape from the loneliness
that isolation brings.

When we began our language study, three months had seemed
like a long time to have to live out of a suitcase. We wanted
to get settled. But the time passed by quickly and now we
were eager to see our new home at Isanzu - our assignment for
service during this first term. We didn't know it then, but
Isanzu was to be the station we would live at and work out
from for the next 15 years of our missionary service in East
Africa.

Isanzu

CHAPTER 7

"Therefore, seeing we have this
ministry, as we have received mercy
we faint not."
2 Cor. 4:1   K.J.V.

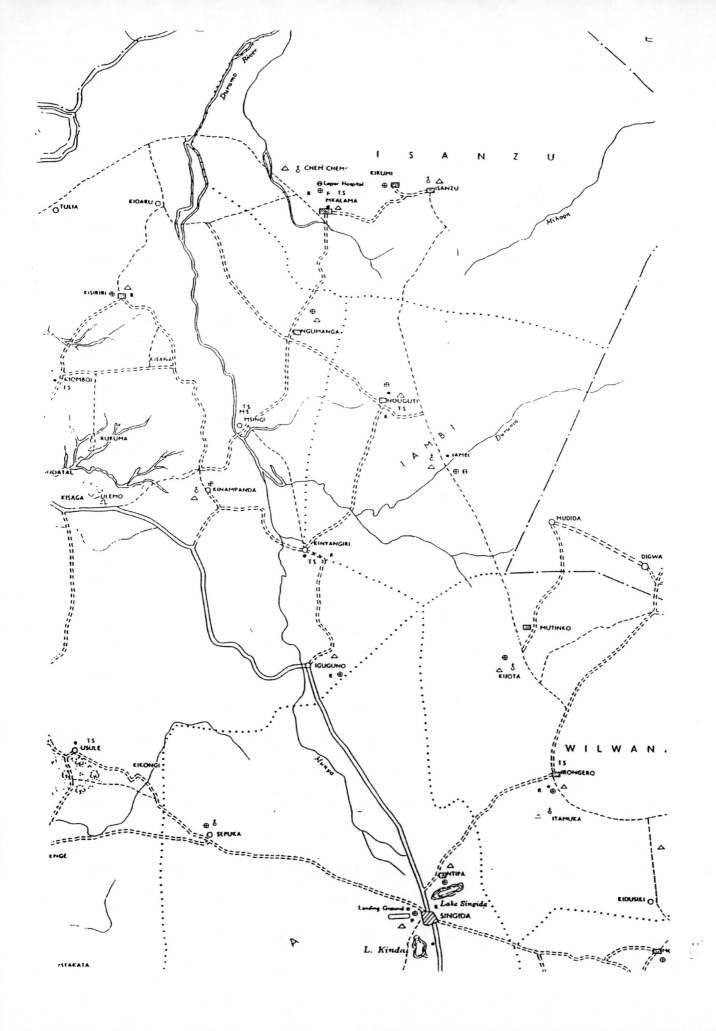

We could hardly wait to see our "new home" at Isanzu. It was located on a plateau and had an elevation of about 5000 feet above sea level.

We had gotten all the information about the area we could glean from the people on the field who knew anything about it. We learned that the location of the station itself was called <u>Kitaturu</u> by the local people. The Wanyihanzu, as the people called themselves, were a different tribe than either the Iramba or the Turu who occupied adjacent areas on our field. They were a rather small group who had migrated, in their distant past, from Ukerewe Island located north in Lake Victoria. They had their own vernacular, but were rapidly accepting and using the Iramba language.

Their tribal structure was very similar to the Iramba. They were of Bantu origin and were farmers. They gave their allegiance to their chief (mtemi). His name was Omari Nkinto. He held his court a short distance from the Isanzu Mission Station at a place called Kirumi. The chief exercised a great hold on the people because they believed he had the power to control the outcome of the rains which would assure a good harvest. No one was allowed to plant the seeds of the new year until he first cultivated with his special hoe(jembe). Some folks told me it was made of gold, but I have my doubts about that, never having proven it to be true. During our residence at Isanzu, the chief pretty much faded from the scene. The British Government's policy of indirect rule was replaced by the new, independent Government's very direct rule. Under the new scheme of things, older customs concerning local chiefs were mostly put aside.

Just before our final farewells were spoken at Mgori, we took delivery of a vintage Chevrolet Suburban Carryall. It had been well used on the field, and was now assigned to us until a new truck on order would arrive. Most cars on a mission field are given names by their drivers. All cars seem to have personalities of their own. Sometimes vehicles have very bad habits. The Carryall we had just been given had a reputation for "throwing wheels." It lived up to its past history. Just a short way out of Mgori, as we journeyed on our first trip to Isanzu, the back right wheel came off. I was amazed that this didn't cause serious bearing or axle damage. I was able to get the wheel and the axle back together using what we call the Tanganyika formula. I would use this formula -- a tried and true principle -- many times in the years that would follow. This formula can be stated very simply in the words: **brute force and ignorance.** In this case it got us into Singida without having to spend the night on the road. Mossum made final lasting repairs. The wheel never came off again as long as we had the car. I had learned on the trip coming up from Dar Es Salaam that travel in East Africa is not reckoned in miles. Rather it is measured in hours -- how long it takes to get from one place to another. With the wheel problem, it took us several hours to cover the 17 miles from Mgori to Singida. Then, while Mossum undertook repairs on the car, we went shopping.

A missionary hardly ever passed through Singida in the '50s without calling in at Manji Dhanji's. This was the store that served missionaries and their needs as well as those of the towns-people. All manner of things were available from this store, from a sack full of sugar, canned goods, hoes, hurricane lanterns, kerosene pressure lamps and 2 X 4 planks. The list was endless. We stocked up on all our needs -- as much as our vehicle's space would allow. Now we were ready for the 68 mile trip north to reach Isanzu.

We drove out of Singida, noticing that the roadbed was built on top of an embankment that had formerly been the roadbed for a railroad track. It made the road very narrow at that point -- one way traffic -- but there wasn't much in the way of traffic to cause concern. The bog on each side of the embankment was thick with scrub thorn bushes and trees. This was a favorite habitat for rhino. The story was told of a rhino who emerged one night after dark, out of the bush, up on to the embankment. He challenged a lorry for the embankment right of way. He charged the truck full speed and came to a crashing halt as he met the Lorry head on. The animal rolled down the embankment, the loser in that contest. He also lost his valuable horn left behind lying on the road bed.

The first part of our trip covered a distance of about

15 miles to a road junction which was called Igugunu. There were tall miombo trees bordering each side of the road as we traveled the road north. At this junction, one road went to the left. This was the main road going west into Sukumaland after it crossed the Iramba Plateau. It eventually reached the western side of Tanganyika. The other road from this junction that turned right was "our" road. It was not as well maintained as the main road, and a top speed of more than 30 mph wasn't a safe speed to travel. We turned right at this junction, and bounced along a rutted road for about 30 miles until we reached a small settlement called Nduguti. There was the usual local court building called a baraza located here. There were also several small shops, the biggest one owned by an Arab whose name was Mohammed Abdulah. The Arab traders usually picked government administrative centers like this one to establish their bases of trade and business. Their business was usually that of buying dried goat or cow skins from the natives. In return they sold matches, razor blades, sugar and rice. They were often seen with their lorries on the road at night involved in what was locally called Magendo -- illegal trading after dark. One could never be sure what that involved.

We then continued on our way and traveled another 27 miles through rocky hills and valleys. This brought us to the village of Mkalama. An Arab -- Ahmed Shams -- had a store located here. He had built in typical Arab fashion -- store in the front, living quarters in the far rear of the plot. High walls connected the store to the living quarters. In the walled-in area, a garden was planted. Ahmed had planted the usual date palms and in addition had a good vineyard. Once a year he sold the produce from his vines after meeting his own needs. We were always overjoyed to be able to buy some of this fruit from him.

Mkalama was on the edge of the end. The road really ended here. If you traveled further you entered Sukumaland -- the Eyasi salt flats, and herds of game animals. Shams was reported to have used his lorry to do a lot of poaching of game animals.

The story is told of his meeting the Government Game Ranger Bill MooreGilbert one day far out on the Eyasi plains. Shams had his lorry loaded with poached wildebeests. Bill stopped him and was ridiculed by Shams.

"What can you do to me way out here?" Shams laughed.
Bill replied, "I'll show you."

At that point Bill is reported to have taken a large caliber rifle and he then shot out each of the tires on Sham's lorry. Bill got into his Landrover without a word and drove away. It took a lot of effort and expense for Shams to recover from that encounter with Bwana Nyama(Mr. Game).

Mkalama was the location of the old Fort that I mentioned earlier. This old fort, built during German times, stood towering over the countryside, and commanded a wonderful view looking far out over Sukumaland. Just across the valley from the Fort was a location called Kinyama. It was very rocky and most of the topsoil in the surrounding area had long since been eroded away. Here the Government, years before, had built a Leper colony. The spiritual care of the lepers living there would be part of my responsibility while I served at Isanzu.

Following a steep and winding road for nine miles farther on finally brought us to our destination -- Isanzu. As we drove up the road from Mkalama we were surrounded on every side by gigantic rocks and huge boulders. When we reached Isanzu, we had truly reached the "Colorado Springs" of Africa. One huge balancing rock a short distance from our house defied all the laws of gravity and maintained itself on just a tiny support surface without falling a good distance to ground level. Eventually, one Easter season, we built a 15 foot wooden cross at its peak. It was a thrilling climb to reach the foot of that cross. Dr. Wilton Bergstrand and his wife whom I mentioned in Chapter one, paid us a memorable visit in the late '50s and made it up to the top where we all sang, "Beneath the Cross of Jesus" together. That was an unforgetable thrill. Another rock resembled a huge bull dog's face, so much so that our kids named it Bull Dog Rock. Another closely resembled a classical Roman helmet and was so named. The rocks and boulders had a uniform color of rust red or brown to slate gray. In the hearts of several huge rocks were caves in which pre-historic people had painted pictures of animals. These pictographs were very old yet amazingly well preserved.

'A heap of Livin'

CHAPTER 8

"But whoso hearkeneth unto me
shall dwell securely, and shall
be quiet without fear of evil."
                    Prov 1:33

There were two Mission houses at Isanzu station, a rather large church, a primary school and a 20 bed dispensary. These together with a carpenter shop, a church office and staff housing for the teachers made up the number of the other buildings on this site. We were welcomed to Isanzu by two nurses: Mss. Edythe Kjellin and Greta Ekstrand. Greta was the one who had loaned me a sweater at the Dodoma hotel. Edythe was full-time nurse at the Isanzu Dispensary, and part-time at the Leprosarium. Greta was full-time at Mkalama Leprosarium. The nurses lived together in one of the houses at Isanzu, just across the way from our house. The area separating the two dwellings had been planted in eucalyptus trees that were now very tall. There were also some flame trees which were strikingly beautiful when they came into bloom.

The house we were assigned to occupy had originally been built to house a family in one apartment, and a single worker in another. Years before our arrival, it had been modified to house only one family. It had been built in 1935 after the fashion of many settler homes in the old style of Deutsch Ost Afrika. Single story, its sun dried mud block walls were purposely built 10 feet high to help overcome the heat problem. The ceilings were of Maninga: 1 X 12" planks 12 feet long.

Maninga is a dense, termite resistant wood. The planks were usually coated with double-boiled linseed oil which gave them a rich mahogany appearance. A high peaked mabati (aluminum) roof topped the structure.

The arrangement for us now, until we got settled, was that we would eat with the nurses in their house but sleep in our new home. They were most gracious in providing for us.

The problem we next encountered was that much of the ceiling wood in our house had been removed because the 20-year-old planks had been riddled by termites called white ants. The missionary who was in charge of our home's renovation had been very relaxed in completing this project. Because of this, there were no ceiling boards in place in the main rooms of the house. In these rooms, you were able to get a full view of the attic beams and could occasionally see a bat hanging from one of them.

The house had a small inside bathroom with a toilet and even a bathtub. The pipes to service these luxuries had long since rusted out, and now they had been removed as well. If one wanted to use these accommodations, you serviced them by carrying in water by the buckets full. Because Isanzu didn't have a well, water was in short supply. It wasn't too long, although it took a lot of pushing, before an order was made up to get some planks and pipes from Kapoor Singh's sawmill in Singida. "Things take longer in East Africa", was a phrase we heard spoken often. We had no trouble confirming this local axiom.

When the lorry finally arrived with our planks and pipes, we then got to work. Using the maninga planks we finished the work on the ceilings. I had help from our local carpenter/craftsman, Orgenes Manya and his young helper, Ndrasio. Working with them, I began to experience the joyful and warm feeling of working together with the people I had come to live among and serve in a variety of ways.

I appreciated the plumbing experience I had brought to the field with me as I began designing a water system for our house. Just outside the back door a cistern 8 feet wide, 16 feet long and 7 feet deep ran along the back wall of the house. I installed a hand driven semi-rotary pump into this water supply and routed an $1\frac{1}{4}$" pipe up to the attic. I put a 750-gallon zinc receiving tank in the attic which the semi-rotary pump would first fill and then top up each day. Pipes from this tank were run down to the kitchen and the bath. We used a wood range for all our cooking, so I ran a pipe through the range's firebox into a hot-water receiving tank and piped this supply to the bathtub and sink. We now had all the amenities. We could begin in earnest with the drama of living in this fine old dwelling we would call home. The cement floors were ideally suited and very practical for families with small children. All the milk spilled at mealtimes just disappeared as it was absorbed into a thirsty cement floor.

Edgar Guest, a popular American poet of some years past, wrote: "It takes a heap a livin', to make a house a home."

We were to find that our house had a personality that was as changeable as that of any presentday teen-ager. Most of the time our home was very loving and caring, but then--there were those times -- .

For example, we moved into our new home enlisting the aid of many cardboard boxes. Because of the design of houses built back when...our house had no built-in closets in which to store clothing. It was the custom to use very heavy, free-standing closets, called wardrobes, for storage. But the space they provided in spite of their large size was quite limited. We made up for this lack of closet space by storing some of our clothes in cardboard boxes shoved up against the mud block walls of the house in out of the way places.

Imagine the shock we got, when some months after moving in, we began to unpack our supplies of extra clothing stored in the boxes. When we lifted the boxes away from the walls, we saw that the side of the box next to the wall had been completely eaten away, and worse still, the clothing inside the box had become excellent fare for the ravenous termites. All their eating had been done in strict secrecy and silence. They hadn't given us a clue as to what was going on. Out of necessity we continued to use boxes for storage but from that time on we were very careful about their locations. Mostly, they were placed on top of the large wardrobes. Each leg of the wardrobe was seated in a container of kerosene that discouraged the ants from attempting to get at our boxes again.

As we began our work at Isanzu, we were asked to follow the usual practice of hiring a number of workers. We had one for cooking, called an <u>Mpishi</u>. Jeanne enjoyed cooking very much, so Wazaeli Kiula was <u>mpishi</u> in title only. He was rather Mama's helper in the kitchen. We also had an <u>Ayah</u> -- Waza Andrea, whose job was to care for the children. She usually did this by tying the smallest of her charges onto her back, African style. Next in line of importance was the <u>inside house boy</u> in charge of cleaning and helping with dishes in the kitchen. His name was Mattia. The <u>Dobe</u> followed him in the order of workers, he was the laundry man. His name was Jeremiah. Prior to the advent of gas washing machines, clothes were taken to a stream. With the use of some soap, and then being pounded on rocks they were sun dried and clean. Finally, a worker, who had a dangerous task, served by gathering firewood which was called kuni. Scorpions love to hide in wood, and snakes often make their homes in the boxes or enclosures used to store wood. Our <u>kuni</u> man's name was Obed Mkilanya.

Why so many workers? Did we come to Africa to live like nobility? Some of us questioned this. The answers we got were: salaries of all these people totaled to a very small sum. Work provided employment for these people who were all our church members. The logic was also given that in new areas, people had many questions about <u>these</u> missionary foreigners: what they ate, how they lived and acted in their homes. Hiring all these people meant that a whole team of public relations folks would communicate to the community what and who the missionaries were and what they were like. In practice these workers became part of the missionary's family. You were responsible for them and their families in many special ways.

*   *   *   *   *   *

Even during daylight hours, danger could find its way inside our home's thick walls which seemed to promise security. Parallel to the rear wall of our home was the large cistern. Rain water, which was usually plentiful during the rainy season from January through April, was our **only** and **very precious** water supply. This rain water collected on the roof of our home, flowed through a series of gutters and pipes to renew the supply in the cistern. The pump located on our back porch, with its pipe leading into the attic, supplied the gravity fed water system we had installed.

Early one morning, I had gone through that porch and on outside to work in the garden. A short time later I heard Jeanne urgently calling me. Her voice had that quality of emergency in it that made me drop my hoe and come on the double. A very large cobra had been coiled around the water pipe, high up, in the porch. It was trying to gain entrance to the attic. The snake was hunting for rats or mice. Jeanne had walked onto the porch after being outside, and the snake then dropped from its perch to the porch floor very close to where she stood. She screamed and ran outside, the snake ran into the kitchen. The door leading out of the kitchen into the rest of the house was shut fortunately.

When I arrived, our kitchen helper, Wazaeli and I entered the kitchen. With Wazaeli's encouragement, I grabbed a long handled cleaning broom which had a large wooden head. I used it to try to knock the snake senseless, and I landed some pretty good blows. But I didn't faze the creature one bit. It got tired of our efforts and the chasing we were doing. It then turned and started chasing us around the kitchen. This game continued for several rounds until the snake, seven or eight feet long, spied the cleanout hole in the brick chimney next to our wood stove. It made a bee-line for the refuge that the hole promised. I saw what was going to happen, so I shouted for Jeanne to bring my gun. She brought me the only gun she found in her rush, and it wasn't a very practical choice for snake hunting. It was a 375 H & H Magnum, a gun which I used for elephant hunting. I knew that if the snake could get into the chimney, I wouldn't be able to get at it. It would hide there in safety until nightfall. Then it would come back out and be loose in the house. It was halfway in, disappearing slowly into the hole when I shot it, cutting it in half.

Unfortunately, I then became liable to my wife's criticism, which would be often repeated. I had "ruined" her chimney, and it would have to undergo major repairs.

Once again I used the Tanganyika Formula with effective results.

*   *   *   *   *

Although our bathroom was located through the kitchen on the opposite side of the house from the bedrooms, it was

PLATE II

OUR "HOME" AT ISANZU

THE ISANZU CHURCH

THE KITCHEN SNAKE

ONE OF ISANZU'S MANY LEOPARDS

vastly more convenient than having to travel outside in the middle of the night. That would have meant leaving the safety of the house. Safety means the absence of danger: danger from snakes, scorpions, and the ever present leopards and hyenas who prowled our yard after dark. Hyenas, in particular, took over the outside area as their domain with the onset of darkness. Though we were told these animals were cowards, that was just partly true.

I remember one night lying in bed listening to the bleating of a small goat some distance down the valley. It had been separated from the flock as they came home at dusk after a day of grazing. The youthful shepherd had been too anxious to get home to eat and rest. He hadn't kept a count on his many charges. The goat probably wandered into some choice grazing among the rocks and remained contentedly feeding until darkness set in. Finally it became aware that it was alone. Then it began to bleat, hoping to hear some answer that would give it direction so it could reach home in the darkness.

As I lay listening, I debated whether I should attempt to go and rescue it. I knew it would be foolish to try. The goat didn't know or trust me, and I would probably succeed in chasing it away into greater danger. The choice was taken from me when I heard two hyenas calling from across the valley to each other. Having heard the goat's cries, they were closing in for a kill. I heard the goat give one last bleat in terror and anguished pain. All, then, was total silence until a few moments later.

Finally, in typical hyena fashion the two animals celebrated their victory. They began to laugh. It was horrible to hear. It sounded like two demented women laughing hysterically at some obscene sight.

A hyena's jaws are said to be more powerful than the jaws of an adult lion. It is easy to frighten them away, but they generate a lot of courage if they think their prey is helpless or disabled. We had some cases of hyenas attacking hospital patients. The patients exposed themselves to danger by lying outside the hospital on a ramp on warm evenings.

Another favorite target of the hyena was the cow. A cow is helpless to defend herself from a hyena's attack. The attack is always centered on the cow's udders and milk bag.

*   *   *   *   *   *

I got into work at Isanzu, and found that I had a wonderful man to introduce me to many of the tasks I would be doing. Pastor Paulo Mkali was my colleague in the work. We shared the ministry at the Mkalama Leprosarium and of Isanzu Parish. Every Friday was **shauri** (affairs) day. The Elders of the church and the two Pastors sat in Sessions, beginning after breakfast and often times lasting until well after dark. Members of the congregation would sit patiently outside the church door, sometimes waiting for hours to have their **shauris** come before the Elders. Many persons involved in drinking or adultery or other infractions of Christian conduct were put on church discipline. This meant they suffered the loss of church privileges such as receiving the sacraments. They were restored to complete fellowship after they showed signs of repentance.

Isanzu had a number of out-district points which were served by evangelists. Once each month these workers came into the station, some from far away. They received their monthly salary for the work they were doing. They were also given instruction for the following month's preaching. Pastor Paulo and I took turns preaching at the Isanzu station church. When I did not have the responsibility at Isanzu, or the Leprosarium, I tried to visit out-station bush schools to check the work being done there. The evangelist's job was to teach children the 3 'R's during morning hours. His afternoons were spent contacting potential church members. Sundays he preached.

Once a month the congregation at the Leprosarium was given communion by either Pastor Paulo or myself. I recall my introduction to the Leprosarium and its people. Nurse Ekstrand took us on a tour of the treatment center. The dressers were in the process of changing dressings of the very large ulcers on the lepers' bodies. These came as part of the disease. Before the coming of the Sulfone drugs, Hansen's bacillus (named for the Norwegian doctor who discovered the germ in 1874) was treated by using Chaulmoogra Oil. Although the Sulfones do not cure leprosy, the disease becomes inactive after prolonged drug treatment. It becomes active again if the patient does not continue to take the drug. There have been very few reported cases of remission of leprosy without the use of medications. Leprosy is contagious. However, most people have little chance of contracting it unless they live in the same house and come into continual close contact with a person who is infected. I didn't have any fear of becoming infected. Therefore, I touched patients who were being baptized, those receiving communion, and I shook hands with those who participated in worship services. I learned later that my very warm reception among the lepers of Mkalama was the result of this. We had an evangelist there whose name was Nalingigwa Mpya. He was an avid Christian and did far more in his patient status to minister to lepers than either Pastor Paulo or I could ever have hoped to do as outsiders.

When the Church began its work at Mkalama, sufferers who were admitted for treatment came from homes where everything had ended for them. They were considered by their relatives and families to be, in a real way, lost to them and dead. The requests came from some of these patients to be allowed to remarry after they joined the colony. In sympathy, the Church authorities allowed remarriage. With the advent of Sulfone drugs, it now was possible for most patients to return to their homes as inactive cases. Ironically, this good development caused great problems for a Church that espoused monogamy as one of its principal tenets.

*   *   *   *   *   *

Isanzu had five primary schools, and the administration and maintenance of these schools was my responsibility. All of this work required a lot of the handling of funds. Each station missionary was given a set of double entry financial books to keep, and a quarterly report to the Field Treasurer was required. Most bookkeeping was attempted at night, under the poor light of a kerosene pressure lantern. This light was responsible for many entry errors that later took hours to find. A cause of great frustration. On the other hand there was a lot of satisfaction to be gained by getting a trial balance each quarter.

*   *   *   *   *   *

There were those special meeting times, called Mkutano wa Kiroho (Spiritual Life meetings), resembling Bible Camps held in the U. S. Our people were very receptive to "getting away" and into a Bible Camp setting. They built thatch booths at a location called Yindi, just down the valley from the Station. Our camp had programs filled with singing, preaching, fellowshipping and eating together. We ate ughali (cooked corn flour), and added to this fare, tea and the meat of a wildebeeste freshly hunted for the occasion. We were fortunate to have Pastor Lud Melander and his wife Esther join together with us one unforgettable year. Lud was one of the pioneer pastors who was still on the field at that time. He played his violin to everyone's delight, and brought candy for all the kids.

*   *   *   *   *

Our house was located on the main path that the local people used for travel to the valley below the station. The path ran behind our house and where it passed our bedroom windows, it was hemmed in on the opposite side by our garage. The passage between the buildings at that point was pretty narrow. This usually posed no problem, because all the trips were done by travelers during daylight hours. People were afraid to travel at night. Snakes enjoy lying on paths which have soaked up the sun's heat during the daylight hours. So the people who could, avoided after dark travel.

We hadn't lived in our home very long before one problem became a bit troublesome. Once or twice a month some unstable characters, two or three, would get drunk on "pombe"(native beer made from sorghum or honey). Then at about midnight, they would decide it was time to return to their homes in the valley below -- a place called N'gwa Middo. They would charge into our station area following the path which led home, singing, yelling, and shouting back and forth to each other in their drunken ecstasy. This never failed to awaken us, and to scare our kids half to death. We found the solution to this problem by using the **WISDOM OF SOLOMON,** -- although we didn't realize how wise Solomon could be.

I had initiated making evangelistic foot safaris into Sukumaland to the west of Isanzu, across the Sibiti river. I began by using porters to carry supplies. I soon learned that when I took them along, they had very big appetites. I was also short on the number of tents needed to shelter them. I decided then to "do it" like the locals "did it". I purchased a donkey to carry a safari tent and loads, and back-packed the rest without porters. The grain the donkey needed to supplement the grass he ate on safari breaks was a fraction of the amount of ground corn needed to make "ughali" (native porridge), for 6 or 8 porters. I didn't have to provide a tent for the animal either. We could either keep him in a hastily constructed thorn enclosure, or lodge him in a Sukuma cattle corral. I looked far and wide for a beast that would be docile and a hard worker at the same time. The search turned out to be long and hard. Even so, I finally acquired a donkey whose name was Solomoni. The kids mounted him and he consented to give them both free rides. You could even walk in close behind him without getting the swift kick most area mules awarded the unwary.

Now that I had purchased my new found helper, the next question arose, where could I house him? I've already alluded to the danger for an animal left outside unprotected after dark. The solution to the problem was easily found. The garage behind our house was used for storing everything except our pickup. Solomoni found his new home to be the garage as soon as he arrived.

Not long after Solomoni "took up residence", the time came around again for the appearance of our drunken revelers. Midnight came and the shouting, singing, swearing band drew near, approaching our house on the path. Closer and closer they came, and the noise (kelele)of their revelry on the silent night air swelled in volume as they approached us. Finally they reached the point between the bedroom and the garage in a crescendo. At that precise moment, Solomoni put them all to shame.

He **BRAYED!**

Not a quiet, docile bray, rather an ear-splitting spine-chilling bray of a volume I didn't believe he was able to produce.

Like King Beltshazzer of ancient fame who, when he saw the hand and fingers writing on his wall was changed from drunkenness to the point where "the joints of his loins were loosed and his knees smote one against the other," so it was with our small band of drunks. Shrieks of terror and fear came first, then followed a stampede down the dark path as the group stumbled, fell, and sprang up again to fight for a continuing flight in their mad dash to escape.

The next morning I was certain that Solomoni winked at me when I let him out to pasture. Be that as it may, from that time on our drunks chose another way home after their nights out. They had received some very wise guidance from a source that stood solidly on four legs.

Reflections

CHAPTER 9

"...For whither thou goest, I will
go; where thou lodgest, I will
lodge: thy people shall be my
people, and thy God, my God."
                    Ruth 1:16

There are those blessed, especially at the beginning of their adult life, to find that special person who will share their life and work. The two together can accomplish much more than either could alone. As Christians, we believe God has a plan for us, and that it is His will that we find **that** special person. I had received my call to service at the Youth Convention in Los Angeles. I was yet to learn how greatly the Lord would bless me in giving me that special person who would be willing to become a missionary with me in my/our calling.

After returning from the Los Angeles youth conference to Portland, I was aglow with the call I had gotten. My pastor told me I had a real case of "convention-itis". My parents also had a lot of reservations about my decision to become a pastor. I worked for a little longer at my job in Portland before I set off for Augustana College in Rock Island, Illinois.

I arrived at the college in time to experience a beautiful summer. I roomed that summer in the college dorm with a young man who was a pre-law student. He was a hard working student and spent a lot of time studying. He knew how to study -- I didn't know the first thing about it. My light course load did not encourage me to apply myself either. My roommate cautioned me, "If you don't get busy soon, you're going to be in trouble here; this is an egg-head college."

The summer session ended. I stayed in Rock Island, not

having the funds to return to Portland. The fall quarter began, and now I was ready to begin studying. I signed up for too many courses for a new student: beginning Greek, Latin, and German, together with the usual freshman load of courses. I wanted to finish my undergraduate work in about three years, coinciding with the end of the funding from my G.I. bill. I got into serious academic difficulty at once. In just a few weeks I had to drop the German course, and even then I was still overwhelmed in my new life as a student. I had also taken a part-time job in a restaurant, and had to give that up, too.

It took the whole of the first year, and even into the second for me to learn how to study. There was no time for social life, but since I was on the G.I. Bill, I had no money for dates anyway.

The Christmas holidays came and I remember being very lonely when my classmates left for the vacation period. However, I planned to spend the following summer going to Portland, and also to take a summer church assignment. That expectation kept me in good spirits.

The end of the spring quarter came quickly. In an arrangement with three other students who were already in the Seminary, I drove out to the Pacific Northwest in the car of one of the students. His name was Douglas Pearson. He was married, and he and his wife were already in Portland to spend the year to fulfill their internship requirement serving a church there. Douglas had returned to Rock Island to get his car. Marie, Doug's wife, had remained in Portland, where she had been joined by her younger sister, Jeanne. Jeanne had just finished her training at Swedish hospital in Minneapolis to become a registered nurse. She then traveled out to join her sister Marie, who was now pregnant with the Pearson's first child.

Our car trip out to Portland in 1947 was uneventful until we reached the Columbia Gorge in Oregon. There we found the Columbia river to be in very high flood stage, and were grateful when we were finally able to reach Portland traveling by an alternate route over Mt. Hood, rather than trying to follow the Gorge Scenic highway which was now closed.

My church assignment for the summer was at Elim Church in Hokenson Washington, located about 25 miles northeast of Portland. Jeanne had taken a job at Emanuel Hospital in Portland. I met her there once or twice during that summer, but neither of us were particularly attracted to the other.

The end of summer came and I returned with the other students in Pearson's car to Rock Island. We arrived in that city tired and hungry, after driving practically nonstop from the Northwest.

Marie and Jeanne had flown back to Rock Island because Marie was having a difficult time in her pregnancy.

When we pulled in at the Pearsons' home, Jeanne met us at the door with a smoldering skillet of meatballs in her hand. For me, that was a very eventful meeting. In a short time we became well acquainted. I had offered to help Douglas paint his house, and Jeanne was often in their home. She was making the decision about whether to return to Minneapolis to work at Swedish Hospital from where she had graduated, or whether to remain in Rock Island, close to her sister. She also was considering the possibility of doing midwifery work in Appalachia, and what further study she would need to make to enter into that work. I had been able to put aside some money during the summer, and she needed a loan to make a trip north, which I was able to provide. We still had not yet developed anything more than a very casual relationship. Her trip to Minneapolis was primarily to see a young man whom she had been seriously dating. She thought a great deal of him, but he wasn't a Christian. This was enough, after a lot of prayer and heart-searching, for her to decide to end her serious affection for him. After visiting Minneapolis, she returned to Rock Island and began to work at Moline Lutheran Hospital. A short time later, we started dating, and by the middle of January, 1949, I gave her an engagement ring.

Our love blossomed in the Pearson's home and in the Music building of the College, where I had frequently gone during my "lonely" days to play on a small organ. Now Jeanne played for me and we both enjoyed those hours so much.

Because we loved the out of doors, even during the winter, we often went for long walks. Lincoln Park was next to the College. One January evening found us sitting on one of the benches in the park, oblivious to the cold. I had been to Rock Island several times examining jewelry shop display windows looking for an engagement ring that I might be able to afford. On this particular day, I finally put my anxiety behind me where it belonged, and marched through one shop's entrance. I told the man at the counter that I wanted to buy "that" lovely ring but that I would need to make the payments on "time". I made the down-payment· and to my great surprise, no questions were asked about my credit rating. Then with a heart overflowing with happiness, I gave the box containing the ring to Jeanne as we sat together on a park bench, and told her that I loved her very much, and asked her to marry me. I remember her first response was:

"We've been going together such a short time."

But she consented to my plea that she be my wife. We then started laying plans for our wedding date and where we would hold the marriage ceremony. This wasn't the first time I had told Jeanne that I was in love with her, so I imagine my proposal was not totally unexpected. I would have been heartbroken had she refused.

In June we were married in the Augustana Seminary Chapel. I still had another year to complete before I finished college (I finished college in two summers and three academic years.) Jeanne took a job as School Nurse at Augustana College, a job she continued to hold for the next three years.

We left Rock Island at that time to go on our year of internship. This is the year of practical work for seminary students. We were assigned to intern at the Trinity Lutheran Church of Minnehaha Falls in Minneapolis. We left Rock Island

and planned to spend the summer in Portland before our work in Minneapolis would begin. Jeanne had one month left before the birth of our first child, Kristine. Her doctor was concerned about her making such a long trip by car at that late date in her pregnancy, but all went well on our drive to Portland. On July 11th, the happy event took place when Kris came to join us, and to begin our family. In the fall we drove to Minneapolis from Portland. We then began our year of internship.

We spent a blessed time at Trinity, serving in a Spirit-filled church, with its pastor, Rev. Carl F. Danielson. Trinity was a church which had a heavy emphasis on Missions, and was home ground for a Missions group called the "World Mission Prayer League." This group would become our sponsoring agency in our later years of service overseas.

I had already made overtures to Augustana Seminary, expressing a desire to go to Alaska as a missionary. I received the reply that our Synod had no work there. So my proposal came to naught. While we were at Trinity, and as a part of its commitment for Mission outreach, a week of meetings was held there in the fall. One night toward the close of that week, the speaker asked all those who would be willing to dedicate their lives to Missions: "Would they please stand." Jeanne's hand crept over into mine and, holding tightly to each other, we stood up together.

At that time, our first born, Kris, was just five months old.

Our Augustana Board of Missions office was located right in Minneapolis, where we were then in residence. So I contacted the Director, Dr. S. Hjalmar Swanson, and gave him our names as candidates. The Board had a great emphasis on work in Japan at that time. They wanted to send us there, citing my service background in the Orient. I, however, felt a strong leading to go to Africa, and the Board kindly allowed us to have that freedom of choice.

We returned to Rock Island in the fall of 1953 to finish our final year of Seminary. That turned out to be a very **lean** year. Until we had left in 1952 for our internship, I held a job as a nightwatchman at the Minneapolis-Moline farm equipment plant in Moline. The income from this work, together with Jeanne's salary as school nurse had kept us going very well. The nightwatchman's job was now no longer available. Jeanne wasn't able to work now that we had a youngster in our home, and we had another one on the way. To complicate things, in 1953 the entire country was undergoing a severe recession. Part time employment was almost impossible to find. I finally got work for a period of that year as a part-time elevator operator/night watchman in a bank. I also sold toys door-to-door during the Christmas vacation.

We had a jar in the kitchen of our apartment where Jeanne kept change to buy bread and milk and other necessities. Sometimes the bowl was empty when we picked it up to see if it would rattle, but we always managed to have bread to put on the table.

Our second child, Daniel, was born right after Christmas of that final year of Seminary.

Ordination of the Senior Graduating Class was scheduled to be held at Los Angeles, California, in June 1954. We had the largest graduating class in the Seminary's history.

We closed our apartment and then drove to Colorado Springs on our way west. Jeanne's sister Marie and her husband Douglas were now serving a church there. We had a short visit with them. When we left, Jeanne took a twenty dollar bill from our funds to help them with the expense of our stay. But this over-taxed our tight budget, and as we traveled on, we got as far as Flagstaff, Arizona, and completely ran out of funds.

As I drove down the main street of Flagstaff, wondering what I should do now, I saw the office sign of the New York Life Insurance Company. I remembered that I had my policy, issued by that Company, with me in my papers. I stopped at the office and spoke to the Manager. I told him my story, that I was a seminary graduate on the way to Los Angeles with my family to be ordained and had run out of funds. The kindly manager made this reply:

"Here's fifty dollars. Leave me your policy as security. If we can't trust a minister, we can't trust anyone."

Fifty dollars in 1954 was a lot of money. It got us to our destination.

Following the ordination service to which my parents from Portland had come, we got a loan from them. We traveled on to Portland and spent the summer months with them there in their home.

Upon my ordination, I was on salary from the Board of Missions for $ 2,400 a year, so I couldn't take work during that summer in Portland. But Jeanne was employed at Emanuel Hospital for the months we were there and I baby-sat. We were commissioned at our home church, First Immanuel, to serve in Africa. Pastor Carl Sodergren, pastor of First Immanuel, and Pastor Ralph Lindquist from our Board of Missions officiated.

*   *   *   *   *

At the close of the summer we traveled by train back to Minnesota to bid farewell to Jeanne's mother. Her mother strongly felt that we should not go to "far off" Africa. This made it hard for us to leave, particularly so for Jeanne. Even so, we continued on to New York City. There a dear lady, Miss Constance Shaw, from our Board of Missions office, received us and guided us through what was necessary in order to get our things and ourselves on the Queen Elizabeth for our voyage to London.

On the day of our departure, we were bid farewell on the deck of that great ship by the pastor who had been responsible for so much that was important in my life. He had brought my parents into a saving relationship with the Lord. At the time he had performed this ministry for them, Pastor Nels Lundgren had been pastor at Zion Lutheran Church in Omaha Nebraska, where our family lived. He had been my role model when I was a small child. It was very fitting that he send us off to begin our work for the Lord overseas.

Hunting

CHAPTER 10

"He causeth the grass to grow
for the cattle, and herb for
the service of man; that he may
bring forth food out of the earth.
...These wait all for thee, that
thou mayest give them their food
in due season." Ps. 104:14,27

It wasn't simply a matter of sport, it was a matter of supply for the table. I began hunting as soon as we reached the field in Tanganyika. While we were still involved in language study at Mgori, there was a need to provide meat. The fact that I thoroughly enjoyed getting into areas that provided game was an extra plus.

Some very frightening stories were told to me about the experiences some of the missionaries had while hunting. For example, Donald Flatt, a British Government District Officer serving at Kilosa and one of our field's doctors, Dr. Stan Moris, were out one day hunting guinea fowl in the bush. A buffalo appeared and in its charge pinned Don to the ground as he straddled its horns. Dr. Moris, who had only a shotgun, in desperation bravely fired at the buffalo and hit it behind the chest. The shot did little more than partially penetrate the buffalo's very thick hide.

Then while the animal ran off, Don and Stan ran for the safety of a nearby tree, but the buffalo returned, cut off their escape and charged them again. It attacked Don who again grasped it by the horns, and carrying Don forward it also swerved to attack Stan at the same time. Stan fired from his hip, again at very close range. This time the shell penetrated the animal's skin and passed through the beast's liver into its lungs and it died. To penetrate the very tough hide of a buffalo was a miracle that Dr. Moris said was the result of a full choke shotgun fired at the beast at very close range.

Sometime later, Don lost his first wife through death,

and met and married one of our single missionaries, Ruth Safemaster. He then joined our mission and was subsequently ordained a Lutheran Pastor.

Almost all of Africa's game animals provide tasty meat. Even the zebra, shunned by most nationals because they consider it to be of the donkey family, has delicious meat if the marbled fat portions are removed prior to its being roasted.

After we were established at Isanzu our first term, every five or six weeks, it became time to replenish the 33-pound capacity of the freezing compartment of our Servel Kerosene refrigerator. I would drive carefully down the escarpment on a track to the plains area: either in the Yaida Swamp or lower still to the Eyasi Plains. At these locations, herds of wildebeeste, hartebeest or impala were there for the hunting.

It was necessary to purchase a yearly game license from the Government. The license had a liberal listing of animals of almost every variety. As they were shot, one entered them as harvested on the license. Quail and guinea fowl were also allowed without limit. We enjoyed them roasted and the guinea fowl was very special meat when used in the preparation of spaghetti sauce.

We lived a full day's drive from the nearest store located in Singida which could supply us with food, mostly available in tins and therefore expensive. This compelled us to rely on our garden and our hunting to supply most of what we ate. Mr. Shoten, an old man and a relic out of the early ox cart days in Tanganyika now long past, lived with his African wife

a short distance out of Singida at a place called Kitatimu.
He grew vegetables in his shamba in small raised beds which
he then harvested and used to make up baskets of mixed
vegetables for sale. He had a theory that all the leaves and
tops of the plants he grew must be returned to the ground that
grew them. He did this without fail and produced very good
results in his gardening.

It was a real education in wildlife to simply be in the
wilderness areas and to keep your eyes and ears open. We were
on a trip to visit the Bushmen one time and camped on the fringe
of trees that bordered the Eyasi plains. During the night
a large herd of wildebeeste moved into the area all around
our camp. It was pitch dark, but the bleats and baa's of the
animals surrounded us as they fed on the grass of the area.

I was awakened by the coming of dawn and as I lay on my
cot looking out through the screening of our tent's door,
a snake came slithering along. As it passed the doorway it
stopped every now and then to try to poke its head into the
screen in order to gain entrance into the tent. The screen
held, and the snake went on its way.

Sometime later in that same area, Heidi, our daughter,
brought us news that a big puff adder was sleeping in her tent
under her cot. Wazaeli, Jeanne's helper, shot the snake with
a bow and arrow.

We had many snake experiences in Africa, but most of
the time the creatures were more anxious to run from us than
to accost us for an attack. Only during a short portion of

each year did one find snakes looking to attack. I believe this was during the mating season. Snakes can hear and sense your approach by the vibrations of your feet striking the earth. This was their signal to escape into their holes or into the surrounding bushes. I was once told to keep my eyes up off the ground and watch just a little up and ahead. Then I would see snake movement as it sensed our approaching footsteps on the ground. I found this to be true.

Almost every African I have ever met has considered snakes -- all snakes -- as a scourge, and all snakes they say, without exception, are deadly poisonous. The nationals give no credit to the reptiles for all the good rat control work they constantly do. Very often when a snake is killed, the natives start a fire and burn the snake's body. They claim this is the only method that will ensure the snake's complete departure from this world. It is very true that "dead" snakes have bitten a number of people. Their muscle reflexes carry on after they die. It is also true that when snakes are killed, rats multiply, and the danger of an outbreak of bubonic plague increases alarmingly in areas where it is endemic.

An animal that could always be counted on to provide trouble was the rhino. A number of times on our foot safaris we had a very hard time avoiding contact with this dangerous beast. When it became aware of our presence, it would lower its head and charge at great speed (some claim a rate of 30-35 mph). Authorities on the rhino believe it cannot see well at all, so if you dodge the charge, the animal just keeps on going in a straight line for some distance. We experienced this a number of times, but we also could count on the rhino's reaction when it reached the end of its run. It would turn to swing about and "come looking" for its target again. It has a very acute sense of smell to aid it in its quest.

My hunting and safari guide, Justino Nzugika, had a very great dislike for Rhinos. On one of our safaris we came to the end of a long, hot day of trekking. We were in the Kindera Mountains where water is very scarce. It usually outcrops in artesian fed pools in the hills. The place we had reached was called Majimaruru. We set up a hasty camp on a hillock some distance from the water. Since there was still some time before it became dark, it was still safe to go to the outer pools of the water hole for a much desired quick bath.

Elephants are notorious for becoming enraged if they find any one, animal or human in "their" water holes. But they usually wait for the advent of darkness to begin arriving at their watering places. Justino witnessed an angry elephant pick up over a ton of rhino that had intruded into "its" pool and pitch the animal bodily out into the surrounding forest.

We quickly stripped off our clothes and wetting down, we thoroughly soaped our bodies to get rid of the day's dust and sweat. Then into the pool for a quick rinse and back into our clothes so that we could escape to our campsite and the relative safety of our camp fire that most animals fear.

From our camp we had a good view of the pool in which we had just bathed. We had left the meager supply of water in the pool being almost more soap than water.

Soon after we left, a lone rhino trotted into the water hole. He was in a hurry too, to drink and get out before the elephants started arriving. He chose our outer pool to drink from. He hastily gulped down a big supply of water, without even stopping for breath. Then the soapy message got through to him -- he stopped gulping, and at that moment seemed to explode. He jumped up and down, backward and forward, seemingly trying to rid himself of this strange unexpected thing he had drunk. Nothing seemed to help so he galloped off into the bush, snorting as he went.

Justino doubled up in mirth, and laughed about this event for the rest of our safari. It was something he would recall again and again in the future.

At another location called Maaungu there was a massive boulder that towered high over the water. We took guests there every now and then, and slept on top of the rock. Its sides were vertical, so that the elephants couldn't get to us. It was always a thrill on the night of a full moon to arrive early and enjoy the show.

The elephants would come in regular shifts, group following group in what seemed to be a well ordered succession. The first animals to arrive would "fungua" -- open -- the hole, that is to uncover the water which was covered by sand. We experienced the huge animals taking a trunkfull of water and squirting it high into the air. This caused us who were watching to get well sprayed.

Each group of elephants took about an hour or so to drink. Succeeding groups waited off in the bush and never intruded until the time for their group's entrance into the water hole. They were very patient awaiting their turn.

With the coming of the first light of dawn, the last group of elephants which had come to the hole would "funga" -- close -- the hole, by using their trunks to cover over the water with sand. This activity was always punctuated by a huge bellow or two from one of the group. It was as if the animals were issuing a warning for all to stay away from "their" private hole.

When we first attempted to contact the Bushman tribe, called Hadza, living in this area, we were never successful. We could find their camps, even with campfires still smoldering, but no one was ever around.

We finally made contact when we shot an elephant, and a few men of the group came asking our permission to eat the elephant's meat. Thus began a long relationship of love and trust that would culminate in many of these people receiving Christ into their lives and being baptized into the Christian faith.

I was very sensitive to the pleas for help when we began to live at Isanzu. Elephants would raid the fields of corn and maize the people had worked all year to grow. It was their food supply for the coming year. A herd of elephants can simply erase a whole year's work by a farmer and his family in one night. Leopards making night raids on a family's herd of sheep and goats could bring disaster again in one night. Leopards have the bad practice of entering a native's corral and instead of choosing a goat or sheep to eat, they kill everything in sight, then drag away their choice and leave the rest.

One day a group of farmers from the valley below Isanzu came and pleaded with me to help them. They had been using fire and banging on empty five gallon cans throughout the night, but the sweet smell of ripening corn was so overpowering to the elephants, they paid no attention to the farmers' threats. The herd was devastating one or two shambas a night. Soon the farmer's said there would be nothing left of their food supply for the coming year. "Would I please come down with them and bring my **BIG** gun?" Elephants are truly afraid of the sound of a rifle. I went down with them but explained that I couldn't do more than try to frighten the animals away. I was not empowered by the government to do control work. It would be better for them to call in a government Game Scout. They said they had repeatedly called for government help, but their pleas simply fell on deaf ears.

I went with the men to where the elephants were reported to be. The herd had not even bothered to move away from the shamba area during the daylight hours -- they were just into the forest a short distance.

I carefully positioned myself down-wind from the herd knowing that frightened elephants always run into the wind allowing them to smell what danger might be in their path of escape. I fired off two or three rounds from my 375 H & H

Magnum. A Magnum makes a big, big noise. The forest around me and my friends exploded. The animals did not follow the rules, rather they charged in the direction where the farmers and I were standing. I had to pick one of the lead animals and fire point blank at it to divert this charge. This caused the rest of the herd to veer away from us. Unfortunately, the animal I had shot at, was mortally wounded and died. It had very small tusks. I had a current special license to hunt an elephant. It had cost me over sixty dollars to purchase, and I was intending to shoot an elephant that would more than return my investment. I took the very small tusks to the Government's District Commissioner in Singida, and in telling him what happened asked that I be allowed to turn the small tusks in to the Game Department. The District Commissioner, Mr. Ian Norton, refused. He informed me that it was a good thing for me that I had a current elephant license to cover the shooting of this animal, or I would have been severely fined, and my hunting privileges might have been suspended.

However, all's well that ends well. Shortly after this incident happened, I received the news that I had been appointed by the Government to be an Honorary Game Warden. I could now do Game Control work without getting myself into trouble.

When it became general knowledge among the people that I had been appointed as an Honorary Game Ranger, they didn't take advantage of my appointment to bring petty reports or calls for me to come and assist them. When I got a call it was usually one of a very serious nature.

Early one morning, a messenger came with the startling message that a leopard (chui) in making a raid on a cattle corral had been frightened into the owner's house. This caused the occupants of the house to flee, and they said that in their hasty flight, they had left the baby behind inside.

"Please come at once to save our child!"

Of course, I dropped everything and left immediately, guided by the messenger. When we arrived at the house, I talked with the owner, and he sheepishly admitted that the "baby story" was just a ruse to get me to come. There was a donkey left inside and the leopard had clawed him. So, there was no baby inside, but there definitely was a leopard in there. This leopard had a long history of making the owner and his neighbors' lives miserable by his repeated raids on their manyattas.

The house in which the leopard was trapped was of typical mud and wattle wall construction. It had the usual earthen roof called "tembe." The house had some places on the walls where the adhering mud had flaked off leaving holes through to the inside. I noticed a larger hole about four inches in diameter, and decided to try to use it to see into the house. Possibly I thought, I might be able to spot the leopard who was located inside.

I very quietly crept up to the hole and put my eye to it.

Lo and behold, on the other side of the hole an eye was looking out at me - - that of the leopard.

The animal was lying prone on the floor of the hut, with its head toward me. I carefully put the barrel of my 348 Winchester rifle into the hole and tilted it downward for a shot at the rear of the animal. This was the only target I had with the limited visibility the hole offered.

I fired the gun.

The animal gave me a roar in return, but didn't move an inch. Looking closely, I saw that my bullet had gone true to its mark, breaking the leopard's spine. The animal would never move again under its own power. We went into the house then and put the animal out of its misery with a second shot.

There was a case reported at the village of Igwelambau, not far from the station, where a leopard had seized a baby from the doorway of a hut and successfully killed the infant and carried it off.

As opportunity permitted, several missionaries and their wives would go on an elephant hunt together. It provided a time for a camp-out and a chance to enjoy the pori(the bush) together as well as each other's company. On one hunt in the Yaida Swamp, we had successfully shot a big elephant not far from our camp. The Bushmen got word of our kill and with all the members of several camps, came to enjoy feasting on the elephant's meat. It was their custom to cut into the animal's leg joints which have a fluid oil lubricant in quantity. The Bushmen smear this oil on their bodies. I call this the Hadza "Jergens lotion." They were also after the most select portion of meat, the tenderloin strip that runs along the inside of the elephant's rib cage and spinal column. To get at this meant they had to crawl in through the stomach cavity and cut the meat off the bones.

As soon as an animal dies, its stomach begins to swell. Given a day or so, the size of the stomach is huge; it looks like a balloon ready to become air-born.

The Bushmen have a method, which is almost a ritual, to enable them to get inside this swollen mass of flesh. It's not easy, because the elephant's hide is so tough. One man will climb up on top of the animal which is lying on its side. Carefully wrapping his scanty clothing around himself, he raises his spear and with all his might drives it into the animal's side. An explosion follows when gas, dung, and fluid shoot out of the pierced stomach into the air in all directions. After this, the rest of the Bushmen swarm over the animal's body, in a cutting competition, to see who can be first inside and at the tenderloin. The elephant's skin is porous, and has a lot of sand in it which quickly dulls the sharpest knives.

I had warned our party about the explosion that would come, and that everyone should not talk but keep their mouths closed until the explosion's zero moment was over. One of the wives along on that trip, Helen Johnson, forgot to heed my advice. The explosion caught her talking, and she got a mouthful. She continued retching well through the night.

It seemed like every third month, as if there were a schedule, a marauding leopard would move into the Isanzu area. We were located on the fringe of the thick bush, which might have accounted for this. I became accustomed to expect a call for help at these intervals.

Isanzu had many huge boulders in the area around our location. Erosion would cause these rocks to fracture and split apart, sometimes separating only a few inches following a seam from top to bottom. Sometimes they separated a foot or more. Natural caves were found under some of these boulders. They were the ideal locations for leopards to hide in after or during their raids. The local people would chase the leopard into one of these caves, form a ring around it and then send someone to fetch me.

On one occasion I arrived to find the leopard inside a cave under a very large boulder that was fifteen feet high. A man was standing high on the top of the boulder, motioning wildly for me to come up and join him. When I scrambled to the top of this rock, he took me to a vertical fracture in it that extended down to its base. There, looking up at us was the leopard. It was an easy job to rid the community of him that time.

A number of times the leopard being chased by residents would itself climb some of the larger boulders. These were such big rocks that they would even have a path that circled their crest. One boulder in particular regularly attracted the leopards in that area as they were pursued and fled to escape to their refuge. The natives hold leopards in high respect because of their fierce cleverness. Leopards have frequently turned on and attacked the people who were driving them away from their homes, inflicting very serious wounds. Confronting a leopard was always a high risk operation and very dangerous. I had several experiences with the leopards who climbed this boulder, and would circle round and round the path on its crest until darkness set in. Then the animal would sneak down the rock and escape into the darkness. I learned to climb the boulder and, getting into a prone position on the trail, I waited for the animal. As it rounded the corner in front of me, I would shoot him. The procedure never failed because as the leopard rounded the corner and saw me, in his shock and surprise that I was there, he paused for an instant and gave me a perfectly still target.

One evening I was working in my office and Jeanne was sewing in the bedroom at the other end of the house. Our dog, a large Rhodesian Ridgeback, was outside. Jeanne heard the strange sound of alarm which the dog made. She came running into my office shouting: "Something is trying to get our dog!"

I didn't have anything in the office in the way of a gun, except my 12 gauge shotgun. I grabbed it and went quickly out the door, holding a flashlight as well.

I could hardly believe my eyes as I rounded the corner of the house. There sitting upright on its haunches was a leopard. He reminded me of the vintage Edison Victrola advertisement where a dog is poised sitting on its haunches before an old style gramophone.

Without giving it a second thought, I fired the shotgun at the leopard. A shotgun is not an adequate weapon to use for hunting leopards, but all I could think of was, "You tried to kill our dog!"

The leopard ran off into the night into the bush. We searched for him, but it was too dangerous to continue the search very far until the coming of light. The following day the animal died and he was skinned and salted immediately. Because the pellets entered the skin without leaving any marks, I still have a perfect trophy skin to remind me of the leopard that: 'tried to kill my dog'.

Hunting resulted in many benefits for us during the fourteen years we lived at Isanzu. It was beneficial for the community as well. Time and space will not permit me to tell of some of the other control work which I did with wart hog, baboons, snakes and elephants which posed a perennial threat to the food and safety of the local people. Missionaries are always happy when they can join with the people in the area in which they serve in a common cause. Protection of life and livelihood provide a chance to witness in love by deed as well as by The Word.

First Term Ends

CHAPTER 11

"So teach us to number our days,
that we may get us a heart of
wisdom." Ps. 90:12

Its been said that new missionaries take the whole of their first term to be able to learn to speak the language of the area in which they serve. This may be an exaggeration, but it isn't far from the truth. One never stops learning to speak a language, but you should feel rather comfortable in expressing yourself in the language of the area you are serving after four years of residence there.

By the end of four years you also should have decided whether you are in the right area of the world to serve the Lord as an overseas worker, and whether you have the ability to adjust to living in a different cultural setting. Some people seem unable to make such an adjustment. Then too there was the concern of how the family could tolerate the diseases in the area in which you served. Our family had serious cases of malaria. Jeanne almost died from it during one illness. I well remember kneeling at her bed with Pastor Paulo, my colleague, as we implored the Lord to spare her life. She was in an extremely serious condition. The Lord in His mercy answered our prayers and she regained her health. I was so full of malarial parasites that I had an attack of the disease every third month while I was in the U. S. on furlough.

Our first term had been almost consumed in constructing buildings. We had built and maintained school buildings, dispensary buildings and put up bush school structures, as well as remodeling our house. Many times I felt much more like a truck driver or a builder than a pastor. I had gotten satisfaction from doing these jobs, but I felt this should have had second priority and place in my work as an evangelist, and not become number one. I had just about come to the conclusion at the end of our first term that I simply couldn't put up with another term of "building." As I prayed about this, it occurred to me to ask that we be assigned **FULL TIME,** upon our return from furlough, to do itinerant evangelism among the migrant and nomadic tribes whose areas bordered our Isanzu area to the north and west. The Wakindiga, a small nomadic tribe of hunters and collectors were first on our list. Then the Wasukuma in the vast area to the west were worthy of any effort we could invest in getting the Gospel out to them. There were also the Wambulu living in the highlands to the north, who were farmers and who made their homes by digging caves into the hillsides. They were experts in very steep hillside cultivation. The Wataturu, a cattle herding tribe, lived in both Iramba and Sukumaland. They as well were unreached. We laid out our proposal before the Mission: **"Itinerant Evangelism -- full time."** They concurred to allow us to return after a year's furlough to fill this position as an assignment. The African Church also called us to this work which they called **"Doria"** -- wandering evangelism.

In the first four years of our service on the field, it had been made very clear to me that our field which was approximately 100 miles wide and 300 miles long was wasting a great amount of time for lack of communications. I remember a time when I had a very urgent message for Rev. Howard Olson who lived at Ihanja station, about 90 miles away to the south and west from Isanzu. I climbed on my motorcycle and rode hard for a full half day to deliver my message, and then rode hard again to return home before dark. It didn't take genius to point out the need for an inter-station radio network. I was a radio amateur operator although I wasn't allowed operating privileges at that time in Tanganyika. This interest however made the lack of communications especially galling to me. Before we went on furlough I presented an inter-station radio network as a project for endorsement by the Mission. There were some on the field who simply couldn't agree that this was a priority. Their reasoning was that the "Winds of Change" of nationalism were blowing strongly all over Africa in 1958. Therefore, the work we were doing as missionaries might soon be a thing of the past. It was their idea to continue struggling along as they had done previously. A vote of the Mission was taken, and those who favored installation of a radio communication network endorsed and passed this as a project. I was allowed to go to the U. S. with the mandate to purchase equipment and spares and ship them out to the field. I was overjoyed.

We packed up our barrels of belongings as the field directed in preparation for furlough: some labeled to contain items to be sold in the event we couldn't return, others to be shipped home to us. One is never completely certain that health wise, you can look forward to a succeeding term until physicals are completed during furlough.

Then with our young family of four children we left Tanganyika and traveled to Nairobi in Kenya. There we boarded the B.O.A.C. (British Overseas Airways Corp.) flight to London. How different this was to be from our trip out four years ago on board the Warwick Castle.

This was our first visit to Nairobi, a city we had heard so much about. We felt like country bumpkins walking down Nairobi streets. Our Chevy pickup truck had faulty brakes, but I got around the city well because I was used to controlling the vehicle by shifting into low gear to stop. When I turned the truck over to Missionary Della Brown to drive it back to the field, she had the experience of not being able to stop, and ran into a police barricade at Longido.

As we journeyed home, we had the very wonderful experience of being accompanied by a national. This co-worker, whose name was Rev. Zephania Gunda, was on his way to study at the Lutheran Bible Institute in Seattle, Washington. He kept his large black Bible visible -- it was like his shield as he made his first trip out of Africa.

Now was the time for assessments. How successful had we been during our first term? Had we truly been able to communicate Christ's love in our witness on the field? We were certain that we now belonged to a family -- the Mission Family -- a relationship that is so wonderful and binding but defies explanation. Jeanne had endured a great deal of loneliness which went along with living at an outpost mission station. In spite of all this, I don't think either of us seriously considered resigning as missionaries. It was truly **the life** we knew the Lord had called us to live.

Finally, we were returning to America recounting the Lord's many mercies with which He had blessed us over the last four years. His gift of a return to health after illness among family members was high on our list.

We had come to know and love many new people in our lives, missionary as well as African co-workers: Pastor Paulo Mkali, Evangelist Nalingigwa Mpya, Orgenes Manya, and Justino Nzugika, to name but a very few. All had added so much to our lives. Our children also had their special friends as well: Abeli, Lameki, Loti, and many others.

We praised God for the thrill of the new kinds of service in which He had placed us. Now, at furlough time, we would be allowed to return to our homeland, and share with our friends and indeed the whole Church that had sent us out and supported us, what work the Lord had provided us to do and blessed us and it as we carried it out.

We had arrived in Africa in 1954 when the Lord gave us the promise: "The lines are fallen unto me in pleasant places; yea I have a goodly heritage" Ps. 16:6. Now we returned with rejoicing and exalting hearts with a new message on our lips -- one we felt with even greater urgency: "And the Gospel must first be published." Mk. 13:10

Furlough

CHAPTER 12

"Who has believed our message
and to whom has the arm of the
Lord been revealed?"
Isa. 53:1 NIV

Four years pass by very quickly when you are busy in your work. The first departure from the field is probably almost as memorable as that time which is called your terminal departure, when you leave the field for the last time. The excitement of anticipated reunions with family and loved ones and of your many faithful prayer and financial supporters is nothing short of wonderful.

The time begins with a stopover in the city where Mission Headquarters is located -- in our case it was Minneapolis. Dr. Herb Johnson, who was the Mission's medical director, and his staff gave thorough medical exams to each member of the family. We also had many friends to see in the Twin Cities area where we had interned just six years before. Then we visited Jeanne's mother, her sister and brother and their families in Minnesota.

From those visits, we flew to Portland, Oregon, where my parents eagerly awaited our arrival. When we left them four years before, we had two children. Now we returned with four, two they had never seen except in photographs. We rented a house in Portland and got the school aged kids enrolled in their schools.

I registered for graduate work in anthropology at the University of Oregon located at Eugene, Oregon -- all in quick succession. Then I attended a Pastoral conference held by the Columbia Conference of the Augustana Lutheran Church at a retreat center called Menucha. I gave a missions slide presentation which I had prepared concerning the work we had done on the field during the previous four years. This presentation was given before all the pastors of the Synod who attended the conference.

At the close of the presentation, the pastors filled in my calendar's dates, week after week, so that I could come to their churches for a visit to present missions. This gave me an opportunity to visit the states of Washington, Oregon, Montana, Idaho and Utah. I requested a full day at each place, generally scheduled on a Sunday. I would begin by preaching at the morning worship services, then holding sessions for the Sunday School and finished up with an evening slide presentation which usually followed a potluck supper at the church. When it was possible, Jeanne and the family accompanied me. She took over the Sunday School sessions, and the family would often sing together in Swahili at the worship services.

When deputation entailed long distance travel away from Portland, as it did the first six weeks into the new year of that furlough, sessions were planned right through the week. People in the churches were, without exception, warmly receptive and deeply interested in the report of what we, who were their missionaries, had come to tell them about one of the areas of their outreach work overseas. They had supported this work with their gifts and now they were given a report about how their gifts were being utilized. Many people in the churches came with questions about how they might support us more effectively. The emphasis was always on our corporate partnership in the Lord's outreach overseas. It is extremely important for churches to have regular visits from workers in from the field.

A furlough allowed time for our children to experience life and culture in the United States. This was important for their education and development. Because I was gone so much of this period, it made heavy demands upon Jeanne to be both **mother and father** to the family while I was away.

Our younger children sometimes had a difficult time in their new setting away from the freedom of Africa. Once our daughter Kathy, who was a three year old, shocked her mother when after a walk about the neighborhood, she came home with a hat full of fresh tulip blossoms plucked from someone's yard. Another time she followed the older children to their school and was found walking around the halls. The authorities at the school had no idea who she was so they asked the police to help locate her home. When the police queried her about where she lived, she responded, "Africa."

Furlough is not a time of vacation for missionaries. The stresses and upset of moving, making new friends for the family, and the heavy deputation schedule, make the return to the field more and more desirable as the year wears on. When that return takes place the kids get together with their

African playmates -- Abeli and Lameki, and others, and talk for hours about all they have experienced on their visit to America. Please understand, missionary kids are not American kids, nor are they African -- they are somewhere in the middle culturally. The place where they feel most at home is with their peers -- the sons and daughters of other missionaries. This is a bond that lasts for the rest of their lives.

Because our children are the products of two cultures, sometimes the contradiction of language is amusing. We experienced these language problems even as adult missionaries learning a new language.

One pastor tells about how he was preaching a sermon on the coming of Christ taken from the account in the book of Isaiah, where Isaiah states: "Behold a virgin shall conceive and bear a son..." The word for teapot and the word for virgin in the Swahili language is very close: **Virgin** is the word **Bikira**, and teapot is the word **Birika**. The pastor preached a whole sermon repeatedly using the incorrect word, but his African congregation was very gracious in not laughing openly at his mistake. Another time a missionary greeted the local chief and mixed up the word for chief, **Jumbe**, and the word for hoe, **Jembe**. Our kids talked of **Collie** dogs with wonder. People here in America assume that everyone knows what a **Collie** dog is. In Swahili however, **kali**, which is pronounced the same as Collie, means fierce and dangerous. It may mean any animal, or even a human. The kids really came apart when they saw the **TACO** resturants. **TAKO** is the Swahili word for buttocks.

Once, one of the children's uncles wanted to be 'African' and give them a true African welcome greeting. He approached them saying: JAMBA, JAMBA. He couldn't understand why the kids were overcome with laughter. He should have said: JAMBO, JAMBO, which means "hello" in Swahili. JAMBA means to pass flatus.

On the field in Africa all adult male missionaries are called Uncle by all children unless that missionary is your father. All adult female missionaries are called Auntie. It wasn't hard to understand then, when we came on furlough, that Dan my son, repeatedly called my father: "Uncle Grandpa."

If our first term went by quickly, furlough went by at top speed and we were soon headed back to Tanganyika again. I had only three weekends to spend with my family during that year. All the rest of the time I was either at the University or traveling on deputation. This turned out to be the usual schedule with each succeeding furlough as well. I know the grandparents experienced a lot of sadness in seeing us return to our work on the field. But they gave us into the Lord's hands, knowing we had been called to His service in that place so far away from them.

OUR FAMILY GROWING UP
1963
L-R: Kristine, Joel,
Dad and Mom,
Heidi, Daniel
and Kathryn

Interstation Radio Communications

CHAPTER 13

"Call unto me, and I will answer thee,
and will show thee great things, and
and difficult, which thou knowest not."
                    Jer. 33:3

"A-L-M TWO - QUEEN ROGER KING - - TWO . . . QUEEN ROGER KING?"

"Does anyone know if TWO is on safari?" "TWO - TWO -....."

The control station of our 14 station radio network was taking roll call using procedural signals/words to expedite handling traffic, which saves a lot of time. QUEEN ROGER KING in radio parlance are the phonetic words for the letters Q R K, and these letters stand for the query, how are you receiving me and my transmission. The reply was QUEEN ROGER UNCLE (I HAVE TRAFFIC FOR) and the station numbers were given, or QUEEN ROGER UNCLE - NEGATIVE (I HAVE NO TRAFFIC).

A-L-M ONE was the control station located in the town of Singida (Kitatimu), where lived Dean Buchanan, our business manager, and his wife Marilyn, who was our net control.

In calling A-L-M TWO, Marilyn Buchanan was asking the station at Barabaig, where the Harold Fausts lived, to respond with a Q-R-U affirmative or negative. Marilyn began calling each station at 7:00 AM each morning. The same opportunity for exchanging message traffic was available at 7:00 P.M. each evening. For medical help, both hospitals on the field, Kiomboi and Iambi, monitored the frequency at 1:30 P.M. every day for incoming medical traffic. The air waves were available for our use twenty-four hours a day. We were licensed on the frequency of 33.54 Megacycles. But since the radios were powered by station light plants, our operating time was limited to the AM/PM schedule except by special individual station agreement.

When Marilyn completed the role call, she signed off all stations that had neither incoming nor outgoing messages. Then she systematically directed the stations having messages to proceed with their traffic, one station at a time. The net operated in the Very High frequency band. This meant that every station could reach every other station in the network directly (line of sight), or in a very few cases by using one relay through another station. Because these were FM sets, even during the heaviest rain storms, communication was unaffected by the weather.

In 1959, during our first furlough I went to Lynchburg, Virginia, to the General Electric factory. Mr. Warren C. Light was the G.E. co-ordinator to make our field net dream become a reality. We received fourteen 100 watt transceivers that were re-conditioned new/used equipment. We learned that many state police units in the U. S. used this same equipment. We also were supplied a C. S. K.(Critical Service Kit) that had a very complete inventory of all the electrical and mechanical parts for any replacement repairs that would be necessary on the field. This, together with 14 omni-directional vertical antennas and one hundred feet of coaxial cable for each antenna, completed our supply that the General Electric Company shipped out to the field in Tanganyika.

I went to school during that week in Lynchburg. Building on my past study of electronics, I was given a complete orientation at the G. E. Factory on servicing and trouble shooting the new equipment. I was also given suggestions about the service meters and equipment I should get for analysis and alignment of the sets. I purchased a number of test instrument kits from a company called Heathkit. These had to be constructed and assembled. I did as much of this as time would allow before we returned to Africa, and finished this work after our return to the field.

These kits included: a vacuum tube voltmeter, capacator/ resistance bridge, a scope, a tube tester, a grid-dip meter and a watt output/standing wave ratio meter. We now had all the necessary equipment to set up and maintain our inter-station net, except for one very important item, antenna towers. We wanted our omni-directional antennas to be elevated at least sixty feet off the ground.

In the area where our field was located, an Italian family was involved in a gold mining operation. Mr. Bicchieri was the owner of a gold mine at a location called Sekenke. His family lived at a place called Kirondatal, located close to our Kiomboi station. I had a close friendship with Mr. Bicchieri's two adult sons, Marco and Mickey. Mr. Bicchieri, using six inch, four inch and two inch pipes from his gold mine supply, bolted these pipes together, and fashioned masts that were about sixty feet in length. We fitted them with two sets of guy wires. Then they were based in between two 2 X 6 inch wooden posts. The wood itself was embedded in a 4 X 4 X 4 foot block of concrete which we poured at each location. Mr. Bicchieri seemed to have an inexhaustible supply of used pipe stock to meet our needs.

The installation at the 13 station locations was a very big job that fell almost completely to Justino Nzugika, my African co-worker and to myself. We traveled around, arranged the delivery of the antenna poles, dug the pits for the concrete bases and the guy wire ties, mixed and poured the concrete with the wooden posts in place. We then were able to raise the sixty foot pole after we mounted the antenna to it at its top end.

After we installed the guy wires one-third and two-thirds of the way up the pole, we attached one of the guys from the one-third level to my short wheel base Land Rover. The car provided the motive power to pull the pipe into its vertical position. We always back-tied the poles being raised with the opposing set of guy wires in the opposite direction so that the antenna mast would not be able to come past its vertical position and then fall on the car which was pulling it up. We had only one near accident in all the raisings of the poles, but the guy held!

As the network became established, it proved to be a tremendous boon to the work of everyone on the field. The only real problem we had was when someone on the net used too much time for general conversation while the rest of us were waiting for our turn to pass traffic. This was soon sorted out by some pointed remarks by Net control who did a very good job in the role of Net policeman. The network saved many lives of our church members by getting medical counsel from the hospitals and field doctors. We had no postal service, of course, on the field. Arranging meetings, which before had to be done months in advance, or by sending a runner on foot, was now made possible immediately by radio.

I remember when our missionary co-worker, Rev. Douglas Lindell, who was located at Ihanja in the southern area of our field was reported on the net in the morning as having a very severe headache. Dr. Joe Norquist at Kiomboi was informed and gave some medical advice to Ihanja. Some of us came on that noon to learn that Doug had died of what appeared to be a cerebral hemorrhage. The radio had not been able to save Doug, but we all knew about our loss the same day.

Our daughter Heidi was very ill with measles that would not advance to the breaking-out point. Although the Nduluma river was in flood stage, the Doctors at Kiomboi advised us to bring her there. We feared the over 100 mile trip would be very dangerous in her condition. So we as a family gathered around our Christmas tree in prayer and felt led not to go. We received frequent advice from Kiomboi as they monitored her condition throughout the day. Jeanne, who was a registered nurse, was able to provide the care at Isanzu that advanced Heidi into the next stage of the disease. What a great source of help and encouragement the radio contact had been to us at that critical time.

Many of our African friends would get reports by word of mouth that a relative a long distance off was dead or dying. In Africa, this meant that you would drop everything, and travel sometimes for long distances by foot in dangerous country, often after dark, so that you could respond to what often might be only a rumor. They would bring a request to us to inquire into the report they had received. Sometimes this would involve sending a runner out from a distant station to an even more distant location. In almost all these cases we could check out the report within a day or so.

How gratifying it was for a wife at a remote station, whose husband had not returned from a safari, to learn on the evening broadcast net that he had been delayed and she should not worry, that he was not somewhere enroute stuck with car trouble.

Every third month I toured the field's stations and checked out the performance of the radios and rarely had to make anything except minor adjustments. Given this maintenance, the units gave us practically trouble free operation. When a station lost its volume, generally it was because the ground wire to the microphone had been broken off.

We had one mobile set that was mounted in my vehicle. It was a great aid in servicing other sets. It was also very useful to us in our itinerant safari work. We were often in the middle of the bush doing our work and could use our car during the dry season. With our radio, we weren't cut off from the rest of the field, and it was always nice to have in the event of an emergency. We are grateful that we, in all our travels never had need to use it for this.

I left the Iramba/Turu field for other work in 1969. Later in 1977 I returned to the field in answer to a request from Rev. Zephania Gunda, President of the Central Synod, to check out all the sets which were still in operation. They had been in use for almost twenty years and had paid for themselves many, many times over.

Our missionary neighbors to the northeast, the Norwegian Lutheran Mission at Haydom, also asked for my help in setting up a radio network between their hospital and their other stations. We didn't have special antennas for their sets, so we just used half wave dipoles -- a long wire cut to the frequency they were using and fed at the middle of this wire. We installed the equipment and the antenna masts at a station called Kansai, where the nurse serving the area was by herself and frequently urgently needed the contact with Haydom Hospital and Doctor Olsen there.

After we completed our installation, we returned to Haydom Hospital and waited eagerly to hear how our antenna would work. However, the time for radio call came that evening and went by without a sound coming out of Kansai. The next day the nurse from Kansai brought an emergency case to the hospital. Dr. Olsen and I were very anxious to learn about why Kansai hadn't been on frequency. We asked the young nurse what had gone wrong. She replied:

"I didn't try to use the radio because I didn't think it could understand Norwegian."

I mused later that the radio was very quick to pick up a new language because I heard the nurse at Kansai use it speaking Norwegian that very evening to Dr. Olsen. I held that young Norwegian nurse in special regard as she gave her life to Christ serving Him at a lonely place.

The Barabaig

CHAPTER 14

"...to many peoples of a
strange speech and of a hard
language, whose words thou canst
not understand. Surely, if I sent
thee to them, they would harken unto
thee."   Ezek. 3:6

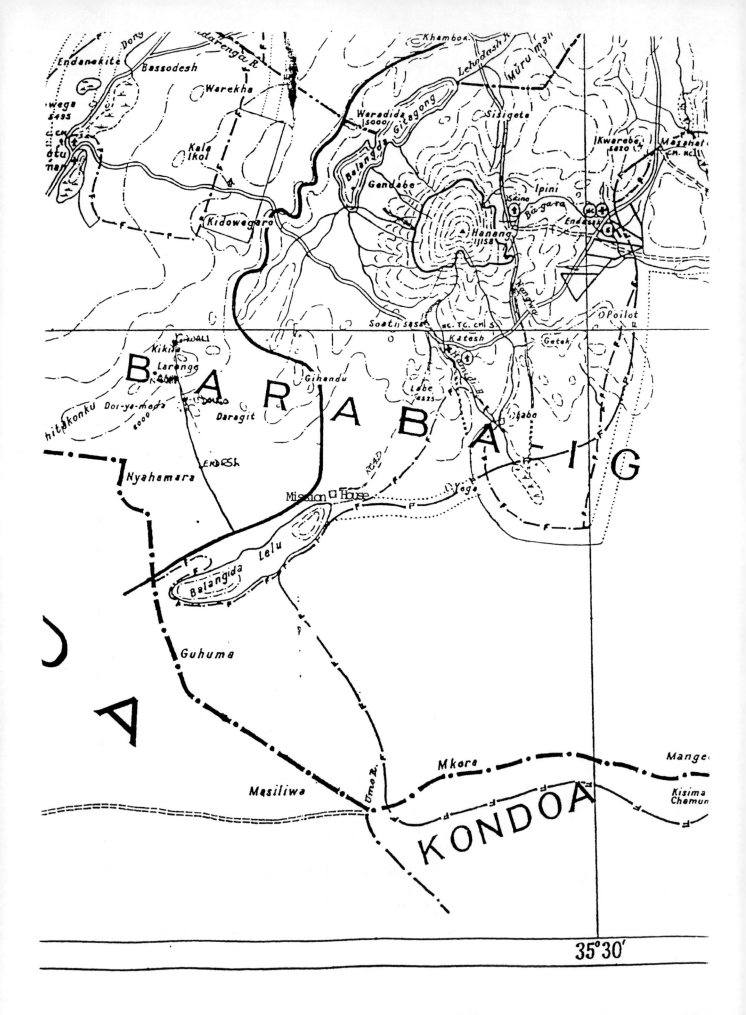

"Yesu - Agabarinyesha muuch"

("Jesus loves us very much" - Barabaig Language)

We returned to Tanganyika in 1959 looking forward to beginning our new work called Itinerant Evangelism. But this was not going to take place yet. Instead we were told that Rev. Harold Faust and his wife Louise, were going to go on furlough. It was important that the brand new work they had begun in the Katesh area at Balangida Lelu among the Barabaig tribe not lose its forward momentum. So we were asked to take over the work among the Barabaig and live at the new station, a place called Gitagababoi by the people. It was on the shore of Lake Balangida. This lake dried up for a portion of the year and became a dry mud flat upon which you could drive. It reminded me of the Great Salt Lake flats in Utah.

The Barabaig were a tribe of people who proved to be very difficult neighbors for the other tribes living on their borders. Like the Maasai tribe, the Barabaig believed that God had created them and then He created cows. He had given them the right to all the cows He had created. Therefore they were within their right to take cows from any other people who had them. A second name for the Barabaig was "Ma'ngati" -- the Maasai name which means "thief".

Living in Barabaig country was plainly "at risk" living.

Each Barabaig elder routinely carried a bundle of staffs. The number he carried with him indicated the number of people he had killed. If you went on safari in this country and slept overnight, you would be safe as long as you stayed within the circle of thorns that made up an owner's manyatta or corral. Otherwise you would become fair game for a Ma'ngati's foul play. I heard reports of several youthful foreign travelers walking through this area who disappeared and were never heard from again.

It had taken a lot of courage and love for Hal and Louise, who was a nurse, to open up this new mission area. Everything seemed to be against beginning this new project. Water -- a matter of key importance -- was very hard to find in this whole area. Apparently the granite under the whole countryside was fractured and cracked to a great depth and would not hold water to provide a supply for wells. Mr. Holmes, a well driller employed by the Mission, after sinking nine holes to reach a water table, finally gave up in despair. There was an artesian spring just below Gitagababoi. It was heavy with minerals, so much so that if you drank from it and it alone, your system could handle it. But as soon as you left the area and drank other water you could expect several days of stomach cramps.

At the time the Mission was seeking the registration of the plot for mission work and ownership, the British Colonial authorities were exercising a heavy hand over a local Tanganyika school teacher whose name was Julius Nyerere and his political organization called TANU. The authorities made registration of the new Barabaig station contingent upon our Mission not allowing our teachers to become involved in TANU.

In spite of all these hindrances, Hal and Louise went ahead, refusing to take "no" as an answer. They built a beautiful house on a knoll adjacent to the lake. They installed a hydraulic ram, the closest thing I have ever seen to perpetual motion, to pump water from the spring up the hill to the location of the house. The principle involved in a hydraulic ram is the utilization of water pressure generated in the ram by a small fall in the elevation of the water coming into it. Then an internal spring fires again and again, like a mousetrap, to provide the rest of the energy for the ram's work of pumping water. The amount of the flow out of the ram is conditional upon the force of the fall of the water coming into the ram and the ram's physical size. Long term operation is guaranteed as long as the operator of the ram cleans the screens through which the incoming water flows, and also replaces the diaphragms in the unit periodically.

Stories are told about the eagerness the Fausts had to take up living in their new house before construction was completed. One morning they awakened to find a visitor in their bedroom scanning them from the foot of their bed. While we lived there, people often were seen peering into the windows. When we first arrived, before we learned to lock the doors, tribesmen and women would often just walk in unannounced, even though this was culturally unacceptable in their own homes.

We allowed the folks free reign into the house until one day I caught a small child using our kitchen as a toilet. Then we drew a line of separation.

We had many wonderful experiences during the year we lived at Barabaig. This nomadic cattle herding tribe had a culture that was very brittle and had a high resistance to change. But because of some very able diplomatic work by Hal and Louise, the tribe had allowed the Mission an entrance into their heartland.

At the time prior to our year of service in Barabaig, something happened between the Barabaig and their neighbors to the southeast. These neighbors, called the Wasandawe, were always important to the Barabaig because the Sandawe were a hunting and collecting tribe who supplied the Barabaig with a great amount of the honey. The Sandawe were very capable bee keepers as are all those in hunting and collecting cultures. The Barabaig used a lot of honey in their making of beer, and in their social contracts between each other as well. For some reason, the Barabaig had become angry with the Sandawe living on their border. The Barabaig made raids on them, driving them out of a large section of Sandawe tribal area. The Sandawe had fled in terror, rightfully fearing for their lives.

They had left their famous hives hanging in the trees because they had no time to recover and move them to other safer locations. We made a trip into this area together with some of our workers who were from the Turu and Iramba/Isanzu tribe. We picked up a number of these abandoned hives. The hives were large hollowed out logs, some of great size. None of them had bees or honey in them, but they represented many hours of work by the Sandawe to hollow them out. We came back from our trip and reached Balangida with a car full of hives. Eventually my share of the hives was taken to Isanzu and placed high up on huge rocks having vertical sides. These rocks made the hives safe from the threat of the honey badger and the ever present hyena.

Later, the Barabaig, possibly missing that important supply of honey from the Sandawe, recognized that peace must be restored with their very useful neighbors. This new peace was created by the Barabaig placing one of their baby children in a Sandawe home, and the Sandawe ratified this covenant by placing a Sandawe baby in a Barabaig home. The children remained in these homes as a peace symbol to both tribes.

The long slope from the house at Balangida to an area of forested lowland, was an area without trees. It was virgin territory that had never seen cultivation of any sort. During the year of our stay, I hired a tractor from the Mbulu area to come in and cultivate several acres. I then planted a large garden of sweet corn, watermelon, and many other kinds of vegetables. I had never before -- nor have I since -- had a harvest in Africa like we got that year. We had a small trailer that we pulled behind our Landrover. At harvest time we picked sweet corn and took a full trailer load to Kiomboi to our School for Missionaries' Children where it was eaten very soon.

The Barabaig often had disease and famine affect their herds. When cows became weak because of disease, it was very important to keep them on their feet. If in their weakened condition they laid down, the chance of getting them on their feet again was almost nil.

One day I was driving across Lake Balangida after it had become dry. Out of the haze on the lake I saw a Barabaig running toward me gesturing wildly. I stopped when I got close to him and listened to his plea, which was very plausible to him, impossible to me. He was asking me to put his sick cow in the back of my short wheel-base Landrover and then take it home to his manyatta. At that moment, that was the most important request in his life. I showed him that I couldn't honor his request by opening the back door of my car. There was just no space to grant his wish. He kept on pleading and I had to drive off without helping him, his urgent words falling on sympathetic but incapable ears.

Our outreach among the Barabaig was in line with what we hoped to do in our future work among the Bushmen -- going out into the country- side and meeting the people where they were, doing what they normally do.

Dan my son, was a six year old. Because he had the unfortunate birth date of December 27th, he had to delay his school entrance. So he and I went out into the countryside together. We came to a place where a number of morani -- warriors -- were holding a dance. They let us preach to them.

Them we put up our tents to spend the night. Justino my Isanzu
helper was with us. Dan and I got ready for bed after supper.
Justino then came into our tent saying, "Ushafu mno," which
was his Isanzu Swahili saying, "The greatest of filth." I
asked him what he was talking about and he warned me to keep
Dan in the tent and that I shouldn't leave it either.
Apparently, the dancers and the girls present were involved
in some orgy acts that Justino had never seen before. The
next morning two of the girls followed me around insisting
I come off into the bush with them. I told them in Swahili,
which one of them seemed to understand, that I was a missionary
from Jesus, and I only had the message of His salvation to
share with them. They were very persistent and it took me
the better part of the morning to get them to accept my emphatic
"no."

Dan and I went off on safari very often that year. One
day driving on the main road into Singida in the hills above
Balangida, we saw a snake -- a large cobra -- in the center
of the road set to strike at us as we came upon it. There
is a certain time of the year when cobras will become aggressive
challengers. As I came upon it I swerved so that my car wheel
would strike it, and then I slammed on my brakes hoping to
kill the snake by sliding the wheel over its body. In doing
this, Dan flew off the front seat and very painfully landed
squarely on top of the four-wheel-drive gear shift levers.
The fall must have really hurt him, but I didn't hear a whimper.
By the time I was able to look for the snake, it had

disappeared. It was a big one. I heard later of a case where someone had tried to kill a large snake in this manner and later in the day when they lifted the hood of their car to service it, found the snake nestled in the motor waiting for them.

Another time a close call was much too close for comfort. Dan loved to stand with his face out the open window of the car and feel the cool breeze blowing on him as we sped along. There were many thorn trees with very sharp needles along the border of the twisting and curving road going into our mission station. On this particular day, the dust on the road which was very dry was almost like sand. As I rounded a curve, the slippery dust surface threw the car into a large thorn bush. I stopped and was almost beside myself fearing that Dan's eyes had been injured. Fortunately, he only had a few facial scratches. Once again, not a whimper came from him.

The home at Balangida had a lot to boast about. It was well built, it was attractive, and it had a very nice fireplace in the living room. Sometimes during the year it was chilly enough to warrant a good roaring fire. But the wood available locally was not the best, and required a lot of coaxing to burn well -- usually by adding a bit of Kerosene. We had a small lamp which I used to pour the kerosene over the wood. Just a little was enough to serve the purpose. One night after getting the fire started I neglected to screw the wick and top back on to the small base of the lamp which was the reservoir for the kerosene. The base looked like a cup with a handle attached to it. The following morning Joel our two year old son, got up early and went to the living room. Jeanne met him coming back down the hallway and smelled kerosene. The way he was acting gave no doubt as to what had happened. She took him to his crib, and his eyes immediately began to show the effects of drinking the fluid. She got him to drink some milk hoping to make him vomit. We later learned that this was dangerous therapy. Joel lay in his crib for about an hour semi-comatose, then he stirred, vomited, and cleared his stomach. He had been in a very serious and dangerous condition until he vomited. He very easily could have died. We all praised the Lord for delivering him.

We hadn't been in residence at Balangida very long before a curious event took place. We saw a young morani come out of the forest accompanied by several young girls who were singing as they traveled along their way. The strange thing about the morani who was in the lead was that his head was snow white -- obviously covered by clabber milk or "butter". We learned by asking that the young man had done one of three things. Either he had been in on an elephant hunt and had been the first one to spear the beast, or he had been involved in a lion hunt, and it was his spear that killed the animal, or he had killed a man. In all three cases he was visiting all the manyattas he could to announce his victory. The expected response was the receipt by him of a gift from wherever he visited. Most gifts were in cows, or of something of similar value. We had no cows to give, so we tried to honor the culture

PLATE III

BARABAIG DANCERS

VICTORIOUS MORANI

PASTORS MAKALA, WARD & EVANGELIST
GIMBI WITH SOLOMONI ON SAFARI

WATER WATER EVERYWHERE
EVEN IN THE CAMERA

by a small gift of money -- a gift that was never refused. At that time in my ignorance of cultural customs, I really believed I was honoring a valiant lion hunter. I later learned that this may or may not have been the case. During our year in residence these victorious morani appeared several times.

The Barabaig had another cultural celebration replete with all kinds of practices that we were allowed to view. I took the opportunity to preach at these gatherings and my request to do so was met with a positive response from those in charge. This celebration might be called the Celebration of Death. To qualify for this great honor, you had to be a very wealthy Barabaig man, who in this life had amassed a large herd of cows. Now, with the man's passing, his cows were divided up among his children. What followed this took a lot of preparation stretched out over a number of days and weeks. It even extended into the year that followed the man's death, as his relatives cared for his grave.

There was the practice of building a grave/house out of tree limbs, sticks and the red earth mud so characteristic of the volcanic earth in that part of the country. It appeared to me to resemble a large ant hill, pointing heavenward with a large index finger. This "house" attained a height of eight or ten feet or even more. At the culmination of the ceremony, the eldest son of the deceased climbed to the top of the structure and planted a sprouting green branch on it. Honey beer and tobacco were left in the grave as well as the corpse. The tribesmen and women gathered from near and far for this ceremony and there were countless hours spent in dancing and feasting. The ceremony is called "Bun'gade," and undoubtedly provided among other things, a way of remembering and highlighting the passing of certain years.

Although we lived on the knoll which made for clear vision and observation of the approach of danger, it wasn't always foolproof protection as we learned to our dismay one evening just after sunset.

Jeanne was the first to hear the almost silent approach of the enemy -- a kind of a hissing -- scraping noise. Then the enemy appeared, SIAFU -- ARMY ANTS! They covered the concrete wall on the outside of one side of our house and came inside over the rafters, aiming directly for our kitchen and refrigerator, exercising an uncanny sense of direction. They forced their way into the frig past its door's rubber gasket. When we became aware of this invasion we set out to "return fire." I had in stock a supply of potent poison called Diazanon. We were using it to spray the huts in which our workers lived to control bugs and mosquitoes. I sprayed the wall covered with army ants, beginning from the top to the bottom. I was in enemy territory however, walking on the ants which gave them a chance to start making their way up my legs. The ants also started responding to the poison, at first one or two, then dropping off the wall in large numbers. About that time it was as if a bugle call, silent to us, had sounded "retreat." Ants turned around and formed into lines leading away from the house. Those already inside got the message and they too all beat a hasty retreat to join their comrades outside. The battle had gone on for an hour before we declared ourselves the victors. But the battle had not been without casualties. A number of the SIAFU had crawled up my legs inflicting painful bites and would only let go when I literally tore them away from my body. I have heard about some families who just moved out of their homes for a day or two because of an ant raid. The army ants then cleaned up all the edibles in the home and left as quickly as they had come. However before they left, the ants killed and ate everything living in the home: insects, roaches, mice and rats. Nothing that stayed survived.

We have been invaded by ants as we camped in our tents on safari. One night we were awakened shortly after darkness set in and had to spend the remainder of a very long night trying to sleep in our vehicle with our kids.

One evening, about supper time -- roll call time -- we discovered that our youngest, Joel, was not to be seen. Our German shepherd also was missing. We looked in all the usual places: the African workers homes in the usual play areas, still no sign of Joel. It had begun to grow dark, a darkness that always comes to East Africa at seven P.M. the year around. As the evening came down upon us, my concern graded into beginning panic. Our search now turned into a frantic quest for our little boy, and we pressed everyone around into the search. Hyenas and lions were our very close neighbors, and we knew a two year old was no match for them, even less once it became dark. This incident took place during the heavy rains, so the ground was very damp, but there were so many foot prints around our house that finding a track to follow our lost boy was impossible although we desperately tried. There was one direction going out from the house that really went nowhere. There were no houses off in that direction. The way, although there was no path, led eventually down to the shore of the lake. This area had a lot of small catchment areas that would fill with rain water. After checking out **all** the other possibilities and coming up with nothing, I decided to try that direction. I was becoming very desperate now. Just a short distance over the brow of the hill which hid this area from normally being seen, I found my son sitting knee deep in a big pool of water. He was thoroughly enjoying himself, tossing handfuls of water into the air. His companion, Rex our dog, was equally as happy, jumping into the air after the fistfuls of water. Neither of them had any idea of the fear and desperate concern they had thrust upon the rest of us. Be that as it may, we were overjoyed to return our wandering son to his dry, warm home just about the time it turned completely dark.

Our year among the Barabaig went by very quickly. I had spent a lot of my time away from the area installing radios at our other mission station locations. The time soon came when a lorry arrived to receive our things for the move back to Isanzu. This would begin the next chapter of our service -- work among the Tindiga.

Augustana School

CHAPTER 15

"Train up a child in the
way he should go,
And even when he is old
he will not depart from
it." Prov. 22:6

As I think about Augustana School, I always remember first several of the stories about the students who were returning to the school from their vacation. These stories have to do with the difficulties encountered by the students who had to travel by bus down from the northern area of Tanganyika as they returned to school.

One time, while we were serving our year at Barabaig, I got a radio message that the bus had not arrived in Singida on schedule. We were located on the stretch of the road where the bus probably was stuck. It was during the rainy season. The request was that I go and see if I could locate the bus. The road out to the main road from Barabaig was just about impassable, but I made it out through showers of mud. Then I saw what I believed to be bus tracks heading south from our turnoff, so I followed them. At the top of the escarpment I came on the bus. It was in the process of being dug out of a nasty stretch of mud. I got out of my Landrover and heard some noise off to the side of the road. Going over to investigate, I saw several of our school children from the bus sliding down a wet ant hill slope on their stomachs. When I was a kid, we used to call this doing a belly-buster, but we always used a sled with snow to slide on. About that time, the chaperon from the bus arrived and herded her charges back inside the bus. They were covered with mud.

Another time I got a radio report at Isanzu that the bus had arrived at Singida, but could not proceed to the school because of high water in one of the rivers. I was on the Singida side of the river, and I was asked to accompany the bus to the river. The bus would return, and I would be responsible for getting the students across the river and into the waiting vehicle which would come from Kiomboi. Everything went according to plan until we reached the river just past Iguguno. The water was waist deep on me and flowing swiftly. I tied a rope to the car on the other side of the river, and secured it to my car. Then we allowed the older kids to cross the stream as they grasped the rope. This went well, until it came time for the "tichies" (the little kids) to cross. Most of them had no trouble, but one of them lost his footing, and in panic let go of the rope. I was close enough to avoid what surely would have been a disaster, and caught the child as he was swept by in the current.

*   *   *   *   *   *

The Augustana Lutheran Mission in Tanganyika began by establishing work on the Iramba plateau in central Tanganyika in 1927. The missionaries who went out at that time solved the problem of educating their children in one of several ways. Some children were taught at home. Some families left their children behind in the U. S., to live with relatives or close friends in order that these children be educated in the States. No matter how this problem was resolved, it was always crucial.

There was and is no satisfactory solution if one agrees that a child's parents must serve the Lord without reservation -- many times in very remote areas. There is no sacrifice greater, to my mind, than that of sending your children off to a school where they and you must endure that separation for several months at a time. This is often, however, a necessary commitment in order to serve the Lord overseas.

Sometimes parents go out to a field and **limit** their service to where it will be possible to serve and still be near their children. This may limit their commitment of service to the Lord. On the other hand, home schooling is not always a viable answer to this need. Children are separated from their peers and do not get the stimulus of learning that a group provides. Then too, many mothers may be unqualified to successfully teach their children. The best answer may be to provide a school that will also truly be a "home away from home" for your children.

This became a concern and dream of the missionaries on the Iramba/Turu field in Tanganyika in the latter '40s. These concerned parents gave this need into the hands of a mission committee, and by November of 1951 the Mission Conference on the field approved the building of Augustana School.

Rev. Marvin Palmquist, in his unpublished autobiography -- A Personal Odyssey -- gives a complete account of his being given the responsibility of building this school. The first teacher/houseparents, Rev. & Mrs. Arthur Anderson, were already on call and arrived on the field late in 1952. The school was scheduled to open in February of 1953. Building was not finished, but the school did open on time. Like any project, this one showed, in its first year of operation, many additional needs. The original buildings provided: dormitory rooms, washrooms, a dining and fellowship hall, kitchen and utility rooms. At this point Marv advanced from being the Mission's overseer of the Indian contractor, Lachman Singh, to actually becoming the building contractor himself. This change took place in order to meet the school's needs on a very limited new building budget. This forced upon Marv a burden that was overwhelming. The school building continued, and by the time that Rev. Palmquist and his family left the field on furlough in 1956, just about all the necessary buildings were finished. This involved a new classroom building and school offices. To accomplish this, all those involved in this project led by Marv had pushed themselves to the limit. They, together with Marv, had paid the price so that in spite of grossly limited funds, our children truly now had "a home away from home." Marv and all those others who were involved had earned our unending gratitude.

Our family began to experience this benefit when we returned to the field after our first furlough in 1960. Kristine our oldest daughter, was seven years old then. She had always been very mature in her actions and life. During our furlough year in Portland Oregon she had attended first grade. Now the time had come for her to be the first of our children to attend Augustana.

Living at Barabaig meant that we lived the farthest away from the school of those who were on the Iramba/Turu field. Other students lived in the northern area of Tanganyika which involved extended travel for them. Their trips down from Arusha during the rainy season were often monumental as I have already described.

The school was located at Kiomboi station, and we made arrangements to arrive there a day early in order to drop Kris off. She was to spend the night before school opened with one of the families living at Kiomboi, the Hults.

As we reached Kiomboi, we all made a joke of how soon the time would pass, and then we could all be together again. Then we kissed Kris good-bye. As we drove off I looked back and saw a sight I shall never forget. She was standing alone by a tree in Dr. Hult's yard. She was sobbing and weeping. I wanted to stop the car and run back, take her in my arms and then carry her back to our car and take her home with us. But I couldn't do that. This was the price I had to pay for the commitment I had made to serve the Lord as a missionary. Kris was paying her part of the price of being a missionary's daughter. Each of our children had to pay this price when their time came to go off to school. But Kris was the first, and I believe it was tougher on her because of being the first who went off all by herself. I may be wrong. I know God will honor and redeem these payments and I apply His words to all who endure these separations by reading in all three of the Gospels Jesus' words: Matt. 19:29, Mk. 10:29-30, and Lk.

18:29-30

> "Jesus said: Verily I say unto you, There
> is no man that hath left house, or brethren,
> or sisters, or mother, or father, or children,
> or lands, for my sake, and for the gospel's
> sake, but he shall receive a hundredfold now in
> this time, houses, and brethren, and sisters,
> and mothers, and children, and lands, with
> persecutions; and in the world to come eternal
> life."   Mk. 10:29-30

The program at Augustana School followed the Minnesota State Board of curriculum and prepared the students to return to their homelands and compete without difficulty wherever they might live. The teaching was excellent, and the house parents were completely dedicated to being surrogate parents. The children bonded well with their peers at the school, and even now years later these former students will travel great distances to attend the weddings or reunions of their former classmates. They are lifetime members of a very extended family which includes European as well as American members, which is the literal fulfillment of the words of our Lord quoted above.

Because Augustana was a Mission School, there was a great Christian emphasis in everything that was done. The hymnal "Youth's Favorite Songs" was used at the devotional worship services which were held daily. The kids came to know this hymnal so well that when one of them quoted just the number of a song without the hymnal being at hand, everyone else knew the words and melody to sing by heart.

There were discipline and adjustment problems at the school

similar to the problems children experience when they are at home. But these problems were resolved very well by the teachers, the house parents and the students together.

Augustana school was not just the making of a better adjustment from a difficult situation; it was rather an institution that became a **home of love** and excellent instruction and nurture for our children. The students graduated at the end of the 8th grade then went elsewhere to get a high school education. Most of the Augustana School graduates attended Rift Valley Academy in Kenya.

Students attended school for three months at a time, and then returned home for a month's vacation. There was a long weekend in the middle of each term. The students living close to the school invited those who lived far away in the northern area of Tanganyika to their homes and played host with their parents to these guests. At Isanzu we set a record of 22, including several sets of parents, who came for one long weekend. What a time we used to have during these breaks. I remember the loss I felt once when I overheard one of our children remarking to a friend about the fact that they had only two days left before they went home -- Home was Augustana School!

The end-of-term events were always something very special for the parents who could attend. The school offered piano lessons for those students who wanted them. Recitals were a big part of the end-of-term activities. The school also had a choir, and one year it even made its own record of choral music. The school also had a full sports program and usually at end of the term there was competitive team play before cheering parents. Scholarships were offered as we were financially able to fund them for national students.

An institution such as Augustana School caused some nationals in positions of authority in our Church to have misgivings about its legitimacy. The national president of our Central Synod, where the school was located, was a critic of the school. These misgivings led the Mission Board in the U. S. to have doubts about the wisdom of the continuing viability of operating the school under these circumstances. This led to the closing of the school at the end of the school year in 1971. At that time there were fifty-six students enjoying this facility. One of the justifications for closing the school was that there was a diminishing number of missionaries in service, and it would be expensive to carry on with our school. However, Rift Valley Academy in Kenya, where we were compelled now to send all our children following Augustana's closure, continued to have burgeoning enrollment problems with a great increase in its number of students. I was chairman of the Augustana School board at this time and to me the closing of the school was a disaster.

Augustana closed at the end of the school year in 1971. It had served us faithfully and with excellence for 18 years. May God richly bless all those who had a part in it.

The Missionary Affair

CHAPTER 16

"Yea, and all that will live godly
in Christ Jesus shall suffer per-
secution." II Tim. 3:12   K.J.V.

It was drawing close to the end of November in 1964. Several of us from the field had gone to Dar Es Salaam on a shopping/supply trip. We were all in a rush because it was so close to Thanksgiving, a holiday we celebrated even though we were far from the U. S. We wanted to return to Kiomboi station where the Augustana school was located. There we would pick up our children and take them home for their Thanksgiving vacation. So on the day we finished our various tasks in Dar, we planned to set off as early as possible the following morning. Our two Landrovers were filled with our purchases, some of which would enhance the beauty and comfort of our up-country homes: new linoleum for the kitchen, lots of wholesale canned goods, and many other items.

We set off from Dar at once the next day, after finishing breakfast. Jeanne and I drove up in our car. Rolly Renner, our field agriculturalist, his wife, Marjorie and Jon, the son of Dr. Stanley Moris, all rode in the other car. Jon, a doctoral student, was out from the States doing work on his thesis.

I had made certain the previous day before our departure, that the spare "jerry can" of gas that I routinely carried on safari was full of gas. I had not talked with Rolly about what he had as a reserve. It was close to 260 miles from Dar

to Dodoma, our destination for that day's travel. This was
beyond the range of the fuel capacity or our Landrovers.
So a 'jerry can' filled with gas was an important item to have
along. I assumed that Rolly was also carrying a reserve supply.
We drove through the morning maintaining a distance apart from
each other because of the dusty road. Around midday, Rolly
pulled to a stop on the road ahead. We stopped as well when
we came up to his car. He told us that he hadn't brought along
his reserve can, so he didn't have enough fuel to reach Dodoma.
He asked if I was carrying my spare supply. I replied that
I was, but I didn't think it had enough fuel in it to enable
both cars to reach Dodoma.

Rolly had a solution to the problem. Just ahead a few
miles off the main road, there was a small town called Kongwa.
He had visited the town several times in connection with his
work. We were very near to a short cut road that would take
us to the town. I agreed to follow him in just in case his
fuel ran out before he reached the town.

We turned off the main road on to an unmarked track.
We were later told that a warning sign had been posted at
this entrance which prohibited travelers its use. We later
showed the authorities that there was no sign of warning posted.
This road had two entrances, the one which we entered coming
from Dar, and another which entered coming from Dodoma. The
Dodoma entrance was posted, the Dar entrance was not.

We could see the village of Kongwa on a hillside some
miles away as we traveled down the track. We were glad that

our side trip would be a short one. But we hadn't driven in but a short distance from the main road when we came to a pile of logs blocking our way. To the left of the road, in the pori appeared to be some sort of camp with several temporary buildings.

As we stopped, we were immediately surrounded by a group of young men dressed in what appeared to be military fatigue clothing. They demanded that we all get out of our cars: "AT ONCE" (MARA MOJA)! They didn't have a gun among them, but had sticks that resembled weapons. We got out, one by one, and began to ask what this was all about. We said again and again that we just wanted to carry on to Kongwa. Apparently we had stumbled on to a Frelimo Freedom Fighters training camp. The men in the camp were insurgents being trained by Chinese instructors to overthrow the Mozambique government. There were supposed to be Chinese personnel inside the camp training these recruits, but we did not see anyone except the youths who surrounded us like a swarm of bees, and who seemed to be getting more excited with each passing moment. After repeated attempts to explain ourselves out of this situation, we were unceremoniously loaded on a Chinese flat-bed truck and taken to Kongwa.

At the village of Kongwa we were individually interrogated. Jon had a camera slung around his neck which he was carrying because it was so fragile. It had a large telephoto lens attached. This was viewed as an implement for spying. In our car I had a transceiver used as a mobile set on our field inter-station V.H.F. radio net. This as well indicated to our interrogators that we were spies. Those questioning us became very impatient with us because we wouldn't confess our guilt.

After they had passed their hands a countless number of times through Jon's blond hair -- I still don't know what they hoped to find there -- they decided to drive us on to Dodoma under guard. We arrived in that city very late at night, and were taken to the Police Station and shown to the second floor. The Regional Police Commander apologized to us. He said that the cells in his jail were in a very untidy condition. He therefore would lock us up on the second floor of the station, which had no beds or facilities. The police officers brought in curry and rice for us to eat. We also had a generous supply of armed police guards at all the doors. So we settled down on the floor to sleep, or tried to sleep on chairs.

The next morning, Rolly and I were taken to our cars in the police garage. The cars had been stripped of all their contents. These things were laid out in display on the garage floor. We were asked to show the police any secret compartments in our vehicles. Since we weren't able to do that, we were returned to join the rest of the group on the second floor of the Station.

Then we were taken from the Police Station to Mr. Mwakagali, the District Commissioner, for individual interrogation. He was the first national to be appointed to this rank in Tanganyika. We were ushered into his office, one by one. I took note of his surly attitude and stood before his desk until he said, "Sit down!"

Jeanne was taken in after I had left, and made the mistake of leaning her elbow on the District Commissioner's desk while he was questioning her. He blew up: "Blatant disrespect" he shouted at her. "Never before has anyone shown me such a lack of respect."

Restraining tears, Jeanne apologized, saying that she was simply exhausted from the previous day's trip and from not having slept the past night.

We were taken back to the second floor of the police station. Later that day, Mr. Mwakagali came to the police station and announced to us:

"You are all lying. By law, you are in the custody and under the authority of the Police until tomorrow. Then you will become my prisoners. At that time I am going to get the truth out of you."

The C.M.S. -- the Church Mission Society's office in Dodoma -- had gotten word of our arrest. Canon Ron Taylor came in the late afternoon of that first day we spent locked up in Dodoma. He brought food and blankets and pillows for our use. He apologized that they had no camp cots available to loan us. We were very grateful for this first outside contact and their kindness in providing what they had for us. The second night at Dodoma, we were still sleeping on the floor, but at least we had blankets and pillows to make a good night's sleep possible.

Very early the next morning, the Regional Police Commander appeared. He said:

"Get up quickly -- we don't have time for breakfast. I am taking you on my authority back to Dar Es Salaam. I must get you away from this D. C., the man is a maniac, he's crazy"

We were later told that the D. C. was a very resolute Communist, and ideologically much farther "left" than Tanganyika's new socialist government.

We were rushed to our cars that had been reloaded with all our things. Police drivers were supplied. The cars had been filled with gas, presumably with the idea of proving whether or not with our size gas tanks we could drive straight through to Dar without running out of gas. If the cars could make it without refueling, our statement that we needed gas from Kongwa would be proven false.

I remember two impressions I had as we drove back to Dar through the hills and valleys on our way. Always before, this country I loved, had seemed to smile back at me as I passed through it. Now it seemed to be hostile.

The second impression was to want to strike out at the fact that I wasn't "suffering all this" because of obviously doing the Lord's work, I was just a seeming victim of circumstances.

As we drove on, I noted the driver pushing in the clutch of our car as we coasted down the lengthy hillside descents. I complained to the Police Commander who was riding in our car. This tactic would use far less fuel than we had had to use coming upcountry. The practice was stopped by the Commander's order to the driver.

We drove onwards and some distance before reaching Dar, both cars ran out of gas.

When we arrived in Dar we were taken to the Central Police Station, which was popularly called The Tank because of its concrete walls. We were booked in and placed in cells in solitary confinement. The Provincial Police Commander from Dodoma announced in a loud voice as we were being put inside, that he was certain we were innocent of any wrong-doing.

I did not get his name so that I could have thanked him later for all he did for us, which I regret.

Our watches, belts, glasses, and shoes were taken from us. Jeanne and Marge were placed together in a cell with a very young national girl.

The Administrative Officer from the American Embassy appeared while we were being processed, but he was not allowed to come near to us, nor to ask us any questions. The reason given for this was that the Officer in Charge of the Central Police Station was absent.

"All right," he shouted loudly enough so that we could hear him, "but I'm coming back this evening, and at that time **I will talk with these people!**"

The cells were filthy and had an overpowering smell of human feces and urine. We were given a blanket, but the cells had no beds or toilets. We were taken to the common Asian type toilet upon request.

Rolly was very near-sighted and couldn't see me when he and I both looked out of our cell doors. I could see him, but was not allowed to communicate with him by voice.

Food was brought in for us to eat individually in our cells.

As the evening wore on and it became quite late, the Administrative Officer from the U. S. Embassy came again. The Embassy had been alerted by our friends in the C.M.S. at Dodoma about what was going on. This time, we were all allowed to meet with him together.

He said very apologetically, "I'm sorry I can't get you out of here tonight. They insist that the Commander of the Central Police Station is out of town, and no one else can give permission for your release. But I will get you released tomorrow. Will that be all right? Can you put up with a night in here?"

We were very encouraged by his words. We agreed that we could survive another night in detention. We were then returned to our cells.

I tried to get some sleep. By this time I felt like I was walking in a daze. I was exhausted both physically and emotionally. But about every half hour, a police officer appeared at my cell door, all through the night, and awakened me by shouting, "Are you all right?"

He would not leave until I replied, "Yes, I'm all right."

So there was no sleep allowed that night!

The next day, about mid-morning, the police officials

came in a big rush.

"Come out, you are all released" they said.

There was a problem even they hadn't anticipated in setting us free. The cell door of the cell which held Jon Moris refused to open when it was unlocked. The wardens told Jon, "Kick the door open!"

Jon tried -- too hard -- because without having his shoes on, he hurt his foot. The door finally opened and he joined the rest of our party.

As we assembled in the central hall of the police station, we were given this ultimatum by the authorities. "The World Press reporters are waiting outside the Station's front door. Leave by it and talk with them and then go home and pack to leave Tanganyika, because all your residence permits will be canceled. However, if you choose to leave the Station by the rear door and keep your mouths shut, then you can go back to your stations and your work."

We as a group chose the latter course.

It was several blocks from the Central Police Station to the American Embassy. As we walked those blocks the press corps followed us like a pack of hounds.

"Why are you afraid to tell us what happened?"

"Are you guilty of spying for the C.I.A.?"

"Tell us the truth, don't be afraid!"

"You must be guilty, or you would talk with us!"

It was very hard not to turn and reply to some of their taunts. We were grateful to reach the Embassy. The American

Ambassador, Mr. William Leonhard, invited us into his office. He expressed his sincere regret for the ordeal we had just experienced. I stood and asked our small group to stand in order to show our appreciation for the fast way Mr. Leonhard and his staff had come to our rescue.

The reasons for the Tanganyika Government's over reaction to our explainable mistake of driving down an unmarked road could have been several in number. Mr. Nyerere's Government was very sensitive to the possibility of being overthrown by a coup. Just prior to our experience, a reported preparation for a "Putsch"(German for coup) as it was called, had been discovered in a document. This document had allegedly come from some kind of C.I.A. connection. The report of this had become public knowledge, and its poison was dangerous enough for Ambassador Leonhard to go to President Nyerere, and request that the President make an official denial of the rumor so that everyone would know there was no U.S.-C.I.A. connection in all this. In spite of the Ambassador's request, the Tanganyika Government had remained silent, and had not disclaimed the untruths of this rumor. The morning of our release, Mr. Leonhard caught President Nyerere just as he was boarding a plane. Mr. Leonhard chided the President by saying, "You see sir, I told you that unless your government told the truth about this false information, it would turn out badly for some of our people."

President Nyerere responded by instructing his Aide, "Let them out".

Another possible cause for this affair might have been that right at this time the former Belgium Congo was undergoing its insurrection by the Simbas - Congo nationalists. The British and French Governments had intervened by sending troops to rescue their nationals serving in this troubled country. Other African Governments were enraged that European Governments would intrude in an "African affair," and were set for any opportunities to show that the Europeans in their areas were indeed subversive. In our case, the name Congo and Kongwa, pronounced similarly, provided a useful linkage. The World Press was given the information by the Tanganyika Government, that we missionaries:

--Had gained access to a Freedom Fighters camp.

--Had taken pictures inside the camp.

--Had interviewed and made tape recordings from the trainees.

In mail we subsequently received from our supporters in the U.S., we were counseled that as missionaries, we should not have done these acts we were reported to have done. Unfortunately, in our Church Periodical published in the U.S., called The Lutheran, an article appeared some months later by an author who began his article by saying,
"Some time ago, some of our missionaries tried to get into a Freedom Fighters camp. They didn't succeed, but I did....." This gave further credence to any who might have believed that we indeed were attempting to enter the camp.

In summary, the document that caused all the fear in

Tanganyika was discovered to have been written on the typewriter in the office of a high Tanganyikan Government official, whose name was Oscar Kambona. He was very popular with many of the rank and file in the country, to the degree that citizens were naming their children after him.

We had a meeting of our Missionary group right after our release and return up-country to our field. I was so upset emotionally that I excused myself from attending many of the sessions. I was in turmoil.

Our Church President of the African church had instructed us when we returned from Dar, "Go back to your work but say nothing to anyone about what happened."

Jeanne became very incensed, and replied to him, "Rumors have been spread that America is trying to overthrow the Tanganyika Government and that we missionaries are the agents of the C.I.A. You want us to remain silent about this as if we are involved. I will not keep still. Anyone who comes to me with questions will get "The Truth!"

Sometime later I learned from Jon Moris that the police had confiscated all his reasearch notes that he was using to write his doctoral thesis. Originally we heard that these notes were never returned. Years passed before I met Jon who told me the true story of what happened. After we were released from custody, the head of Tanganyika Intelligence approached Jon and gave him a packet of papers.

"Are these yours?" the officer queried.

Jon was overjoyed to regain all his lost research material.

"Yes," he joyfully replied.

"All of them?" asked the officer.

Jon examined the papers he had been given and in the center of the pile there was a map of the training camp at Kongwa.

"I've never seen this before!" Jon told the officer.

"That's what I thought," replied the offical.

Nothing more was ever said to Jon about this map which the Offical kept. The question might well be asked, should we have walked out of the front door of the Dar Es Salaam jail? Shouldn't we have spoken out for the truth and justice of our actions? As Messengers of Love, we decided we had to pay the price of silence in order to return and be useful to the Lord in our work as Messengers where He had assigned us. We hadn't been asked to pay the price that Dr. Edgar Carlson, a faithful missionary in the Congo had been asked to pay. At the same time we were being arrested, he had been shot in the back and killed when he tried to escape over a fence. He became another missionary martyr. This kind of commitment is one which all Messengers must be prepared to make as they follow the Lord's path for their service. It seems that this kind of missionary witness is becoming increasingly necessary in these later days. Our Lord told us very plainly, "Remember the words I have spoken to you, no servant is greater than his master; if they persecuted me, they will persecute you also." Jn.15:20

This same Lord also said, "Be of good cheer, I have overcome the world." Jn.16:33

Itinerant Evangelism

CHAPTER 17

"Behold upon the mountains
the feet of him that bringeth
good tidings, that publisheth
peace!"   Nah. 1:15

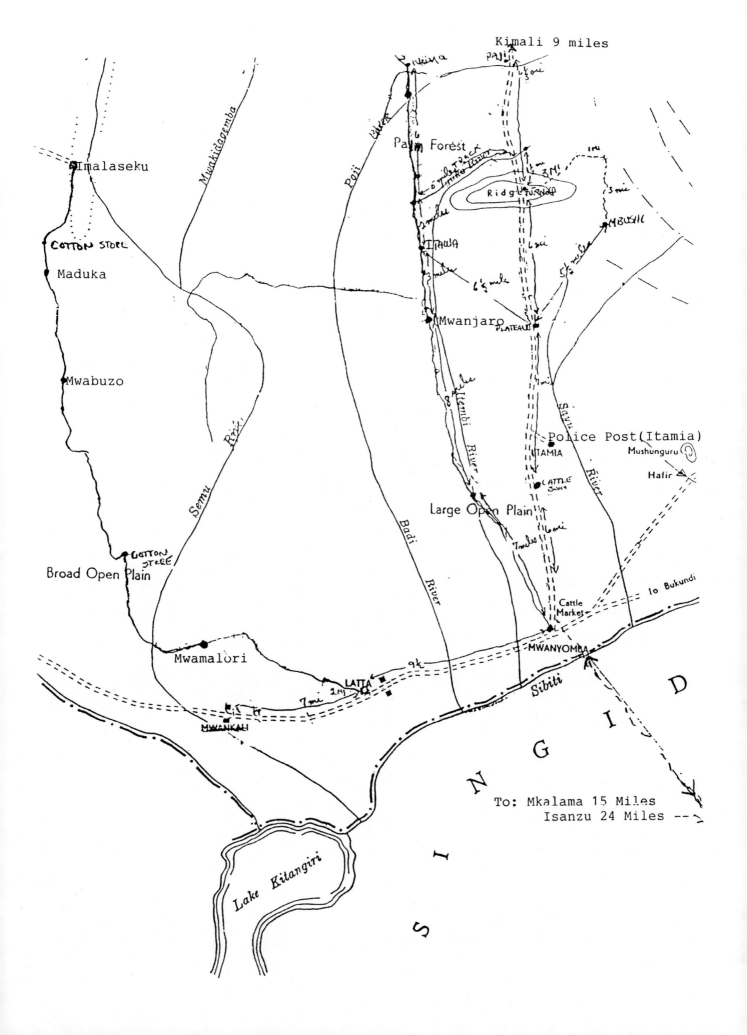

It was October 1957. We had just come around a corner of the winding road that descends through the hills from Isanzu to Mkalama. It was **hot!** A heat that even up in the hills gave a forecast of imminent rain. But even the heat could not detract from the beauty of the panorama that stretched out to the west before our eyes. We were just beginning our first itinerant foot safari into Sukumaland. There were three of us: Pastor Danieli Makala, Evangelist Lutheri Gimbi and myself. Solomoni my donkey, was carrying our tent, food supply and blankets. He didn't have a proper pack saddle so we stopped very frequently to retie the loads that were constantly threatening to slip off his back.

As we looked toward the west, the sky was a brilliant blue without a cloud in sight. It was a temptation to return to Isanzu, now about six miles behind us, and to transfer our loads to my pickup truck. It would save days of walking under the hot scalding sun. Sukumaland had a lot of black cotton soil on the route of our travel. That soil seems to suck in the sun's heat and then re-radiate it back to anyone on its surface. The very intensity of the sun's heat gave silent but stern warning to anyone who would pay attention. A change in season was about to take place. The monsoon winds had turned around and were now blowing from east to west. Soon the massive clouds of moisture arising out of the Indian Ocean would appear on the horizon. Then in just a day or two, the dry, cracked earth scorched by the sun for months now would undergo an incredible change. It would turn into a quagmire of mud. There were also the Sibiti and Durumo rivers to consider. Now they were only ankle deep and flowing along silently. They too would change into dangerous obstacles, ready to make vehicle passage next to impossible, ready to destroy a car as they forced it -- end over end -- to be swept away.

NO! Forget the temptation to drive. It was too much of a risk in a land where the unwritten rule is: "Never willingly get yourself into a situation you can't control, there is no one else around to help you."

Pastor Danieli, Lutheri and I had been looking forward to this trip for a long time. We were always committed to serving the Isanzu/Mkalama parish, and it was very hard for us to get away from our responsibilities. Now we had accomplished the first part of our goal. The whole Sibiti-Eyasi-Sukuma area we had in sight was without a Christian witness. We bore this evangelism need in our hearts whenever we looked to the west from Isanzu that was located on an escarpment one thousand feet in elevation above the Sukuma plains.

Our descent was from Isanzu, past the village of Mkalama where our leper colony was located. Continuing on down, we walked out onto the flat level, an area that stretches for miles and miles to the west. This area in Tanganyika is called "The Sukuma hardpan." On our way west we passed the small Catholic Mission Station called Chemchem which is located just a short distance from where the two rivers join together to flow on into Lake Eyasi.

On we journeyed, into the late afternoon when the heat in the land reaches its peak before it tapers off no longer fueled by the sun. By now, my face was a rosy red. I had tied a bandanna on it and looked like a bandit. This was to protect it from further radiation and also from the flies. They are torture on a sunburned skin. A Sukuma Boma now came into our view. Because we were all very tired, we asked for permission to camp there for the night. As it happened, the elder (Mzee) of the Boma was suffering from a high fever caused by an attack of malaria. I treated him from our supply of medicine. Then we pitched our tent and started supper. We prepared ughali, but we had no meat for making mchuzi (meat sauce or gravy dip). The Mzee's family brought us a large calabash of clabber milk. That was our delicious "dip" for our ughali that night. After the sun had set, the evening was simply beautiful. It was cool and the stars came so close to the earth, it seemed you might gather them like wild flowers into a basket.

We presented the Gospel message we had brought to everyone

there in the Boma. The Mzee's malaria was now controlled, and he was feeling much better. He listened to what we had to say very attentively. Then all the members of the Boma began an evening's activity. Mzee used a one stringed instrument which appeared to be a small, strung bow (almost capable of shooting an arrow), except that the bow string was wire. Along the course of the bow's handle, about two-thirds of the way down, a gourd was attached. It served the purpose of a sounding board. The gourd was alternately held against the player's body, then held away for a musical effect. The wire string itself was tapped with a small stick in a rhythm providing the beat for dancing. Each time the player's finger from his other hand touched the wire the sound from the instrument rose a note in pitch. Each time it was taken away, it went down a note.

Married women of the Sukuma tribe have the custom of wearing a heavy amount of wire coiled around their legs up to their knees. Dancing involves standing in one spot, stomping the ground in position, in time with the music. This dancing carries on well into the night, as the group forms a single line standing shoulder to shoulder.

On this night, we -- the visiting guests -- were not able to observe this merriment for very long before our eyelids closed in sleep. The following morning we, like our hosts, were up before dawn. The Sukuma were getting their cows milked and off for another full day's grazing, anxious not to miss a moment of light.

We ate our uji heavily sweetened with sugar and covered with another gift from our hosts -- warm milk, fresh from the morning's milking.

We started off, and in a very short time we came to the rivers, and walked across without delay. There was a police post, Itamia, we had heard about far to the west, and we hoped to reach it in our travel today. That hope was not to be realized for several reasons. The first was that after crossing the rivers, we would spend half a morning hunting. The area by the river had a flock of spur-winged geese feeding on its banks. I crept up on them, but had no cover to hide behind. They saw me and spooked, flying away. I had to follow them to get the opportunity for a chance to shoot one. This all took time, but it was a successful effort, and now we had meat for several days along our way.

We noticed heavy clouds massing behind us to the east. We were grateful because they reduced the intensity of the sun's rays most of that day. That night we camped at another Sukuma Boma. Again we were treated like visiting royalty, even though there was no one ill who needed medicine. We exchanged a cup of sugar for a lot of milk. It was always my practice to carry along a small portable radio on safari. At that time E T L F, the Radio Voice of the Gospel was regularly broadcasting from Addis Abbaba each evening in Swahili to East Africa. After our supper, and after our presentation of a Gospel message, we listened to the world news, and then shared the program of singing and preaching with the group in the Boma. The group listened attentively to every part of the broadcast. Dr. Daniel Friberg had a regular question/answer series in which he responded to queries sent to him from East Africa. He responded to the questions in Swahili, and this program blessed everyone who listened to it who could understand that language. Many of the women and children who could not enjoyed the programs choir music.

It was then time for another night's rest. I hadn't been sleeping for very long when I was awakened by a tremendous fight going on in the Boma between some animals around our tent. The Boma had a herd of its own donkeys. These animals didn't like guests and picked a fight with Solomoni. The Sukuma Mzee took measures to protect Solomoni. The local animals might have seriously wounded or even killed him otherwise.

Again we were up early and after breakfast went on our way again quickly. During the night, flashes of lightning had been seen in the eastern sky **far off in the distance. The rains were coming --**

NO -- THEY WERE HERE!

Mid morning, the rain came with a vengeance. There wasn't much in the way of shelter out there on the plains, though we did find some trees in a river course that were good for a little bit of cover. The old saying, "You can only get wet once," applied to us then. We were soaked to the skin in short order. The rain poured down, covering the countryside. It just kept coming as the heavens opened and dumped an unbeliev-able amount in a very short time. Then the rain stopped, but the land was flooded. Even so, we had to proceed on our way. To go on meant walking ankle deep in water. The water carried fine sand in suspension; as you walked along you were also "sanding off" the skin from your feet. Even so, we walked for hours, alternately in water ankle deep, or in mud to clutch at our soggy feet. I was amazed at how quickly the landscape could change. As I looked around the plain, I noted that the Sukuma were not unaware of what happens when the rains come. All of their Bomas had been built on little raised places even though to my untrained eye the landscape seemed perfectly level.

My African colleagues were not used to having lunch at noon, so on this trip I went without eating at noon as well. We were making very slow progress in our march even without taking a lunch break. I tried to set a schedule of walking an hour then resting for ten or fifteen minutes. It's surprising how the hours go by quickly by following this schedule.

It was almost dark when we saw the police post off in the distance. That was a very welcome sight. Our pace quickened. I was very hungry now. We were all very tired -- exhausted would have been a better word to describe our party.

The police post was able to merit this name because of the officers who served there. It had typical Sukuma dwellings, roundels with mud and wattle walls, and high peaked vertical roofs of grass. This post was part of the Tanganyika Police campaign of an anti-poaching/cattle rustling operation. The officers at this post knew that once the rains began, they would be completely isolated for some months to come. They would also have to be completely self-sustaining. At that time, they didn't even have a radio to use to call for help in case the Maasai made a raid. This happened frequently. Both the Masaai and the Sukuma had been known to engage in some bitter battles and rustling operations in this buffer area between the two tribes. The post had a five man contingent which seemed to be more for show than effectiveness.

After our arrival, none of us felt up to preparing any kind of food. We did get the tent up right away, and while my two colleagues rested I looked for the Sergeant in charge of the station. He was pretty drunk by that time of the evening. I gave him some rice from our precious supply. I had been saving this for a special occasion. I asked him if his wife could prepare it for us because we were too tired to do it for ourselves. I also said I would be glad to pay her for her work.

"No problem," came back his reply with a smile.

By this time I was so hungry I almost fell over in gratitude. I knew there would be no problem getting water for cooking, the whole countryside was full if it. What a difference from just a few hours ago.

I looked at my watch, and in spite of being soaked with water during the day, it was still working. It was 7:30 P. M.

Good! Half an hour to get the water boiling; then about

12 minutes to cook the rice. We should be eating by 8:30 P.M. at the latest.

I returned to the tent and I was 'out' on my feet. I sat down on the floor of the tent and dozed off at once. When I awoke, it was after 9:30. I asked my traveling companions if the rice was cooked yet. The startling reply came back to me, a dejected, "no."

"Well," I said, "the wood must have gotten wet with all this rain. That's the cause of the delay."

10:30 came and went. Still no food appeared. I was too numb to follow up on what was happening.

At 11:00 P.M. a shamefaced Police Sergeant appeared with my bag of rice in his hand and said, "I'm sorry, my wife has never prepared rice before."

By common but unspoken agreement, our group said a courteous, "Thank you, Good night."

We unrolled our wet blankets, wrapped up in them and went to sleep.

As often happens, after the initial deluge at the beginning of the rains, they disappeared for several days. We were able to preach at the Post and in the surrounding community. Originally our target had been to reach Imalaseku, a village that many of our Isanzu people often talked about. We asked directions at the Post about how far we were from this village. We learned that it was about 30 miles to the north and west. It was decided that our schedule wouldn't permit us to make that safari on this trip because our time was limited. Our work at Isanzu compelled us to return now. But I promised myself that at some future time, I would ask to be placed full time in itinerant work as my assignment in the Church.

We took leave of the Police Post and its families, and went on our way to reach Mwanjaro and Itawa before heading back toward the Iramba Plateau that was visible off in the distance. Now the heat was more noticeable because it was so humid. On the last day out before reaching the Sibiti river, we camped at a Sukuma Boma where we again encountered a sufferer from malaria. This home will always be vivid in my memory. The Mzee or head of this Boma was just simply enthralled with the message of Christ and his offer of salvation. He couldn't get over the wonder of it! He wanted us to baptize everyone in that home. However, because our Iramba-Turu church did not allow polygamy, we told him that we could not baptize his whole household without his agreeing to take only one wife of the several he now had. As we left that Boma, he was considering what kind of a commitment he was prepared to make. He pleaded for us to stay longer. The Bible's teaching on monogamy is a real stumbling block for those living in cattle herding cultures.

There is always a special thrill to one's soul to publish the Good News. Even going to one's neighbor anywhere in the world, there is that special blessing given to the go'er by the Holy Spirit. The dictionary definition of itinerant is, "traveling from place to place - - to a series of places to fulfill official duties." We had been commissioned by the Lord

Jesus Christ. Our official duty was to tell all those with whom we visited that Christ died to redeem them from their sins and the curse of darkness. In Swahili the word for itinerant is: kuzunguka-zunguka, (to go round and about), kutembea-tembea, (to walk and walk), kwenda huko na huko, (to go there and there).

As we made our way back to Isanzu we sang as we walked along:

YESU, YESU, NIMFUATA YESU,	JESUS, JESUS, I WILL FOLLOW JESUS,
POPOTE, POPOTE, AENDEAPO.	ANYWHERE, ANYWHERE, THAT HE GOES.
YESU, YESU, NIMFUATA YESU	JESUS, JESUS, I WILL FOLLOW JESUS,
NITAMFUATA ATAKAPONITUMA.	I WILL FOLLOW HIM, WHEREVER HE SENDS ME.

And we rejoiced in our hearts that He counted us worthy to bear His GOOD NEWS.

We reached the Sibiti river and by its height realized that Irambaland had continued to have good rains. Our anticipation grew apace with our climb up the Isanzu hills. Mzee Lutheri Gimbi left us at Mkalama. This was the place in which he was assigned to work regularly and his home was located there. Pastor Makala and I were left to complete the final climb of 9 miles to Isanzu with our faithful donkey, Solomoni. Our spirits were high and we weren't disappointed by the loving welcome home we received from our wives, Eliwandisha and Jeanne, and our kids.

This was a beginning. Subsequent trips both on foot and by car during the dry season brought the establishment of outpost evangelistic stations at Imalaseku, and at several other locations in Sukuma land reaching west and north into Masaai territory. These areas were good for cotton growing, and many Isanzu people migrated to capture this promise of work and wealth.

Imalaseku had existed as a very small town on the fringe of Sukumaland for many years. There were some Chagga shopkeepers (Tanzanian entrepreneurs from the Kilamanjaro area) who were located in this town. They insisted that a Lutheran Church be planted there. Since they were wealthy by local standards, their call to establish work was received by the Central Synod, and the Synod encouraged me to reach out in that direction. I had already begun to do this. Pastor Dean Peterson located an evangelist from his parish to go, and we assigned him to live at Imalaseku. It wasn't very long before a congregation was established and a church was built.

The Wakindiga

CHAPTER 18

"And other sheep I have, which are
not of this fold: them also I must
bring, and they shall hear my voice;
and they shall become one flock, one
shepherd." Jn. 10:16   K.J.V.

36°

SUKUMA LAND

MANGOLA RIVER

TINGIDA

MBULU

3°30'

LAKE EYASI

KINDIRA MTS.

YAIDA SWAMP

TINDIGA

ISANZU

I had just set up camp on a hill close by Maaungu, a water hole used by many elephants regularly throughout the year because it never dries up. I was trying to get into contact with the Wakindiga who were located somewhere in this area at this time. My mode of establishing contact was always to visit the water holes in an area where these Bushmen might be. If they were around, they would come into the water hole and leave tracks. It was late in the afternoon, and we had just arrived at Maaungu after a long, hot safari. We had been there only a short time, when wonder of wonders, we heard another car coming into the area. Our tracks, which we had so painstakingly made as Justino my guide had walked in front of my Landrover and guided me in slowly, were now the guide for this other car. Very soon a typical "White Hunters" type of Landrover came into view. It was traveling a lot faster than it should have been in this country of thorns and hidden holes. The vehicle had a canvas roof supported by aluminum poles fitted to the car's body. The lower part of the car extended half way up toward this roof. It had easy access doors designed as a part of the chassis to provide for the fast exit/entrance of excited hunters. The car came racing up to our camp and out jumped a man in typical bush attire. He wore a khaki shirt and shorts, tennis shoes and a wide brimmed bush hat which had a leopard skin band around its crown.

My visitor turned out to be Brian Nickolson, a man well known in Tanganyika and Kenya game circles. He introduced himself and in the same breath told me his reason for coming into the area.

"I came here to have a look at these Bushmen," he said.

He was referring to the Wakindiga, (whom the Germans called Das Tindiga), who were the objects of our itinerant evangelistic outreach.

Mr. Nickolson went on to say, "I've just visited one of their camps, and now I understand, they're just like Baboons."

I replied that I was attempting to evangelize these people. Nickolson looked at me as if I were out of my mind. Without another word he climbed back into his Landrover and drove off retracing his tracks back to the Eyasi valley below.

It would soon become dark. Elephants then would begin arriving at Maaungu. They considered the water hole their private property and as far as they were concerned had posted it with **"NO TRESPASSING"** signs everywhere. Heaven help you if they discovered you on their property. No matter if you were a small insignificant human or a huge rhino, they would pick you up like a sliver of wood and pitch you out and away from their possession. For in this land, water is more precious than gold to all.

We had just enough time to check out the sand of the hole, identify human footprints freshly made that day, and to snatch a supply of water for our camp before the sun's light disappeared completely. Then we retreated to our camp on the hill and built a large fire. This located our position for the incoming herds and the occasionally passing rhino. They all gave us a wide berth because we had located far enough away from the water so that we were not a threat to them.

The Wakindiga are a Bushman tribe who live off in the far reaches of the bush, areas shunned by other tribes for several reasons. The animals that live in these areas are predators. The areas are often in the tsetse fly zones that are a threat to men as well as domestic animals. The Tindiga, or Hadza(which is the word in their language meaning people) as they call themselves, are to my mind a half step up in physical stature from the Pygmies found in the Congo, and a half step down from the size of the typical Bantu African who is generally a farmer. The Bushmen are hunters and collectors. They normally do not plant, cultivate or herd animals. They represent the Xhosan tribal group who speak using clicks.

I believe it's risky to imitate the early anthropologists who used a measure called the cephalic index to classify people into tribes. It is risky because of some inter-marriages that take place between tribes. There are also too many contradictions in fact. I have taken courses in Anthropology where all Bushmen to qualify as Bushmen had to have the characteristic of Steatopygia -- abnormal growth of fat on the buttocks.

The German Colonial rulers of Tanganyika who held the country's rule in the last part of the 1800's, who were followed by the British, were all interested in learning about the

Tingida. But it has always been very difficult to research this group because of their secretiveness. They have always wanted just to be left alone to live in their hunting and collecting culture. Although they are valiant and brave hunters, they have tribal prohibitions refusing a member the right to use force against any human. To cope with some of their aggressive neighbors like the Maasai, the Sukuma and the Barabaig, their only course has been flight or to become masters at hiding. When I first tried to get into contact with them, I managed to spot one of their scouts in a lookout tree, way off in the distance. But whenever I tried to come upon their camps, all I ever succeeded in finding was the still smoldering coals of their fires.

My first chance meeting with one or two of them came at the time I first shot an elephant. The hunt took place in Tingida country, and while we were removing the dead animal's tusks, two men from the tribe came asking for permission to harvest the animal's meat. I agreed to their request. Then I worked pretty hard to convince these men that I was their friendly neighbor who lived "up on the hill at Isanzu." They had a few contacts with the Isanzu, sometimes bartering honey or skins and the meat of game animals for sugar and maize. But I wasn't the first Lutheran missionary to establish contact with them. They have never been a large tribe, estimated to number about a thousand people. So they hadn't attracted a lot of attention, except as being survivors of a culture now almost extinct. To the Christian Evangelist, however, they have the value of being numbered as part of the human race that has been redeemed by our Lord Jesus Christ.

Pastor Ludwig Melander, one of the pioneer missionaries on the Iramba-Turu field, spent some time at Isanzu and learned of the existence of the Tindiga. He wondered how it would be possible for them to come to know about Jesus because of their language barrier as well as their cultural one. He found that during a recent famine, prior to his coming, the whole Isanzu tribe had been forced to come down from their plateau and live in the bush in Tindiga country to avoid starvation. The Tindiga had shown these farmers how to gather roots and to eat the seeds of the baobab tree and be able to survive until the famine passed.

During their stay there, several Isanzu girls learned to speak the Tingida language quite well. These girls, now grown women when Pastor Melander arrived on the scene, were the key to the problem of communicating with the Bushmen. Pastor Melander made visits to the Hadza, but then he left the Isanzu area quite soon after this for other work. Not very much was done in the way of Tindiga evangelism after he left. However, one of the women, Elizabeti, now a widow, made regular trips into Tindiga country to evangelize them.

With the help of Justino, my Isanzu guide, we cut a bush track that allowed us to use our Jeep to at least get close to one of their main water holes, Majimaruru. The Tindiga frequently used this area for camping in their migrations around the Kindera Mountains.

In 1955, we received a request for help in contacting the Tindiga from a group called <u>Gospel Recordings Incorporated</u>. A team of three women were traveling in Africa making recordings on which they transcribed simple evangelistic Gospel messages in the vernacular. This was done on tapes, which were then returned to the U. S. and the messages were pressed on small phonograph records for distribution. In her book, <u>LIGHT IS SOWN</u> (Moody Press 1956-Chap.2), Miss Sanna Barlow gives a detailed account about the team's visit to Isanzu.

It was my responsibility to contact Taa Washi, the Hadza tribal chief, and arrange for him and two others to come up to Isanzu. I had established a good rapport with Taa Washi in the short time I had known him and now he showed no reluctance to answer my call that he come to Kitaturu. The call had been relayed to him by runner sent from the Isanzu chief, Omari Nkinto. What took place then was the beginning of at least 48 hours of hard work by everyone involved spread out over the next several days.

The three Tindiga, the three ladies from Gospel Recordings, Edythe Kjellin,(the nurse stationed at Isanzu), and Pastor Paulo Mkali and myself who were the pastors stationed as well at Isanzu, all had a significant part to play in the making of the tapes. The Gospel messages were first translated from English to Swahili, then into the Isanzu Language which was marginally understood by the three Tindiga. One of the Isanzu women Elizabeti, who had learned Kindiga during the famine was present as well to share her understanding of this difficult language and help in its translation.

Again and again, as a phrase was spoken by the Tindiga into the mike that put it on the tape, a replay was done to make sure the words carried the intended message. Taa Washi, according to Saana's account in her book, "never once had shown the slightest flicker of unsophisticated surprise that such a box could thus relay his voice. We wondered if it ever really had occurred to the gracious old man that this was actually his own voice he was hearing on playback. It seemed to us that he was simply concerned that the recorder learn its lesson well. Now and then he would agree to our suspicion that the box had made a **kosa kidogo** -- (a little mistake). This promptly erased and redone always evoked his special little nod of commendation and **mzuri sana** --(very good).

"The going became extremely difficult during those hot sleepy hours following lunch. After a feast of meat supplied by missionary Bob and his wife Jeanne, the Wakindigas found that their brains were taking a well-deserved siesta. A thought hardly won would slip into oblivion before it could be repeated into the microphone. There was the will to do, but the **nguvu** (strength) was gone. At such a time we presented the old man and the dozing boy with a harmless white pill (anacin tablet) and a cup of water.

"It had been interesting to see the **Mzee** (Taa Washi) learn this immortal passage -- John 3:16 -- and as he learned a phrase, he and his forefinger taught it faithfully to the boy who then spoke it into the machine with confidence.

PLATE IV

TINDIGA VILLAGE

TAA WASHI'S BAND

VISUAL EVANGELISM

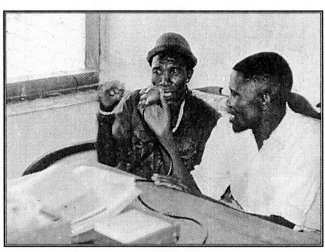

TAA WASHI 'TEACHING' THE MIKE

"Bob had come with a distinguished visitor, the top C.I.D. (British FBI) man of all Tanganyika, an English gentleman of long experience in many parts of Africa. When he heard about a Moslem subchief's opposition to what we were doing, he remarked, "Well, he shouldn't worry! It will be a long time before any of these bush people will be made Christians! They simply can't be corralled. It is impossible to keep track of them. They spend a week or two in a place, and then suddenly, bas! -- they are gone -- leaving not a trace of their existence!"

After the work of translation/transcription was done, the three ladies wanted very much to visit a Tindiga camp and give their work a "trial run." Although it was late afternoon, they wanted to journey down into the pori to a Tindiga camp. Taa Washi (one translation of his name means, "light the lamp") cautioned against starting out so late in the day. The pori is trackless if you get off the beaten path. But Joy, Sanna and Ann had scheduled their departure from the Isanzu area for the following morning. So if they were to visit a camp it would have to be done at once.

While it was still light, the trip down went well. We had to leave the jeep about two miles before reaching our destination at the camp and walk in the rest of the distance. When we arrived, we were very cordially received. I'll let Sanna continue the account of what then happened:

"Presently we found ourselves seated under one of the two giant baobab trees that flanked the small hilltop encampment of these nomad bush-people. Quietly the evening curtains closed us into a tiny parlor -- its near wall, the broad (30 feet in circumference) trunk of the baobab where **Bwana Bob** promptly hung his hunting rifle. Our chairs were the flat rocks neatly arranged by our hosts who now huddled together under the farther baobab where a soft twittering conversation blended with the night sounds of the uninhabited bush around us. Four or five little fires glowed red between the three stones, which made the hob of each -- the usual African stove.

"In silence we watched the pale stars draw brightly nearer, until just clearing the wild branches of the baobab, they dropped silently down and scattered themselves about our own front yard. Pastor Paulus set the recorder gently on a low table of stone; and now the box was ready with eight precious messages which it had been "taught" to speak in the clicks and clucks of these little forest folk, who had never heard one whisper about that Saviour whose seeking love could not pass them by no matter how intractable they might be. This was a sacred hour."

The playback was begun. The voice of Taa Washi came out clear on the night air, "Sch'aari Amu" (the usual greeting for "hello").

The response came immediately out of the darkness from the assembled group, "Sch'aari ya Mutaana" ("All is well today")

By the time we finished playing the eight tapes, it was drawing very close to 10:30 or 11 P.M.

Sanna's account again:

"Saying good-by was quite a ceremony involving each of us to each of them. As we started down the rocky hillside toward the plain and river bottom, two young Wakindiga with bows and arrows preceded us. They had taken log embers from the fire and now as they preceded us they marked out our way by dropping sparks of light along the path. It was now very dark and there was no moon. We followed the sparks as they carefully placed them to reveal a jutting rock likely to trip us or a thorny branch stretching over the trail.

"**Bwana Bob,** who had previously been our rear guard, came crashing past to lead us as we crossed the river bed. This was the watering place for elephant, rhino, and other game.

"Safely through the place of greatest danger, we followed an elephant trail to the jeep."

Now began the true test of my ability to get our small group safely home to Isanzu. Our enemy was darkness and the inscrutable bush that was filled endlessly with "look alike" thorn trees. I was confident that I could follow our tracks in spite of the darkness and not having Taa Washi to guide me as he had done on our trip down. I was overconfident. This part of the pori had been recently burned over and our tracks showed up plainly for some miles. Then we passed the burned area, and shortly came to the all important place where the crossover had to be made back into the N'gwa Sigwa location where Isanzu cultivation began. We had traveled well and made good time until we reached this point. Unfortunately,

without the help of the fire overburn, our tracks just didn't
show.

"No matter," I said to myself, "its just a little bit
farther on."

"No, I've gone too far, I don't see any track now at all!"

"I'd better turn around and retrace our way a bit."

"If only there was a moon, I'd be able to see the
escarpment."

"Ah yes, now I see the track, now let's go home!"

I drove and drove on good tracks, and then to my dismay
recognized I was almost back to where we had left the jeep
to walk into the Tindiga camp on our first arrival.

"Turn around Bob, at least you know which way is **out** now."

We had spent the better part of four hours twisting and
dodging obstacles like boulders and stumps. The only thing
we hadn't had was a flat tire. I could usually count on at
least one or two on each Tindiga safari. I should have taken
Justino with me to guide us back to Isanzu. He had a built
in compass -- I had only seen him really lost once, and then
when he got out of the car, he successfully re-oriented himself.

Now we were back in the "no-burn" area. I stopped the
car and Edythe, who was a knowledgeable student of the stars,
got out with me and pointed us -- direction wise -- to where
the Isanzu escarpment was located.

I stopped looking for tracks then, and we just set a dead
reckoning course, or as we called it then, "bashed" our way
forward. It's risky to do this, particularly at night. There

are unseen hyena holes, stumps, and thorns, as well as overhanging branches that are very hard on the roof of the car. Soon, we came to the edge of the pori, and broke out of the trees and brush into the cleared area of Isanzu cultivation.

"PRAISE THE LORD FOR HIS MERCY AND GUIDANCE!" We had found our way home by looking "UP" for our direction.

As we now climbed the escarpment road to Isanzu, the light dawned in the east. We were all so tired that we said quick, "Good-nights" and went off to bed for some very much needed rest.

The Gospel Recorders rose early the following morning and were on their way to their next assignment among the Wasandawe, many miles to the south and east. Jeanne and I missed seeing them off and having the chance to thank them again. They had given us a very wonderful evangelistic tool to use in our work of evangelizing the Tindiga. A short time later, the records with the eight messages were supplied to us. We played them again and again. The Tindiga liked to listen to them many times through at one sitting. I'm certain these records will never lose their value as long as this language is spoken. They, together with the large charts depicting the **Heart of Man,** and preaching were the three major ways we communicated the Gospel to the Tindiga. It was effective.

The work we were able to do among the Tindiga was limited until we were given our assignment of Itinerant Evangelism in 1960. Then we began to safari into the Hadza area, both in the area of the Kindera Mts., and into Sukumaland to the west of Endasiku, a town located on the Sibiti River. We combined the work among the Sukuma people with the work in Tindiga. There were pockets of Tindiga also living in the Sukuma region.

During the dry season Jeanne and the children who were still at home, Joel and Heidi, went along and were good campers. Jeanne, a registered nurse, held morning treatment sessions each day for all those who were sick. She always had a good attendance. Sometimes she felt that the women who came again and again were there to satisfy a need just to be recognized and to receive her loving care. That was a special ministry she had.

The places chosen by the Hadza to establish their temporary camps were almost always located on hill-tops. This gave them surveillance of anything or anyone approaching them from almost any direction. They also located close to available water. Those holes of the Kindera Mts. as I have already pointed out, were shared by people and animals. During the rains and even well into the dry season, the Digas had some flexibility in possibly locating other places. A few of the mammoth baobab trees had huge caverns caused by their natural growth. These, opening to the sky, were filled with water during the rains. They allowed the Hadza to camp in areas rich in their favorite foods of seeds and tubers, and still have the all important supply of water available.

On one foot safari well into the dry season, we set off on our way early in the morning. Our objective was to reach Mzee Maloba's camp located deep in the Kindera range. I had never ventured into this region before, and looked forward to seeing a new kind of high terrain. There was no water normally found where we were going, but we had been told that it was available "in the trees" at Maloba's location. The day was very hot, but even so we made good time. I had Justino and a party of five Isanzu porters with me to carry loads. In spite of hitting the trail hard, it took us until around 4 P.M. to reach Maloba's camp. We were just gratefully getting to our destination when we saw a line of Tindiga coming toward us setting off going the opposite way. When our two groups met, we asked them where they were going. The crushing reply was:

"We are leaving camp -- we've had no water for the last two days -- we've used up all the water supply from the Baobab tree."

"Are you sure it's all gone?"

"Ndio, imekwisha Kabisa, hata nyani wamekwisha hama!"

"Yes, it is absolutely finished, even the baboons have gone elsewhere!"

We rested for a few moments, and then decided that rather than suffering a dry camp, without any water to drink or to use for cooking, we would return to Majimaruru, the water hole we had left at dawn, eight hours ago.

If our rate of travel was rather relaxed in coming, now

it was a different matter. We were so thirsty it was difficult to speak to one another because our mouths and tongues were so dry. We literally "Hit the trail" with a vengeance. I knew I was over doing by the way my feet hurt, but it was bearable pain as long as I didn't stop too long for a rest.

The sun had set, but with Justino as a guide and a rather well-defined elephant trail to follow, there was no danger of getting lost. We were also blessed by a moon that was almost full and which was shining brilliantly.

Our real danger was from rhino or elephant that we might come upon now. The Lord in His mercy spared us that trial. We reached Majimaruru about midnight. Regardless of the danger that elephants might be in the water hole, we cracked out sounds of joy as we threw off our loads and buried our faces in the water of the pool. Then, with a revival of spirits and strength, we made camp and cooked supper. I took off my boots and I was shocked. In my right boot was what looked like a sole insert pad. But it wasn't, rather it was a complete section of the skin from the bottom of my foot -- the whole thing had come off! I was in real pain now, and it was difficult to walk on that foot. What to do now? My packers had the solution. They said this had happened before, and the treatment was to put your foot in a pot of boiling water. I told them I would sleep on that idea. The next morning, I could hardly walk. I declared a day of camp rest before we began our trip (I hoped) back to Isanzu. That was a trip that would take two days to make on foot. I still don't quite know how I talked myself into those two days. The pain was pretty intense in the morning, but I controlled it with aspirin and as the day wore on, it took care of itself. It was a happy time for me when I reached the station. I took several days off -- to get off my feet completely.

Foot safaris are rarely _routine_. Dr. J. Birney Dibble, who was at our Kiomboi hospital first in 1962, and then again in 1967, has written accounts of safaris he made with us into Tindiga land in his books, "In This Land of Eve," Chap 14, Abingdon Press, 1965; and in "The Plains Brood Alone," Chap. 6, Zondervan, 1973. In the last reference he describes his experience on a safari with us in the Yaida Swamp. They make very excellent reading.

We began by using porters from Isanzu to carry our loads. Then we hired the Tindiga to carry things for us. I must tell of one safari we went on with them. Our destination was Man'gola, many miles north of Isanzu, to the northern border of Lake Eyasi. We were in and out of valleys and up again into the next hills. As we reached the crest of one hill, another valley stretched out before us. There, down on its lowest level, a solitary elephant was making a big disturbance. I believe it must have been in "must." It was throwing its trunk into the air, bellowing, and turning in circles as if it were out of its mind. I cautioned the Tindiga porters to be absolutely still: **"NO TALKING."** We would pass the animal quickly on its left before it could hear or get wind of us. We carefully descended into the valley and started to pass on and out of danger. At that time the porter just ahead of me lost his nerve. The animal bellowed. The Tindiga was just too close to the elephant to keep his head. In getting ready to "run for his life" he said, "Bwana, naogopa sana!" (Sir, I'm so afraid).

Saying these words he dropped his loads, which happened to be all our metal cooking pots that were tied on his back wrapped in a blanket. They fell to the ground with a crash and a clatter. I reached down and picked them up, catching him at the same time, and put them back on his back. Then I whispered to him, "Usiogope, twende" (Don't be afraid, let's go.)

I fell out of line and covered the group holding my gun ready in case the animal charged. We weren't all that far from where it was standing. The group of porters continued up the next hill, and I then followed them. Fortunately the elephant was so involved with itself, it just continued to bellow and twist and turn and it didn't charge.

During the dry season, Jeanne and the family would come along by car to visit the Hadza camps. One day, Taa Washi gave Kathy and Joel, our kids, a gift of two baby ostriches. Taa Washi said that either we took the birds or they would wind up in his cooking pot. We were delighted, thinking we might take them to Isanzu and start raising them. Our delight turned to chagrin very soon. The birds simply had no common sense. They were enthralled by our open camp cooking fire and went over and sat in it. The smell of burning feathers didn't seem to faze them at all. We ran shouting for them to "get out." Rescuing them, we thought they had learned their lesson. Five minutes later they were back sitting on the fire again. We then returned them to Taa Washi and told him they were too much for us to handle.

Another experience we had in camp was one that might have had a disastrous ending. One morning, Heidi, our youngest daughter came with the report that she had a snake in her tent under her bed. At first I thought she was kidding me. But on looking, there it was -- a puff adder -- serenely curled up under her cot. Wazaeli, our helper from Isanzu, had his bow and arrows along, and killed the snake. We had become careless about zipping up the tent doors, otherwise the snake could not have gotten in.

As the work progressed, and folks of the Hadza tribe came to know the Lord and make professions of following Him, the next question was: when should we baptize our first Tindiga Christians? It was a big question for me to consider. I had heard of the Neuen Dettelsau Mission to the headhunters of New Guinea. This Mission was working with people like the Hadza. They were illiterate without any Christian background to build on. The German Mission had worked out a pretty thorough system of requirements to be fulfilled by new converts before they could be baptized. Converts were required to learn 100 Bible verses. They were also required to wait a number of years to show that they could live a Christian life. They were also required to bring in at least one other convert as well.

I had written to our Seminary at Makumira asking their direction. No response came. My prime concern was to avoid the charge that I was simply baptizing converts too quickly.

Taa Washi, the chief who had done so much to provide us with an opening for the evangelization of his tribe visited me one day at Isanzu. He wanted me to baptize him. I didn't go into detail when I refused his request, but I did say, we were waiting a little longer for a ceremony to baptize the whole group together.

Some weeks later, a runner came to Isanzu saying:

"Come quickly, Taa Washi is very sick".

I told Jeanne, "I must go at once".

I had just gotten into my car when another runner arrived with the news, "Taa Washi has died".

Some months later at the beginning of 1965, we had the big baptism service at Munguli when over 80 men, women and children were baptized. We invited all the missionaries on the field as well as our Isanzu Christians, and the President of the National Church to attend. I'm certain Taa Washi was there in spirit. Had he been there to be baptized, I think he would have taken the name **Abraham.**

Before the baptism ceremony, I wasn't sure how long to wait before baptizing a new convert -- I believe I know now.

One elder in the group, whose pre-baptismal name was Sumuni and Danieli after baptism, came to me one day for a long talk. The burden of what he said was that he would like to settle down in one place and plant a shamba, but he was afraid that if he failed to get a harvest, he would starve. I made an agreement with him. I would supply him with the seed he needed. Then if the year turned out badly, I would provide the food he needed for his group to survive until the next harvest. Thus began the settlement which the Hadza called Munguli. It was a totally voluntary project and it worked.

A good harvest was forthcoming the first year. The only complaint I heard from Danieli was that tribal members came in from all directions and they were taking the harvest he had laid up for the dry season. It's impossible for one Tindiga to deny another in need if he makes a request for help. I told Danieli that anyone who got grain from him should promise to be responsible for cultivating at least a part of Danieli's shamba for the next year.

The Munguli project became known to the Tanzania Government. Several years after things really got going well, a team of Government Officials visited Munguli. They brought a work crew with them who constructed ten grass-roffed houses in a line on the edge of the shamba. They also brought bags of grain which they gave out to everyone, and along with these gifts, lots of second hand clothes were given to anyone at Munguli who wanted to take them. All this was combined with a big celebration and the Officials made a lot of very long speeches. In them they said:

"You Tindiga have lived in ignorance and poverty from the beginning. Now the Government is going to settle you permently here at Munguli, and at Yaida Chini, and at other locations we choose. Now you will live in peace and plenty."

There was a heavy accent placed on the ignorance and the inability of the Tindiga to survive without the wisdom and help which the Government was now offering them.

After what seemed like hours of speeches given by the Government Officials, a response was offered by Danieli. He said:

"We people here in the pori sincerely appreciate the gifts you (the word used was 'Serakali') Government have brought to us. You are very wise, and we do not have your wisdom. We are not able to get along without your aid."

Danieli went on at length to express the Tindiga's appreciation for the many bags of grain, and the gifts of clothing which the visitors had brought with them to Munguli. As he finished speaking he said the following:

"Friends, you are our guests. You know how to live in the city. We know how to live here. You are now at Munguli. It is growing dark, and you will have to spend the night here. If anyone among you has the need to relieve himself during the night, please call one of us to go out with you. We have many snakes, elephants, rhinos, lions and other dangers from which we will protect you. You must not walk out from camp without one of us to guide you or you may be killed."

I don't know if the last part of Danieli's speech registered on the minds of the Government listeners. It would prove to be true wisdom in just a short span of time.

The District Commissioner had instructed the Police to see that all the Hadza in the Munguli area were in this camp now, and that they must stay there permanently. I was very disappointed at this turn of events. I was certain that this was the beginning of the end for our volunteer village. As soon as you tell someone: **"You Must,"** just that quickly they begin to react: **"I Won't."** The Government may have anticipated this. They took me aside and made it very plain that I was expected to support them in their formation of this Ujamaa Village scheme. After all, they said, it was a political requirement that was going to be enforced upon the whole country. Therefore, I was expected whole-heartedly to make the Hadza see this was in their best interest.

I knew that I could not be responsible for reporting errant groups of Tingida to the Government. The Tindiga insisted that they would still follow the nomadic pori life they loved so well. It was only a matter of time until the Government would see me as openly opposing them.

Sometime later, when the Government made all the Tindiga who lived in the Kindera Mt. Tsetse area live close together in villages it caused an outbreak of Sleeping Sickness of epidemic proportions. This became very apparent to all the Hadza, who then fled into the bush and practiced, with renowned success, their ability to hide from all intruders.

There is the classic expression: **THINGS TAKE LONGER IN AFRICA.** After the big celebration and visit, nothing at Munguli changed much. The Hadza even built several of their normal grass huts very close to the houses which the government work crew had put up. No one actually lived in the Government's mud and wattle houses. The police did not appear again either. So for a time life and Munguli's development by the Hadza went on as it had before.

A Hard Decision

CHAPTER 19

"In all thy ways acknowledge him,
And He will direct thy paths."
Prov. 3:6

By 1967, the work among the Hadza had developed enough so that we placed an evangelist, Wilson Muna, to live permanently at Munguli. He was an Isanzu by tribe, but had a real heart for evangelizing the Tindiga. He wasn't able to make safaris into the heart of the country by himself without a gun, he claimed, but he was faithful in working at Munguli and agreed to live there with his family. By this time we had built a rest house there which we frequently used now in our visits, instead of our tents. He built his own house as well.

The Munguli community still consisted of Danieli and his family and several others who lived there permanently. The Government did not put in an appearance again during all this time. However, reports were reaching us about how in many communities of Tanzania, Government bulldozers were literally destroying good permanent houses, because these houses were not in the "lines" that conformed to what the authorities considered acceptable to an Ujamaa scheme. I knew it wouldn't be very long until the promises made when the officials met with us at Munguli would come due.

Our next furlough was drawing near. We were supposed

to go off in 1968. I had been given a call from the Central
Church Headquarters located at Arusha. The Evangelical
Lutheran Church of Tanzania's head office was the administrative
center for all the Synods and Dioceses of Tanzania. They were
calling me to begin a new department for the Church, that of
Audio/Visual. I was very much interested in this kind of work,
and the call had come to me when I was wondering what my future
would be among the Tindiga. I sought the counsel of my
colleagues in the work. One flatly stated that if I left I
was deserting the Hadza and the work I had started there.
Others felt differently. As the time for furlough, and
responding to the Church's call pressed down upon me, I decided
there was only one thing I could do to come to a decision on
these questions. So I went down to a very remote hill in the
Kindira Mts., and leaving Jeanne camped in the valley below,
I carried a tent up the hill and made a prayer camp. I had
planned to pray and fast for three days in order to seek the
Lord's guidance to my question: "What should I do now?" Jeanne
very patiently waited for me to be led to see an answer. She
was in prayer as well.

I had no heavenly vision, no special voice came to direct
me in the course I should follow. But I did receive a great
blessing of the presence and closeness of God's fellowship.
It came to me that I well knew the emphasis the Mission was
placing upon turning over the work into the hands of the
National Church. There were those who, like Wilson, could
carry on a ministry to the Tindiga. It would be modified from

what I was doing but still possible.

On the other hand, setting up an A/V department was beginning something completely new in providing services for the whole Church which they did not presently have. I felt that since the Lord had not specifically forbidden me to leave the work I was now doing, and on the other hand had not directed me to leave, that He was leaving it up to me to choose.

Jeanne climbed up the hill on the third day to see whether I had come to a decision, and I told her I felt we should go to Arusha. She agreed. We returned to Isanzu to make plans for our furlough. We began to say farewell to all our Hadza friends whom we had come to love so much.

The Government did then come to Munguli. They made a large investment in building a school, a large storehouse, and an administrative building. I heard about all of this after I returned to Arusha in my new work. I also heard of the reports from the Haydom Hospital, adjacent to this area. These reports told of a great proliferation of sleeping sickness. Many people living close together in this area were reported to have been infected. It was then that the Tindiga fled.

We returned to visit Munguli in 1993 and found that the area had changed a great deal. The Isanzu people had moved in and taken over the whole location. We visited the primary school and asked those students whose parents were Hadza to stand forward. No one volunteered. Finally the headmaster of the school called out the names of those students whom he knew were from Tindiga homes in the bush. There were a few, and all seemed very embarrassed to admit it.

On this same visit to Munguli we got some shocking news when we asked about Danieli. He had gone from Munguli over into Sukuma land to live. There he had been arrested by the Game department for illegal hunting. This was very hard to understand, because the Hadza exercised a tribal right given to them by the Government "in perpetuity" to hunt wherever they were in the country. Danieli was put in jail for an extended period of time. There is a saying: "If you confine a Bushman, he will die." Danieli died in jail.

E.L.C.T. A/V

CHAPTER 20

"That which we have seen and
heard declare we unto you, that
ye also may have fellowship with
us: and truly our fellowship is
with the Father, and with his Son
Jesus Christ." I Jn. 1:3   K.J.V.

It was 1968. We had been very fortunate after we declared our willingness to serve in Arusha. Our Board in the States agreed to this call by the Ev. Luth. Church of Tanzania. The next step was to enter a study program to prepare for this new work. This would involve going back to college. A number of institutions were considered by our L. C. A. Board of Missions Africa Director, Dr. Ruben Pedersen, as I consulted with him: U.C.L.A., Iowa State, Syracuse, Indiana and Oregon State. Each University had its strong department: one in Journalism, another in photography and cinema, another in graphics, etc. It was finally decided that I would attend Oregon State because they had a very good general department that would provide a foundation in all the disciplines I was interested in studying. I was given a full scholarship funded by the Aid Association for Lutherans arranged through the efforts of the media expert from the Lutheran Church Missouri Synod, Dr. Rudolph Betterman.

I registered at the University in the fall quarter to study in the departments of Education, Speech and Anthropology. Because the University had no degree course in AudioVisual, I studied for a Master's degree under the designation entitled

-- General Studies.

It was a real treat to return to school after being away from heavy course work for so many years. I was now 41 years old. On our first furlough in 1958, ten years before, I had taken half a year of study at the University of Oregon. I had studied Anthropology on the graduate level there. Now, with those courses taken at the U. of O. being credited, it would be possible for me to fulfill all the Master's course requirements for a degree in only one more year at Oregon State. My thesis was to be: <u>Developing</u> <u>an</u> <u>Audio</u> <u>Visual</u> <u>Department</u> <u>for</u> <u>an</u> <u>Emergent</u> <u>Church</u> <u>in</u> <u>Africa</u>.

My mentor and advisor was Dr. Earl Smith, who was in the Education Department and combined a great many of his diverse abilities under the heading of "Industrial Education."

It started out to be a very stimulating year of study. I made an office out of the enclosed front porch of the house we had rented in Corvallis Oregon, providing it with an easel, a desk and the lights needed for all the phases of my study. I had to spend almost all my time doing projects, graphics displays and studying. Except for some necessary commitments of weekend deputation, I studied, attended classes and worked on projects nonstop.

At the close of the first semester, the Education Department came to me and said they were short-handed because of some personnel changes. They asked me to teach the graphics, photography and offset printing courses that I had just taken in my first semester. I agreed, and benefited greatly by firming up what I had just been taught. The pay I received for this time of teaching was considerably more than I received as my mission salary, but following our Board's rules, I turned it over to them. However, I learned a great deal about teaching college students and grading them with Dr. Smith's help and oversight.

That year of study went by very quickly. We were on our way back to the field when I was awarded my degree.

*   *   *   *   *

After our return to Tanzania, I had an office in Arusha on a side street several blocks away from where the Central Church Office was renting space. The E.L.C.T. at that time was just starting to build its own new Headquarters and I was given the freedom to design the Audio Visual Department's rooms which were to be located on the ground floor of this new three story building. This meant that the plumbing as well as the electrical systems would not be compromised, but would be designed for the work they were supposed to do. There were four rooms in the A/V facility: an office which also contained a film library, an electronics service center for audio equipment and projector repairs, a large graphics room, and a good sized, well equipped darkroom.

The E.L.C.T. office took about a year to build. That didn't restrict our program all that much. The recording studio that supplied Radio Voice of the Gospel with choir music taken from all over Tanzania was based in Moshi. We used them as suppliers as well. We contacted the choirs they recorded and made contracts with them to use their music. Then we took the R.V.O.G. tapes that the Moshi people had made as they visited different choirs located in Tanzania to Nairobi. In Nairobi I had a commercial firm press the music on records. The records were brought to Tanzania and the Department sold them. The income from this venture alone supported just about all the work we did in the A/V Department.

A surprising thing happened throughout the country in regard to these records. In towns that had good numbers of people, taverns did a thriving business. They would attract customers by playing music well into the night on their P. A. systems which could be heard long distances away. Many times on visits around the country, I heard songs from our records being played over these systems.

We also printed up a large quantity of Evangelistic tracts for general use by the Church. The dream of having an offset press as a part of the Department's equipment was one never realized.

We had a very useful contact with the East Africa office of the Kodak Corporation located in Nairobi. They supplied us with all our film and darkroom supplies and also with a number of 16 MM projectors which we ordered from them and sold to the Synods and Dioceses.

I had a staff of two: an understudy or assistant and a secretary. My assistant was hired to learn the work of the Department so that he could eventually take over its management.

All the equipment we needed for running the Department

was purchased either in the U. S. or in Nairobi. At that time equipment was imported into Tanzania duty free. The many things we required for our program had all been scheduled for purchase in my thesis, so it was just a matter of staying within the budget.

I was able to buy a large glass cabinet in Arusha. On its six shelves, each camera and its lenses had their assigned places. I was able to tell at a glance whether anything was missing, and I checked on them regularly. We had very expensive equipment like a Hasselblad Camera with a lot of accessories. We also had several Nikon 35 MM Cameras with multiple lenses as well as a 16 MM Cinema camera. Keeping records and finances straight, correspondence flowing, and our inventory accounted for was more than a full time job for us all. We were, at once, in a production mode in our electronics shop doing repair work. I had brought all the test equipment up which I had used in the Central Synod for our Interstation radio network. We were also constantly on call to take pictures at Synod and Diocese meetings.

Taking pictures was sometimes a risky business. There are those, particularly in the Moslem community, who believe that taking a person's picture empowers the taker to run off with the subject's spirit and to gain control over it. All photographers had to be very careful to obtain permission before pictures were snapped. Other unexpected responses were possible.

One time, at the opening of a Girls' Secondary School

in Arusha, I thought it would be a good time to get a number of photos of our Tanzanian President, Julius Nyerere, who would be officiating at the ceremony.

Before the ceremonies began, the President was seated in the school auditorium waiting for things to happen. I approached him slowly, and got directly in front of him for a good close up picture. I noticed that he didn't seem too pleased at my being there. Since it was rather dark in the auditorium, I used my flash. When it went off in Nyerere's face, he sprang up, right out of his chair. I hadn't thought I was that close to him. Several soldiers, probably his bodyguards, came at me as if I were a would-be assassin. I was as shocked by all this response as Nyerere had seemed to be when the flash went off. It could have been that there were some security concerns at that time that I knew nothing about. I beat a hasty retreat with only one picture after my credentials had received a good going over. I was very glad to escape what seemed to be a situation filled with a lot of potential.

It was soon apparent that our film library of over 50 films couldn't keep up with the demands made on it by the Synods and Dioceses. We were constantly in need of funding to increase our film inventory. The Department itself used its own films for film evangelism.

Dr. Daniel Friberg was the Evangelism Director for the E. L. C. T. A number of times I accompanied him on visits to the Synods and Dioceses in Tanzania, Kenya and Zaire to hold meetings. These trips continued to be requested, and later I was invited to come just for a film showing alone. It developed that I was spending about one fourth of my time doing film evangelism. We used the technique of "voice over" presentation. That is, we memorized the sound track on the film and then gave a Swahili version to the audience. It was generally very effective.

Dr. Friberg had a standard procedure he liked to follow whenever we arrived at the place where we were planning to make a film presentation that evening. I would mount the public address system's speaker on the roof of the car. Then as we drove through the town, Dan's voice would echo and re-echo down the streets as he said:

"SINEMA LEO, SINEMA LEO."   "FILMS TODAY, FILMS TODAY!"

"TUTAONYESHA SINEMA PALE"   "We'll show the Cinema at___"

"KARIBUNI WOTE, KIINGILIO NI BEI CHINI YA UPUZI"

"Come everyone, admission is ridiculously cheap!"

"KARIBUNI WOTE -- KARIBUNI WOTE!"   "Come everybody -- Everybody"

We traveled everywhere showing films on the sides of buildings' white-washed walls, or on the screen we brought along, which had to be well anchored to withstand the wind.

On one eventful trip, during the rainy season, we visited the Tana River basin in Kenya. To reach our destination we put our loads, including our electrical generator, into dugout canoes. We floated past numerous hippos swimming in the river, and were told to be silent. The canoes leaked pretty badly, and our sleeping gear got wet from the falling rain as well as from the water in the canoes.

We were bunked that night in a primary school that had no doors to close and very large windows. As night fell, a solid mass of mosquitoes attacked us. There was no escape from them short of closing yourself up in a wet, steaming, sleeping bag. I believe that night was truly the most miserable night I have ever spent in my life. Dr. Friberg covered himself with a sheet and I can still imagine I hear him snoring away, enjoying his night of rest which the rest of us couldn't seem to share with him.

Another trip took us to the coast of Tanzania to a place called Pangani. This area on the coast was predominantly Moslem. During colonial days we would not have been permitted entrance into this area. Now sunset found us setting up our film display equipment in an open field in the town. We showed several films that evening. Once or twice the large crowd became very noisy and I threatened to shut down the screening if the noise continued. It stopped. A large rock was thrown at our screen, but fortunately it missed hitting its target. We showed several of our usual films, from the Cathedral "Life of Christ" series: "Crucifixion and Resurrection." We also showed another filmed by Ken Anderson Films of Anderson Indiana. It was about Sadhu Sundar Singh entitled "Journey to the Sky." This film was always very well received by East African audiences.

After the screening, as the crowd dispersed, several Moslem believers held a spirited discussion with us about what they claimed was the "polytheistic" religion we Christians followed. They said they were monotheists, and we should follow Allah. The message of Salvation offered by Christ Jesus was meaningless to them.

We packed up our equipment and went on our way. I wondered about the impact of our visit on that community. Some weeks later, we got a report that was astounding. You must understand that to an uncritical audience in East Africa, things shown on the screen are to them pictures that were actually taken of the events at the time they occurred.

A group from the Pangani Moslem community went to their Shehe (religious leader and Teacher)with these words,"Why have you lied to us?" The Shehe indignantly replied, "Lied to you? I am an honest man, you know that; I have lied to no one!"

The group replied, "You have taught us that Mohammed and Jesus were both prophets of equal stature."

"Yes, that is what Islam teaches", replied the Shehe.

The group responded, "Last night on the soccer field we saw Jesus suffer on the Cross and shed His blood. Mohammed never did anything like that, therefore, Jesus is superior to Mohammed. You didn't tell us the truth."

Assembling a crowd for the purpose of showing them Evangelistic films imposes a big responsibility upon you. We were showing films to a large crowd in Kalemi, Zaire. There were several hundred people inside the walled compound of the Catholic church in the center of the city. Our screenings had been offered several nights in a row. In the middle of a showing one night, someone stood up in the darkness and shouted, "Nyoka" -- (Snake).

The assembled group went into a frenzy in its haste to escape. Many people were trampled upon, and one child got a broken arm. From that time on, I always placed several floodlights around the viewing area to cover it. Turning on the lights never failed to calm an unruly or noisy or even a disturbed audience.

We were very fortunate to have a gifted artist who volunteered her ability to benefit the Department. Mrs. Sinnika Harjula, was the wife of Rev. Raimo Harjula a professor at the Makumira Seminary which was located close to Arusha. Sinnika gave us a day or two a week for projects that utilized her artistic abilities. When she left on furlough and re-assignment with her husband, we suffered a real loss. We didn't have the budget to replace her. I had an Afro-American lady who volunteered to help us for a lot less salary than she was worth. I approached my Director, the national Executive Secretary of the E.L.C.T., for permission to employ her. He was adamant in his refusal to grant the permission that would allow her to work in the Department.

After we got started, the Department was always under-staffed. We could have used someone full time for our graphics and art section alone.

Right about this time, the E.L.C.T. was attempting to introduce a common liturgy throughout the Synods and Dioceses. Our department served the Seminary and the Church by duplicating tapes of this liturgy in quantity for distribution to everyone in the Church of the material made up at the Seminary.

Our work of Film Evangelism continued. On one trip we were coming back from a visit to the Mbulu Synod, located in north central Tanzania several hundred miles from Arusha. We were returning to Arusha - - Dr. Dan Friberg, Jeanne my wife, and I was doing the driving. Upon his arrival in Arusha, Dr. Friberg was looking forward to setting off on furlough with his wife, Ruth.

We were driving in our Department A/V car, a long-wheel-base Toyota Landcruiser. The three of us were all sitting in the front seat and the balance of the space in the car was filled with an electrical generator, a film projector, large speakers and a lot of other gear. We were about 20 miles short of reaching Arusha, when suddenly, with a loud **"BANG"** the back right wheel of the Landcruiser separated from the car and went spinning off in a different direction.

I began to reduce speed by letting up on the gas, but I didn't touch the brake. The car drove like a boat in the water. It began to veer to the left. I compensated in my steering, and gave the car a little more gas. Then we began to veer to the right, and I tried to respond again. This time I couldn't keep the car on the pavement. It went off the road to the right, but still stayed upright as if it still had all four of its wheels. Then it started sinking to the side which had lost the wheel. I still had some control and kept the car advancing forward. We were dragging a lot now, down on the right, and causing a colossal amount of dust to boil up around the dragging car. Then I saw it looming up ahead of us -- a large, dry ditch! It had been cut during the rainy season. We were headed straight for it. Even though the car was dragging on its back right side, it was still going at a good rate of speed.

On and on we advanced to the ditch. I remember thinking: "This accident is now going to be serious." However, we came to the ditch and our momentum propelled us up -- over -- and down to the other side of the ditch where our car continued skidding and then finally, came to a halt. We were all speechless for a moment or two, and then I turned to Dan and said, "Well Dan, it looks like the Lord wanted you to take that furlough!"

We got out of our car and saw that a car was approaching. They stopped because they had seen all the dust clouds in the air and wondered what had happened. The driver of the car was Dr. Ole Halgrim Olsen from Haydom Hospital where we had just visited on our safari. I stayed with the damaged vehicle while Dr. Olsen took Dan and Jeanne the rest of the way on into Arusha. An hour later a tow truck appeared and the A/V car and I were then taken into Arusha as well. We had experienced again the fulfillment of the Lord's promise:

"Jehovah will keep thee from all evil; He will keep thy soul. Jehovah will keep thy going out and thy coming in from this time forth and for evermore." Ps. 121:7-8. Had we not cleared that ditch, we all might have been killed.

*   *   *   *   *

When I returned from rather frequent safaris away from the office I would get reports I didn't like to hear. My assistant had collected money for repairs supposedly done on equipment brought into our facility, which had not been done. When the owners tried to use the repaired items, they would have to return them, sometimes over long distances, for the proper repair work to be done. I also would get reports about how my assistant had been working in the Department's darkroom after working hours, "moonlighting," developing sets of wedding pictures he had taken for hire using the Department's equipment and supplies without paying for them.

After one trip, I returned and gave my usual glance toward the A/V glass storage cabinet. Our best 35 MM camera and three lenses were gone! I queried my secretary and my assistant. No one knew anything about the missing equipment. But the cabinet was locked and hadn't been broken into, so there had to be an explanation. Finally my secretary came to me and disclosed the following: my assistant had sold the missing gear for practically nothing to a young man whom I had befriended. It amounted to theft involving them both. The youth's name was Robert Daz, a young teenaged Asian boy whose parents were teachers at the Arusha Secondary School. Bob had often visited the Department and had shown a keen interest in photography. We let him help us in our darkroom work. Now his parents had taken work at another school in northern Kenya and Bob had gone with them.

As soon as I found out about this I went to my superior, the national Executive Director of the E.L.C.T. and told him what had occurred. I asked that my assistant be disciplined -- this had gone on far too long. I also asked for permission to travel to Kenya to recover the stolen articles. The Exec made no comment regarding my first request. About the second one, he said, "It will do you no good to waste your time going to Kenya; you'll never get your equipment back".

I pressed him for permission and he finally reluctantly agreed; saying I would have to use public transport to make the trip.

The school to which I was going was located in a remote corner of Meru country, about seventy-five miles northwest of Nairobi. It was a private Girls' school. I arrived there in the early afternoon and asked for directions to the home the Dazes occupied. Mrs. Daz, Bob's mother, answered the door. I could see by the look on her face that she had no doubt about why I was there. She told me Bob was "out." I said that if she didn't mind, I would await his return. She let me come in and before too long, Bob appeared. At first he denied that he had the camera and lenses. When I said that unless they were produced I would have to go to the local police with this matter, he reluctantly went into his room and came back with

all the articles. I told Bob how disappointed I was in him,
for we had, I thought, been good friends in Arusha. Friends,
especially Christian friends, shouldn't steal from each other.
I then hurried to catch my transport to get back to Nairobi
where I would have to spend the night.

When I arrived back at the office in Arusha, I got a smile
of encouragement from my boss, but that was all in the way
of support I got from him in the problem of dealing with my
assistant. From then on, I tightened up on security. I talked
with my assistant about the things he was doing, but I got
no real satisfaction from him other than the promise that he
wouldn't do it again.

Several months later, the office of Bishop was instituted
in the Northeastern Diocese of the E.L.C.T. with the ceremony
of installation of the new Bishop, Sebastion Kolowa. This
promised to be an historic event in the life of the whole
Church. I was unable to attend the ceremonies, so I sent
Naftali with our 16 MM cinema camera to shoot some clips of
footage that we would then have on reserve in our library.
We had been commissioned to make a documentary film on the
E.L.C.T., which was to be funded by a large budget provided
by the Lutheran World Federation.

Instead of carrying out my instructions to shoot some
sequences for later use in our documentary, my assistant went
to Dar Es Salaam. He had some buddies in the Tanzania
Government's photography section called the Tanzania Film
Corporation. He wrote up a contract with them to shoot a full

length feature film of the Bishop's installation. The amount he agreed upon with them was a lot more than the complete budget we had been granted from L. W. F.

I then took the matter to my superior. Again, I could get no support from him. He simply remained silent. So I did something very reluctantly, but which I felt was warranted under the circumstances. My boss was the Executive Secretary of the E.L.C.T., but he was responsible to the presiding Bishop -- the elected head of the whole Church, including our Central Office. I drove to the town of Moshi, eighty miles east from Arusha, where the Bishop had his office. I went there on appointment and explained the problems I was having administering my office. I told the Bishop how my assistant was involved in the dishonest sale of the Department's equipment. Now, I went on to say, he was getting into a very large L.W.F. budget amount and it frightened me.

The Bishop gave me this startling reply, "It is good for you that you brought me this information, otherwise if you had delayed and these matters came up from other sources, we would have held you financially responsible!"

The Bishop gave me the promise that he would look into these concerns I had brought to him. I left his office very much relieved that now there would be a solution to this long standing difficulty.

Returning to Arusha, I shared with the Executive Director about my visit to the Bishop and the Bishop's response. The Director received my information with interest, but again I got no response to my plea that we sit down with my assistant and "restrict" his activity and discipline him for what he had done.

There followed a series of meetings with the Bishop. I would be told by my Director that we had an appointment to see the Bishop on such and such a day and time. We would make the trip in the Director's car. My assistant accompanied us on several of these trips. There was no question of his being guilty of the wrong-doings I brought against him. But there was no real solution offered to resolve the difficulties which he continued to cause. Again and again we found evidence of his late night use of the Department's darkroom and photographic supplies, and his pocketing of the receipts for film rentals.

I had insisted from the beginning of the trips we made to the Bishop and we made a number of them -- that because of the great value of investment in the Department, I could not be responsible for it unless I had full control. This meant that my assistant had to be restricted and disciplined.

I don't remember the number of trips we made to the Bishop's office. The last one was made on the week before Jeanne and I were scheduled to go on a three month furlough to the States. At that meeting, the Bishop said he was sorry, but he would not give me complete control over my assistant. I rode home in silence with my Director. What had been our three month leave, had now developed into a terminal furlough. I had emphasized to the Bishop that his original words to me made it impossible for me to be responsible for a department

I couldn't completely administer.

When I arrived at home, I told Jeanne the outcome of the meeting. She was appalled. We had been packing for a temporary leave, which was far different than the packing necessary when you leave without planning to return to the field. Jeanne quickly tried to re-arrange our preparations. There just wasn't time to do this. We hadn't expected it would be necessary.

During the time we lived in Arusha, Jeanne had developed a very close friendship with a neighbor lady whose name was Christabelle Ouko. Her husband was one of the Ministers of the East African Community organization.

Knowing of our furlough, Christabelle and her husband, Robert, had invited us to travel to their home in Kenya as we made our way out of East Africa. It was just a matter of a few days after I had received the ultimatum from the Bishop that we were due to leave with the Oukos. We were to spend our last night sleeping in their home at Arusha.

Robert made a number of phone calls to me that night, asking me, "Are you ready to come now?" We were not. Finally at around 1 A M in the morning, we decided that we couldn't hope to finish packing up our house. So we agreed that he should come and get us. We had two big piles of things on the floor of the house. One was a pile of things we now wanted to burn. The other was a pile of things we wanted to give as gifts to the worker who had served us in our home.

I find it wise not to bring up this night in any conversation with Jeanne. We simply had to abandon good order that night, and we left our house in a mess, something Jeanne

had never done before and has never been forced to do since.

Farewell to Tanzania

CHAPTER 21

"Jesus said to him, "No one,
who puts his hand to the plow, and
looks back is fit for the kingdom of God."
Lk. 9:62

You might say that in 1975 we had just reached our majority. We had been serving in Tanzania for 21 years. Now it seemed we might be leaving this field of service for good. I was still unable to believe that we had not been able to sort things out in the Department. I had built in a lot of potential plans for the future there. The short time I had been allowed to know that we could not return to this work devastated me.

I had written to our Africa Secretary telling him of the seriousness of the situation I was in, and that I wouldn't return to the department unless things could be set right. I didn't believe I would have to make good on my threat. When it did become reality, the next step was to answer the question: "what will we do now?" I was committed to serving in Africa until retirement.

Unfortunately, the Africa Secretary took my resignation from the Department as a resignation from the Board of World Missions. I was apparently to return to the U. S., serve a year of deputation under the Board's program of "Missionary in Residence," and then be terminated. I repeatedly wrote to the Board insisting that I had not resigned from Mission service. They insisted that I had resigned.

Finally, it was made very clear to me that the Board had no other place they wished to offer me in which I could serve overseas.

When we returned home someone remarked to me, "You and Jeanne have served the Lord well for the last 21 years in Africa. Now you deserve to enjoy life by living here in America."

Strangely enough, we didn't feel -- at home -- as we traveled around visiting churches in 1975-76. We were "Missionaries in residence" serving the Pacific Northwest Synod of the Lutheran Church in America.
We met many old friends on our travels of deputation. This was the fifth time we had the chance to witness to the home Churches for a year's running on behalf of Missions.

At this time I then began pursuing another possibility. I had seen the very great opportunity Film Evangelism offered throughout East and Central Africa. I applied to the Lutheran World Federation, to serve under them in the area of Mobile Film Evangelism. I had great hopes that they would agree to this because it was something needed and wasn't being done except for what we had been doing in the Department. It was true that the Christian Council of Kenya was doing something like this kind of work and called it <u>Cinema Leo</u> (Today's Cinema). However they only showed films in Kenya.

I went to the lengths of designing a fifth-wheel trailer rig, that would have been very useful if L. W. F. granted their approval. They kept me waiting hopefully for some time before their negative answer came through to me. They said the work of Film Evangelism should be done by the local or regional Church in Africa. So that closed another possible door of opportunity for us.

Both Jeanne and I still felt the call to serve as overseas missionaries. As we spent our year as **Missionaries in residence** to the Pacific Northwest Synod, almost every presentation we made caused us to become very 'homesick' to return to our adopted land, and to continue to serve the people there. This final year of service to the Board quickly came to an end, and there were many adjustments to be made. We had been living in housing rented in Tacome Wa., and paid for by our Board of Missions. It had been negotiated on short term agreements with several professors who taught at Pacific Lutheran University and who were away on their sabbatical leaves -- we moved twice during that year. Now while we awaited the next development in our lives, it was necessary for us to find another place to live. Rev. Leslie Larson and his wife Louise were serving Zion Lutheran Church in Everett, Washington. They graciously invited us to share their parsonage. They were making an extended trip to Sweden, and I could help them by filling Zion's pulpit while they were gone.

Dr. A. G. Fjellman, President of the Pacific Northwest Synod of the Lutheran Church in America, suggested that I take a call to a church in the Pacific Northwest Synod. The Church he had in mind was located in Portland, Oregon, and was called Gloria Dei in the suburb of Parkrose. I agreed to take this charge as an interim assignment. So when the Larsons returned from their trip abroad, we moved down to Gloria Dei. We now had the opportunity to continue in the parish ministry in Oregon. But my spirit gave me no peace there, even though I enjoyed the work I had at Gloria Dei as its interim pastor.

In the meantime, I had applied to an independent Lutheran Mission organization with which we had contact in the past: the **WORLD MISSION PRAYER LEAGUE.** We had come to know about W. M. P. L. at the time we served our seminary internship in Minneapolis at Trinity Lutheran Church of Minnehaha Falls in 1952. That Church had a close relationship with the Prayer League. The World Mission Prayer League was a "faith" Mission. It, as a sponsoring organization, gave no salary but promised a monthly stipend to each of its missionaries as the Lord's provision made this possible.

I suggested to Jeanne that we go forward in faith and 'just see' whether the Lord would open the doors to further service overseas.

The response from the Prayer League to our application came back positive. So my time at Gloria Dei was limited to three months. During that time we made many new friends who would become ardent supporters of us and our future work in our new venture of service to the Lord under a Faith mission.

In Transition

CHAPTER 22

"Thank God, the Father of our Lord
Jesus Christ, that he is our Father
and the source of all mercy and com-
fort. For he gives us comfort in
our trials so that we in turn may be
able to give the same sort of strong
sympathy to others in theirs."
II Cor. 1:3-4   Phillips

I had suggested to Jeanne that we go forward in faith and "just see" whether the Lord would open the doors.

First He would have to provide us with several thousand dollars to ship our freight back to Africa. Then we would need money to pay for our travel and other costs in getting settled into whatever would be our new work. Some of our freight was still packed in shipping barrels -- ready to go. We hadn't even gotten into them during the time we had been back on what we called our 'home leave'. But we didn't have any funds now to send them off, nor for any other large expense.

The Prayer League gave a briefing course which was held in Minneapolis at their offices. I went back in the spring of 1976 to attend it. Jeanne stayed with the family in Portland. We had already completed our application forms. We had applied to serve with W.M.P.L. under their sponsorship in Kenya where they worked there with a national church. In the fall of 1976 Jeanne and I both returned to Minneapolis so that we could appear before the Prayer League's Board to be accepted as their missionaries. We learned that there were four areas of service possible through W.M.P.L. to serve in the Lutheran Church of Kenya: Audio Visual, Managing a farm, serving as a parish pastor in a rural congregation in southwestern Kenya, or serving as pastor to the English Speaking section of the congregation of Uhuru Highway Lutheran Church in downtown Nairobi. I remembering thinking that the last opportunity on the list was the one I would least like to receive as an assignment. As it turned out, we were placed to serve the Nairobi English Speaking Congregation.

We returned to Portland, and began packing our things to move out of the Gloria Dei parsonage. Another pastor had been chosen to serve that parish when we had made our decision to return to Africa. The date to vacate the house, and the date to send our things off to Africa drew alarmingly close. We didn't have the two thousand dollars to pay for the shipment overseas. In the Prayer League it was understood that you would not solicit funds, you were to "trust the Lord for all your needs."

Even had we asked friends to help, I don't think we would have been able to get the two thousand dollars we needed in time. That also would have been against W.M.P.L. policy. It now seemed to appear that we would have to accept the fact -- a "faith" mission just wasn't in the picture for us.

Another concern was causing Jeanne not to feel at peace about going back to overseas service at this time. She was very worried about one of our children's difficulty in adjusting to life in the U. S. She then put out a fleece before the Lord. He answered her in a marvelous way. Then she felt the freedom in her spirit to say: "I'm ready now to go to Kenya. I have gotten the answer I prayed for."

Right at this time, I got a letter from Dr. Dave Vikner, he was the Executive Director of the L.C.A.'s Department of World Missions. He wrote that while I was serving in Tanzania and paying income tax there, the Tanzanian Government had given me tax remission. I had been training nationals as a part of our A/V program -- this was the reason the remission had been given. Dr. Vikner explained that the money which had been paid to the Government by the L.C.A. Board on my behalf had been subsequently returned to the Board. He was now turning it over to me.

The amount: two thousand dollars!

I turned fifty that year. The Lord was now about to privilege me to learn how faithful He could be in meeting all my needs, and those of my family as Jeanne, Heidi and I now returned to Africa for our second opportunity in His service there. Heidi was fifteen and the last of our five children still at home with us. She returned to Rift Valley Academy, located outside Nairobi, to finish high school. She had attended R.V.A. during our previous time of service.

I must comment on the differences in serving as a salaried

missionary and as one who goes out in faith without a salary guaranteed. Both situations are entered into by answering a call from the Lord. But in either case, the Lord is completely dependable and trustworthy. He is **Jehovah-Jireh -- The Provider (Gen. 22:14).** I believe that before I joined the Prayer League I took his daily provision largely for granted. Now He was leading Jeanne and me into a new and deeper understanding and appreciation of His personal care for us as we began our next period in His service.

When He issues you His call, never fail to answer Him in the words of the Prophet Isaiah: "Here am I, send me!" Have no doubt about His provision and care. He is **JEHOVAH JIREH!**

Part 2 Kenya 1977-1992

Nairobi - One foot in Africa

CHAPTER 23

"I will return to you if God wills.."
                    Acts 18:21

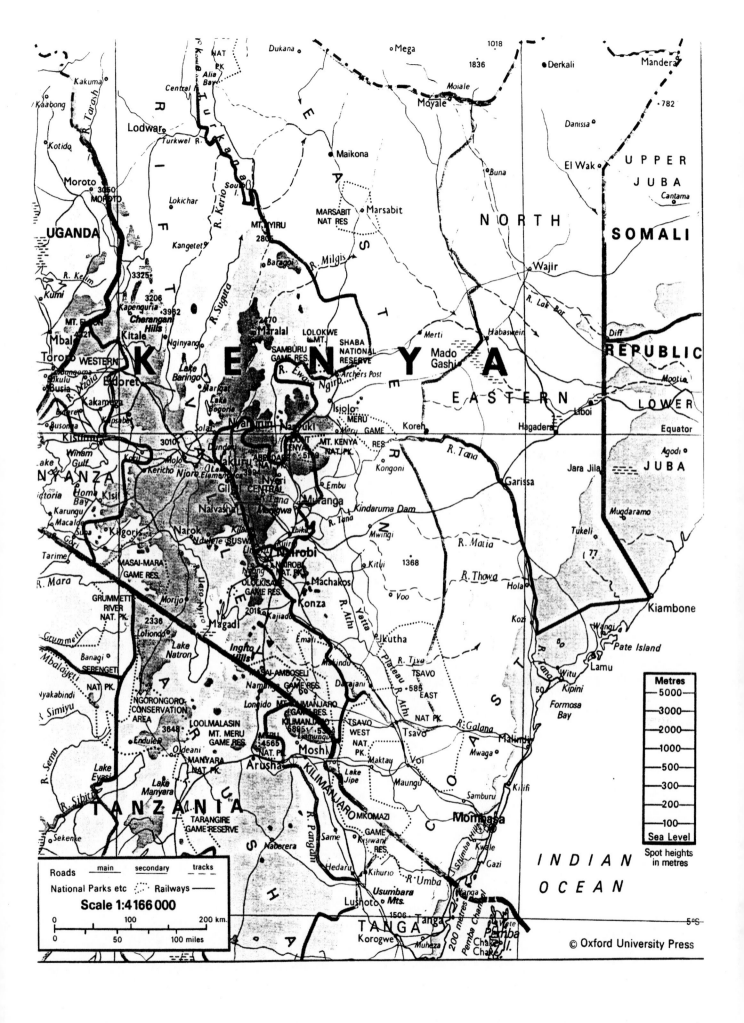

Mombasa is the seaport of the Republic of Kenya and is located on the Indian Ocean. The city of Nairobi, Kenya's capital, is three hundred thirty miles northwest of Mombasa. Nairobi is located on the Athi Plains at the foot of the Kikuyu escarpment. Its population in 1959, near the close of the colonial era, was around 137,000. The city was supposed to have been built on a swamp by virtue of being the place where the hard trek up into the highlands to the west began.

At the time we arrived to begin our service there in January, 1977, Nairobi was a very beautiful place. Called the "City in the Sun," it represented past British Colonial administration at its very best. It was said that every stone or green belt or road in the city was planned. Beautiful green belts (areas of trees and shrubbery) followed the lines of creeks and small rivers which ran through the town. These were supposed to be sacrosanct areas which would not be violated by building housing developments on them. So the city was not lacking for parks or wooded areas. The Nairobi Game Park, located just to the east of the city gave the photographer from abroad a unique opportunity. He could fill his lens with a herd of zebra or wildebeest and have the Nairobi skyline as an impressive background.

Uhuru Highway, a six lane thoroughfare divided in the center by a grassy meridian, is the city's main street. It enters the city limits from the east. It is the continuation of the main road coming up from Mombasa. This road, after passing through the heart of the city, exits to the west. It then proceeds west until it reaches the town of Nakuru. A few miles further on to the west you have the choice to go to Kisumu located on the shore of Lake Victoria. Or taking a turn to follow a road northwest will lead to Eldoret and thence to cross the border into Uganda.

Another road leading off to the southwest in this same general area will eventually lead to the Kenya's southwestern border and crossing it brings you into Tanzania.

At the time of our arrival Nairobi was estimated to have a population of about 500,000. In the years since independence which came to Kenya in 1963, it has always been difficult to get an accurate census of Nairobi because of the great number of people rapidly moving in or out, especially those living in the slums.

In the time following Kenya's independence, Nairobi continued to grow as the commercial center and hub of East Africa. Many international companies and N.G.O.'s (Non-Governmental aid and assistance Organizations) from abroad located their branch offices there. The building of very large hotels and office buildings signaled the quick changes taking place.

It appeared as though there was competition between the Kenya Government and the private sector. The Catholic Cathedral of Nairobi -- The Holy Family Bascilica -- was built in the center of town. As a part of the structure a bell tower rose above the ground to surpass the height of all the other Nairobi buildings. Then the Kenya Government built a conference center not too far from the Cathedral. Its height not only matched that of the Cathedral's bell tower, but surpassed it.

We were very glad to be able to return to Africa again. Even though it wasn't Tanzania, Nairobi was a place where we quickly felt at home. In 1977 Nairobi was a delightful city in which to live. But each succeeding year has brought more immigration from up-country into the city, mostly to the slum areas. These are good rural people but without training to find work in the city. By 1992, the year we left Kenya for retirement, estimates placed the population of the city at between a million and a half to two million souls. This overwhelmed the city's infra-structure. Service facilities like water supply, power, roads, and public transport are unable to cope with the demands made on them. Unemployment was also very high. This has taken away much of the older image of a peaceful and beautiful city that existed in the past. That image has been replaced by one of all kinds of shortages and a big crime problem.

However, even in 1977 Nairobi could be described as a

city which was more European in flavor than African. The expression therefore arose: "When you land in Nairobi, you only have one foot in Africa."

Upon our arrival, we were given living quarters at our Mission's house located in the suburb of Westlands. It was a short distance, about five miles from the town center itself. We shared the housing at the Cedar Road location with Rev. Paul Edstrom and his family. The house which had been built as a fairly large estate house, now had been sub-divided. Our portion of it was comprised of two sections: a narrow living-dining room, a bathroom, and a kitchen plus an adjoining bedroom. Across an enclosed court yard there was another bedroom, a toilet next to it and a tiny storeroom off the court yard.

The grounds were graded in steps from the street level on the upper side of the plot down to a small creek which bordered the low end of the property. The creek, from beginning to end, was called the 'Nairobi River.' During the rainy season it carried a considerable flow of water. There were a number of flowering tropical plants growing on the property. One very large date palm dominated the center of the lower yard, and shared in the beauty which several kumquat trees provided. There was also a guava tree which bore fruit.

Looking across the Nairobi River, one saw a mass of jungle like growth which seemed to be impenetrable as it climbed up the next hillside. The yard, down along the river, gave me space to plant a small vegetable garden. The grounds were completely surrounded with a high chain-link fence.

Shortly after we arrived, I turned the small store next to the second bedroom into an office. The downtown church had none.

The house was located at the end of Cedar Road which was a dead end street. That ensured the location would be a quiet place without traffic noise. The house provided us with all we needed for comfortable living as we settled in to begin our work.

We journeyed out to the Ev. Lutheran Church of Kenya's office at Kisii in western Kenya so that we could be formally welcomed into our new work. Our hearts rejoiced at the warm reception we received from the Africa church leaders. Their sincerity of welcome brought to my mind the warmth of fellowship we had enjoyed in the years we had served the Central Synod of the Lutheran Church in Tanzania. It was like coming home again after being away on a long trip.

Uhuru Highway~ A call to build in faith

CHAPTER 24

"..for great is our God above all
gods. But who is able to build him
a house, seeing heaven and the heaven
of heavens cannot contain him? Who
am I then, that I should build him a
house?" ..... II Chron. 2:5-6

The Lutheran Church in Nairobi, UHURU HIGHWAY LUTHERAN
CHURCH, had two congregations. The English speaking
international section of that Church was partly made up of
expatriates (foreigners). Some of these people were employed
by international firms that had their branch offices in Nairobi.
Nairobi can certainly be classed as the commercial hub of
East Africa. Other members worked for international aid
organizations like World Vision and Bread for the World and
Christoffel Blinden Mission. We also drew congregational members
from religious groups like Life Ministries, an arm of Campus
Crusade for Christ. There were also those who were foreign
employees from Norway assisting the Kenya Government as well
as U.S.A.I.D. personnel. Some others who worked for the United
Nation's large office in Nairobi came from Ethiopia and
Tanzania. The balance of the membership of this section were
nationals from Kenya. I was assigned to be pastor for this
group.

The Swahili speaking section of Uhuru Highway Lutheran
Church was made up of nationals from Kenya and Tanzania.
Originally the citizens of Tanzania who worked and lived in
Nairobi had formed the Lutheran nucleus from which the

congregation had been formed. Shepherding the Swahili speaking section was the responsibility of Pastor Paul Edstrom. He was the leader of the Nairobi District of the E.L.C.K. as well.

Our church benefited because of Uhuru Highway's location -- a high profile corner on one of Nairobi's busiest thoroughfares. Hundreds of Nairobi's residents passed by our church every weekday on their way to and from work.

The Church building had originally been built by the Presbyterians in 1909. It had passed through the hands of another group, the Dutch Reformed Church, before it finally became Lutheran property. The structure itself was small, it had a seating capacity for a little more than two hundred. It was badly in need of major repairs. The walls were slowly sinking because they lacked adequate footings. There were temporary/permanent log supports buttressing the outside walls to restrict their outward movement as they slowly continued to settle deeper into the black cotton soil.

For all of its deficiencies, it was a Nairobi landmark dear to the hearts of a number of Nairobi's older residents. Many of them remembered being married or having their children baptized in this church.

It was reputed to be the first church built in Nairobi. Because it had traditionally western church lines and a steeple with a weather vane at its peak, it was the classic image of a Christian Church for everyone living in the city.

But it had yet another liability -- that of being built

with a portion of the structure extending over the lot's boundary line. There were city plans current to widen Uhuru Highway. With the widening, this building error of long ago would become a serious matter to resolve.

The floor in several places in the front of the sanctuary was "restricted entry." It was unsafe to put any heavy object like a piano there, or even to allow several people to stand together at the same time.

There had been a plan existent for some time, funded by the Lutheran World Federation, to rebuild the Church. They had given a grant of about $ 35,000 to finance a new church building. However, tearing down the old structure posed a great problem. It was considered to be an historical landmark. As soon as plans were announced that we intended to build a new building criticism started to be directed toward us.

Barclays Bank of Nairobi had bought the old Railway Station building several blocks away from our location. The Nairobi Historical Society immediately refused to allow any change to be made to that old building. To this day Barclays regret their purchase of this very expensive property. Even though they are using the building, it isn't providing them with the development which they had envisioned.

We hoped to go ahead with our building plans and believed we could make our plea to rebuild on the grounds that our Church would soon be condemned as unsafe for occupancy.

At this time a very unusual offer was made to our congregation. The large Nairobi Presbyterian Church located just up the hill from us was really the daughter of our little church. They said that if we would give them our old building they would move it from its present location and rebuild it on their grounds.

We were overjoyed. This saved us the expense of demolishing it. This would also silence the critics who said we were destroying an historical building. Their offer was gratefully accepted.

Even today, one can still worship in the old sanctuary which was moved up the hill, literally piece by piece, at a very considerable expense.

My colleague in the work, Rev. Edstrom, had been negotiating with an architect for a long time. One day he came to me and said that the architect who had promised to design and build for us within our current budget now had refused. He said we would have to find more money. This was such a disappointment to Pastor Edstrom who had worked so long on these negotiations that he told me, "You take over Bob."

I had been in residence in Nairobi less than a year when I was given the full responsibility of both sections of the Uhuru Highway Congregation.

When I arrived in January 1977, attendance at the English service was low. By November of that same year we were averaging 92 people a Sunday.

I did a lot of re-organization in both section of the congregation. The Sunday School had classes for both English and Swahili speaking students. A number of new teachers were enrolled.

The elders of the Swahili and English sections of the congregation now met jointly twice a month to plan the church program. I made a promise to these busy men and women that these elders' meetings would only take an hour from their full schedules for each meeting -- a promise which we faithfully kept. This was facilitated by preparing an agenda which was distributed in advance of each meeting.

Both sections of the congregation provided members for our elders' council who were some of the top men and women in their fields in the jobs they held in Nairobi. Let me take this opportunity to list just a few who served over the years:

Mr. John Mamboleo Onsando, Chairman
(Kenya Regional Gov't Development official)

Mr. Albert Mongi
(U. N. Forestry official)

Mr. Nagezy Gebremedhin
(U. N. Habitat official)

Mr. Gene Grogan
(Offshore Oxcidental Petroleum Developer)

Mr. Geoffery Ngumuo
(Shell Oil Co. accountant)

Mr. Geoffery Maoga
(Kenya Posts and Telecommunications)
Professor Joseph Otieno
(Nairobi University - Statistics)

Mrs. Debra Malik
(Professor - American University - Nairobi)

Mrs. Judith Volz
(Husband was director of Norwegian Church Aid)

Mr. Dieter Opitz

(Africa Director - Christoffel Blinden Mission)

Mr. Kenneth Lendh
(World Vision)

Mr. Robert Auer
(Life Ministries)

Mr. Erling Hansen
(Norad - Highway developer)

Mr. Ray Cramer
(Auditor General - U.S.A.I.D. Nairobi)

It was a delight to see the very capable manner in which John Onsando the chairman of the congregation conducted the elders' meetings. He administered the finances of the congregation with great executive ability. Jeanne, my wife, was treasurer of the congregation until Mr. Ray Cramer agreed to take that responsibility.

When the time came to consider the huge step of whether to attempt to build a new church under these very special circumstances the elders were invaluable in their support.

No commercial bank would consider granting our congregation a loan to finance its project. We thought we had the major portion of the funding we needed. We didn't dream when we began to build that the final cost of constructing Uhuru Highway's new sanctuary would come to $ 246,568 - - almost a quarter of a million dollars! We had only about fourteen percent of that amount in hand when we started.

The elders met with me to make a final decision about going ahead with our building program. I shared with the group my conviction that I believed we should proceed with our project "in faith." The council members cast their votes. It was a unanimous decision that we build.

Right at this time, Nairobi's economy was undergoing a recession. This meant that the bids the building contractors were making were very favorable for us. However, we sustained a large penalty when we terminated the original architect and had to pay for the unsatisfactory plans he had developed for the building. In his place we employed an Ethiopian architect whose name was Wubu. He worked closely with Mr. Gabremedhin our elder, who was himself an expert in this field.

The new plans which Mr. Wubu presented were very good.

*   *   *   *   *   *

It might be well to pause at this time to give a short picture of the program at Uhuru Highway in 1977.

With the increase in Sunday School enrollment and with no facilities available in our small sanctuary, a solution to this problem was sought. Across the street from our church stood the recently built St. Pauls Catholic Church which had a large parish building. We asked them to allow us to hold our Sunday School there and they kindly agreed. The Priest jokingly said, "Don't tell anybody." Later with the demolition of our old sanctuary, they kindly allowed us to hold our worship services there also.

The spiritual life of the congregation was not in decline during our upset of building. There were evidences those days of the working of the Holy Spirit in conversion, renewal and empowering. One example of this was when God called a Korean lady to give her heart to Him just as she and her American husband were leaving our fellowship on a transfer of jobs. She had been a Buddhist until her conversion.

Our ministry in the Nairobi Hospital had also been effective by the power of the Holy Spirit in bringing souls to faith. The patients who cried out to God in their physical need received both physical as wellas spiritual health.

The stewardship level of giving among congregational members rose significantly and continued to keep in step with our increasing expenses and constantly growing building budget.

We were also blessed in our program by getting some extra things which would add to and benefit our work. A new 16MM sound projector was purchased. Each Wednesday during the Advent season religious films were shown. Showing films resulted in very good attendance by people from within, as well as of non-members from outside the congregation.

We used a small pump organ for our services faithfully played by a young lady whose name was Laura Volz, which added a great deal to our worship. Later Mrs. Ray Cramer became our organist.

The Lord answered our prayers and made it possible for us to acquire a secondhand minibus which seated nine passengers. It was largely through the support of two former missionaries from Tanzania: Mrs. Veda Magnuson and Mrs. Muriel Lundell from First Lutheran Church of White Bear Lake, Minnesota that we were able to purchase the bus. Veda's husband, Norman was pastor of First Lutheran. The ladies, knowing of our transportion needs in Nairobi started a project called "Ward's Wagon." People at First Lutheran were encouraged to contribute toward the cost of this vehicle. It was a great asset each Tuesday evening as we picked up people around the city for Bible studies. The bus had originally been used to transport tourists to the Game Parks. The study sessions met in our home or in the homes of some of our members. The fellowship of those days was something we all enjoyed and counted as a great blessing. As one of the members told me, "Thank you for making it fun to go to church again."

1978 was spent in strengthening the program of the parish. Weddings, confirmation classes and routine Sunday services together with the participation of our congregation in a city-wide "I FOUND IT" campaign conducted by Life Ministry filled our schedule. It was also time spent in making an appeal for funds to meet our building expenses. We did this by contacting all the Mission agencies directly or indirectly involved with our project.

On May 18, 1979, we held a ground breaking ceremony on the Church site. Both sections of the congregation -- the English/International section, which normally met at 9 A.M. and the Swahili section which met at 10 A.M. -- met together at 9:30 A.M. for a joint bilingual service in the old sanctuary. Hymns were sung as each member sang using his own language. I did the preaching using each language in short segments.

Following the worship service which lasted an hour, the group processed outside to observe and participate in the actual pround breaking. The ceremony continued as the Swahili Choir sang. Then the architect and the nine members of the building committee were introduced to the congregation of over 200 members who were present. Pastor Ward and Elder Albert Mongi ceremonially broke ground using an East Africa jembe(hoe) and a shovel. The service ended with offering prayers for the project's success followed by the benediction.

Redeeming God's Promise

CHAPTER 25

"But my God shall supply all your
need according to his riches in
glory by Christ Jesus."
Phil. 4:19   K.J.V.

Following the ground breaking ceremony, work began immediately by Kehar Singh Kalsi and their large construction firm. Samples were taken of the strata below the surface and it was found that this former swamp didn't have much to offer in the way of support for a building. Because of this the architect planned a very large supporting foundation beneath the new church. Indeed it was reported to me that over one-third of the cost of the building would have to be spent in preparing an adequate foundation. Work also proceeded in the process of moving our old building up the hill. Fortunately this involved a very time consuming process because the attempt was made to salvage every part of the old church down to the last brick. We were able to continue to worship for quite some time in the old sanctuary before we had to move elsewhere. The contract of construction called for a completion of the building by June 1980,a period of eleven months. I kept our donors informed of the building progress by taking pictures periodically of the work completed and sending them out. I did this as each of the four stages of the work was completed and it provided a real stimulus for gathering continued support.

We met with the contractor at intervals that were called Site Committee Meetings, and presented checks of payment for the work completed.

We also employed a Quantity Surveyor who was a Nairobi

University student studying architecture. He kept us well
informed on the building's progress. He worked measuring the
materials being used to build the church, the strength of the
cement, etc, to protect us from being exploited by the
contractor and the sub-contractors. He was a very important
resource to us in this project.

There was a lag in the amount of money we had available
towards the close of the building period. We ended up in August
of 1981 with a shortfall of over $ 8,000 and were wondering
where we could get this large sum. Our donors had all given
once and in a number of cases several times to help us.
Finally, Mr. Gabremedhin in a contact with the Church of Sweden
Mission, was able to settle our deficit. The project had been
a matter of building in faith, but the promise of the Lord
to provide was something we were led to depend upon. He is
indeed: **JEHOVAH JIREH!** Because of His provision, we soon were
able to finish with a Church that was debt free. The Lord
used the following Churches and organizations to make His
provision available to us at Uhuru Highway:

```
            Lutheran World Federation   -- L. W. F.
            Lutheran Church in Bavaria  -- L. C. W.
            Lutheran Church In America  -- L. C. A.
            Swedish Lutheran Mission    -- S. L. M.
            Lutheran Ev. Assn. Of Finland -- L. E. A. F.
            Norwegian Lutheran Mission   -- N. L. M.
            World Mission Prayer League  -- W. M. P. L.
            Congregational giving Uhuru Highway
            Church Of Sweden Mission -- CSM
```

The members of Uhuru Highway gave sacrifically for our
special need to meet our building budget. However they were
not alone in the Lord's personal provision for our church.

As a part of our building we had a lot of room space to be used for Sunday School meetings and as a fellowship hall. We needed to be able to divide all this space up into rooms for meetings, and then to be able to remove the 'walls' for large gatherings. A Rev. Solberg who had retired in Ferndale Washington had been constructing expandable walls or room dividers that ran on overhead tracks. We saw an example of his work in a Seattle church. These dividers pushed together like an accordion when not in use, but when used as room dividers were excellent in every respect including noise control. I arranged for construction of a number of long dividers with Pastor Solberg to meet our needs. The doors were constructed and by hurrying, Pastor Solberg met my schedule and gave them to us at his cost. I picked up the doors in Blaine and sent them on their way to Kenya during our furlough of 1980/81. I later installed them myself at Uhuru Highway after they arrived by sea freight. We closed our program by quoting from Ps. 34:1-2

> "I will always thank the Lord;
> I will never stop praising Him!
> I will praise Him for what He has done. ."

During the project's duration our regular work in the Church went forward. We had a national evangelist whose name was Samson Onditi. He served the Swahili section of the congregation with excellence. We were now blessed by the Lord in receiving three new workers who joined us at this time. Mr. Robert Schmalzle and his wife Denise came out from the U. S. on a two year theological internship. Bob and Denise were very encouraging and gifted people. Bob organized the youth activities of the church as well as serving in many other ways to fulfill his internship.

Miss Tuula Saaski joined our team to serve as our parish worker. She was a Finnish missionary who had already spent a long time serving the Lutheran Church in Kenya in other work.

At this time we began to think in terms of encouraging the E. L. C. K. to place a Kenyan pastor at Uhuru Highway. As a result of our suggestions Pastor Nickolas Oenga was chosen to serve at Uhuru Highway. The projection was that I would remain at Uhuru Highway for a two year period of indoctrination for Pastor Oenga, then he would become senior pastor.

Unreached People: A call to begin new work

CHAPTER 26

"But there are other sheep of mine, not
belonging to this fold, whom I must
bring in; and they too will listen to
my voice. There will then be one flock,
one shepherd." Jn. 10:16   N.E.B.

Along with our busy schedule serving Uhuru Highway, we also had other concerns. The home board of the World Mission Prayer League had encouraged all the missionaries on its fields to explore the possibilities for new work in their areas. The members of the Kenya field were very open to this call. During the month of March 1979, the General Director of the home board, Rev. Al Berg as well as our Africa Director, Theodore Manaen had visited our field. One of their requests was for further information from us about new field possibilities in Kenya.

As a field we determined to attempt to find new unevangelized areas to suggest as new work possibilities. We therefore scheduled a safari on May 9th to look into an area we had heard about - south Maasai in Kenya. This area was located on the border between Kenya and Tanzania. Although the April rains extended into May '79, we set out on safari as a team from Nairobi and picked up a borrowed car from the Finnish Missionaries who served the E.L.C.K. in southwestern Kenya. Rev. Bill Jacobson, Mr. Andrew Wendler, Mr. Mike Koski and I borrowed the four wheel drive vehicle. Our plan was to visit the target area in southern Kenya and assess the needs and possibilities for beginning a new outreach there.

Because the survey was undertaken during the rainy season

several times it appeared that we would have to turn back due to impassable roads; however we did make it through. The conclusion we reached was that the south Maasai area in Kenya was already well and adequately served by several other missions. We believed that we might serve the Lord better if we looked into other areas where no outreach was yet being done.

We then turned our attention northward. The Norwegian Lutheran Mission had asked us to examine the Borana area in the far north of Kenya. It was a field the N.L.M. wanted to serve, but felt at that time they didn't have the personnel or resources to do so. An N.L.M. missionary Rev. Tore Vagness used his car to host our survey party to an area called the Huri Hills. From this location the mountains of southern Ethiopia could be seen far off across the Chalbi desert to the north.

One of the nights on safari in a hastily constructed camp we were sitting in the half light of the camp fire. Jeanne and I were sitting beside each other on safari chairs. I sensed some movement on the dusty ground in front of us. When I turned on my flashlight its beam revealed two very large scorpions marching abreast directly towards us. Their tails and stingers were up at the ready. They appeared to be like two soldiers on a mission. I made quick work of disposing of their threat by stomping them to death with my thick safari boots.

Those making up this survey group were: the Exec. Secy. of the E.L.C.K., Rev. Richard Olak, Mr. Mike Koski, Rev.

Vagness, Jeanne and I.

This area, called the Northern Frontier District of Kenya, was a buffer area and had long been a restricted zone under British Colonial administration.

Our group did not feel that we should enter this area, and as a result the N.L.M. proceeded with their own plan to begin there. They had a background for special interest.

Prior to the time when the Communists took over Ethiopia, the N.L.M. was working among the Oromo people in the southern part of that country. N.L.M. was then expelled by the Communists. As they began work in Borana some of the people they had served in Ethiopia came across the Kenya border to fellowship with the N.L.M. missionaries whom they formally had known and loved.

Our search for a new field continued. I had heard through the material coming out from Dr. Ralph Winter and the publication of a timely book called "Unreached Peoples", that the Samburu in Northern Kenya were a group unreached with the Gospel. I was able to gather more information about them from an Africa Inland Mission veteran missionary, Rev. Earl Andersen. His group was doing work among the Rendille. This tribe lived to the northeast of the Samburu area. Rev. Andersen shared with me that he often flew across 'Samburu' and prayed that they might one day be evangelized.

Living in Nairobi we also had contact with an organization called Helimission. Some of their folks came to Uhuru Highway for services. This was a missionary organization that was begun with the purpose of providing helicopter service to remote mission stations that were unable to construct landing strips for conventional aircraft because of lack of space or bad terrain.

Helimission had been working in Ethiopia when the Communists came to power. When they were told to leave by the new government, they left! The group fled to Kenya with their equipment, much to the chagrin of the new Ethiopian government which expected the group to leave their planes behind.

I felt it was a great gift from the Lord that this Mission was made available to us for surveying the Samburu area. Helimission only charged for their operating costs, even so a helicopter is expensive to operate. I presented this mode of survey as a possibility in a letter to Rev. Berg back in Minneapolis. I hadn't gotten a reply by the time of our next field meeting held in April 1980. A few of our workers on the field did not believe that this kind of survey was possible. It would be expensive!

I was field leader at the time of our meeting and suggested that we make a call to the W.M.P.L. office in Minneapolis for direction. Fortunately I was able to speak directly with Rev. Berg. He replied to my query by saying, "We've already set aside funds for this."

Arrangements then had to be made from the highest office in Kenya -- the Office of the President. My letter of April 22nd, sent to this Presidential Office was answered with permission given just at the time we most needed it. The answer came from the Department of Provincial Administration and Internal Security. It was a copy of a letter sent to the District Commissioner of the Samburu District. It said: "The Lutheran Church in Kenya is very much interested in opening their spiritual operations in the Samburu District. Before they do this they would like to survey the area using the facility of a helicopter between the period of the 1st of May and the 10th of May, 1980. We have no objection to them surveying the area. Please accord them the necessary assistance."

This was in answer to our urgent prayers. Our preparations were finalized and the safari north to set up a base camp got underway at once. Rev. Paul Volz, director of the group called Norwegian Church Aid loaned us their pickup and driver to carry up barrels of fuel. The rest of the survey team either flew up or drove up with me in my minibus. On our trip north we drove well into the night. Then we pulled off to the side of the road and set up a camp in the moonlight. I had no idea where we were except that we were near a town called Wamba.

Morning light revealed that we were camped on the side of the Wamba airstrip built by the Catholic Mission. That day the helicopter arrived and we were ready to began our survey flights.

Our roster of survey members was; Rev. Paul Edstrom, Rev. Nickolas Oenga, my wife Jeanne and myself, my college aged son Dan and his friend Bob Vance and our pilot, Smitty (Mr. Smith).

Since the helicopter could only carry four, we divided
up into parties, some members going out on alternate days.

We had a very good camp with lots of delicious food
prepared by Jeanne. The young men did the heavy work wrestling
barrels of fuel and gathering firewood. We all slept in tents.
Smitty roped off the chopper to keep daytime crowds from getting
too close to the aircraft.

For three full days we made survey trips. We went into
the Matthews Range of mountains along the eastern border of
Samburu. Then up through the central area, stopping to visit
places called Kisima and Baragoi. At Baragoi we were invited
to visit the District Officer's office for an interview with
him. We flew over and landed on the Samburu holy mountain,
Mt. Nyiro, which has a very beautiful forest on its upper
slopes.

On this mountain the fabled 'stargazer' of Samburu lived.
He was supposed to be able to predict an approaching famine
or other events of good and evil. We were told he received
his messages while lying on his back viewing the stars. The
people believed everything he said. We did not get to meet
him on this trip.

My son Dan, along on this leg of the survey was so
impressed with the beauty of the mountain that he vowed, "I
want to be stationed here if you ever build a Mission station.

"Mt. Nyiro borders on Lake Turkana, which is called the
"Jade Sea" because of its beauty. I shall always remember
its shimmering beauty as we flew around the mountain and the

loveliness of the Lake revealed itself to us as we viewed it from the air.

We made trips along the southern border to where small settlements were located like the one called Sukuta Marmar.

The value of this mode of travel is that you can interrupt your trip at any time, stop, and visit with the local people. Some of them were afraid when we landed, and ran off. One man even dived into a ditch out of fear. But most of them were drawn to see this machine that dropped from the sky so effortlessly.

Again and again, when we were able to communicate our purpose for this visit, we were warmly welcomed and assured that we would be well received if we began a Mission in Samburu. In each place they pleaded, "Come to us here."

When we had completed our survey of the whole area to our satisfaction we discovered that Smitty had just enough fuel to return to Nairobi.

At the next field meeting we held, the field accepted Samburu as our opportunity for a new outreach area. Then the call was given for volunteers to begin the work. No one volunteered to go although the Koskis indicated a great interest in going when they completed their current term and its assignment.

Jeanne and I then felt God's call was given to us. We had always been interested in new fields and outreach work. We had also been praying that God would call workers for Samburu and we now felt that we would be in His will if we volunteered.

We were due for furlough. We agreed that after our return from home leave, we would have two years to hand over our work at Uhuru Highway to Pastor Oenga and also have time to survey Samburu again to locate a site to begin work on this new field.

Jeanne was heavily involved in the Sunday School development and work at Uhuru Highway. She would leave her work there with a mixture of joy and sadness. I, too, was thoroughly enjoying our new church building and the fellowship of a growing congregation. Even so we both were satisfied that this new opportunity was God's next call for us.

The time for our furlough arrived and we left the field in Nairobi in August of 1980. The Uhuru Highway Church was left in the capable hands of Intern Bob Schmalzle. My "Samburu" assignment while I was home in the U. S. was to prepare a complete budget for the beginning development of this new work. I set about doing this after our arrival in the U.S. and got it on its way back to the field in Kenya. I also sent copies of my estimates to the Home Council office in Minneapolis. Unfortunately the leader to whom it was sent on the field didn't acknowledge before our group that it had arrived. The field thought I had ignored them. I also sent all the information to Mike Koski knowing of his great interest and commitment for the future of Samburu work. I suggested that we plan on establishing two station/outreach centers at the outset of the work.

On the field in Kenya a special meeting was held on December 26, 1980. The purpose of the meeting was "to discuss further the proposed Samburu Project and act on the capital and recurrent budgets submitted by Pastor Bob Ward in the USA and in recent correspondence with Mike Koski on the field." It was requested that "we give Field approval to the budgets which now have been accepted by WMPL Home Council."

I was extremely disappointed by the first resolution that was made and passed at this meeting: "that in the initial stage of the Samburu Project we limit ourselves to one center only and work out into the area from there, and that such a center be located with an accessibility to roads and communications preferably in a population center near a police post, medical and trading facilities, etc."

I was very troubled by the change from the development method I had suggested and the one decided upon by the Field. I coined a term: Absentee Missionaries, to point up how unworkable I thought it would be to try to live at one place and make your witness and work somewhere else. There was also the question in my mind about one's seeking what I called creature comforts.

In all our past work in Tanzania, we had lived as closely as we possibly could to the targets of our evangelistic effort.

During our furlough I wrote a resume of our past efforts in East Africa and of our future hopes and plans.

".....AND NOW SAMBURU"

As Jeanne and I and our family began our life of service in East Africa, we began by serving a mission station for four years which was truly at the end of the road, called Isanzu.

Then the Lord called us through the Lutheran Church of Central Tanganyika, to reach out in a ministry to people -- migrant tribes -- living out even farther where there were no roads. He gave us a wonderful opportunity for witness among the nomadic cattle herders as well as hunters and gatherers for 11 years.

He gave the increase and called many into His fellowship using us as His tools.

For the last four years we've had the opportunity to work in Nairobi, a very large and international city, pastoring the Uhuru Highway Lutheran Church serving in the Lutheran Church of Kenya. As we now leave to return to East Africa in June ('81) we will return to Nairobi, but our time there will be limited because of our next opportunity -- entering into Samburu -- this is the next thing we see as God's plan for our lives and service to Him, and it is thrilling to anticipate.

As we return the Lord has once again, as He has each time in the past when we have gone out, given us a special promise from His Word to be our emblem for this new period of opportunity.

It is this:

"And the Lord, He it is that doth go before thee;fear

not neither be dismayed." Deut. 31:8

Going out with this promise which was received just the other day, we will enter into Samburu knowing that God will use us in His work and His will there as long as we stay close to Him in repentance and faith.

The Hidden Valley & Open Door

CHAPTER 27

"....Behold, I have set before you
an open door, which no one is able
to shut; I know that you have but
little power, but have kept my word
and have not denied my name."

Rev. 3:8

We returned to Nairobi from our furlough on June 1st, 1981. Kris, our oldest daughter who worked for Northwest Airlines accompanied us so that we got 'pass rates' from her traveling with us. After three days, she began her return trip to the U. S. We deeply appreciated her kindness.

We were picked up at the airport and learned to our dismay that some changes had been made on the field. We were no longer assigned to serve at Uhuru Highway. Housing also was not available for us in Nairobi, we were supposed to go to Samburu at once.

Fortunately during the time when we lived at Cedar Road, we had built a small prefab room -- out back -- to relieve the cramped space that wasn't adequate for our whole family. The small room was known as Heidi's room. We were able temporarily to put that room to good use. Soon after our arrival, Rev. Bill Jacobson got us in contact with a lady, Heidi Bally, who had a large house located on Riverside Drive. She agreed to let us rent a section of her house for a very reasonable rate. We enjoyed getting to know Mrs. Bally, a widow who was a deeply committed Christian lady.

Shortly after our arrival, we journeyed out to the Church office in western Kenya to find out what the Church's wishes were for our service. As a result of that consultation, we were assigned to Uhuru Highway until we could move up to Samburu. To complete that move took about nine months.

Our time now was spent serving Uhuru Highway and in investigating site possibilities in Samburu.

In August 1981, Jeanne and I made a trip up to the Samburu area and did a foot safari into the Milgis River basin, coming in from the east side. The river, which is a dry sand 'highway' most of the year is a corridor that the Samburu use in their yearly migrations. We thought somewhere along this corridor would be a strategic location to establish our outreach center. It would highly visible to all the people who passed by.

The corridor lies adjacent to two mountain ranges, the Ndotos to the north, and the Matthews Range to the east. The surrounding bush country is homeland to many Samburu. The Milgis River serves as a natural passageway for those herdsmen as they follow the sparse supply of grass for their cattle which is the result of a very meager rainfall each year.

We were told there was a track we could follow with our four wheel drive Toyota Landcruiser. However, when we tried to find it we got into trouble because the track hadn't been used for a very long time. It was hard to find, and we got lost. This forced us to make a camp on the sand of a dry river bank. We used our foot safari tent, and spent a comfortable night sleeping on the floor of the tent using the soft sand underneath the tent as our mattress.

Up early the following morning, we resumed our search for the track which was shown on the map we had. With some help from two Samburu lads, we located it. We drove slowly forward, but after eleven kilometers, (about six miles) the track became totally impassable because of ravines and washouts. At that point we put up a base camp right on the lip of a big washout.

Shortly after dark, two young Samburu warriors came along the footpath and happily accepted the hospitality of our fire and a satisfying long drink of cool water. In this country, water is very hard to find.

After supper, I played some gospel story cassettes for them and asked if they would mind if we took their picture. They said this would be all right. When Jeanne took a flash shot, the warrior seated next to me exploded with a leap and a headlong dive into some small thorn bushes bordering on the camp area. After we got the poor fellow untangled from the thorns, things returned to normal. We learned that the moran had been drinking a stimulant made from soaking a certain kind of tree bark in water. This had put his nervous system at flashpoint. This is a Samburu custom, and is encouraged by the tribal elders to keep the Morans <u>ready</u> to defend the tribe. We invited the warriors to sleep on a tarp in front of our fire. They kept the fire burning very brightly for the rest of the night. Jeanne got little sleep though because she thought we might get some trouble from these men who acted so strangely.

Knowing we could proceed no farther using our Landcruiser, we packed our backpacks and set off carrying food, water, a tent, sleeping gear and cooking pots. It was approaching the end of the dry season, so the trees, anticipating the coming of the short rains, were beginning to leaf out with green leaves. Wild flowers were also beginning to appear. The flower called the Desert Rose vies with other flowers because of its outstanding beauty. It is also very poisonous, so it is to be enjoyed from a discreet distance.

As we walked along, animal bones lying along the pathway gave mute evidence of either famine conditions, or of a lion or leopard kill.

The path that we were now following was routinely used by the Samburu circling the Ndoto Mountains. Jeanne and I met some of these people, and when we did we always stopped and talked in our halting Samburu. We told them who we were and what our reason was for traveling here. From these contacts, we gained a lot of useful information about the surrounding country.

The sun was scalding hot as the day wore on. It was a dry heat which can reach 115 degrees during the hottest part of the day. Our throats and arms and faces felt the intensity of the heat. We walked and walked, and it seemed that the Milgis River was deliberately avoiding us. Finally, I suggested to Jeanne that she wait in the shade of a tree -- I would go on ahead and locate the river, then return and guide her to it.

I set off, but the river was an hour or so away. While I was searching for the river's location, Jeanne was growing very apprehensive. Then a Samburu man appeared driving several loaded donkeys. When he saw Jeanne sitting under the tree, he started to get excited.

"Where are you from?" he asked in Swahili.

"From Nairobi" Jeanne replied.

"Who is with you?" he asked.

"My husband -- he has gone on ahead to find the Milgis River, and   then he will come back to get me".

"Well don't you know this is a very dangerous place for you to be. "Don't sit down under a tree, there are lions around all over. Stand up, look around, turn this way and that!"

"Put your loads on my donkey, and I will take you to your husband, I know where he has gone."

"No thank you, I will wait for him here. I know he will come back here looking for me, and he will be worried if he doesn't find me where he left me."

I did return using a different way, and had Jeanne not stayed where I left her, we wouldn't have made contact when I came back.

It took some time before we could finally get to the river. Jeanne was feeling the sun, indeed she was beet-red by now, and suffering from total heat exhaustion. I kept encouraging her -- "just a little farther now."

The river was a very welcome sight for us both when it

came into view. It was almost dry.

We camped on a cliff, adjacent to the river. Our small foot safari tent protected us from mosquitoes -- there were many in the area even during the daytime, it was heavily forested. By digging in the sand of the river, plenty of good water became available. After a rest, just a little farther down the river, we found a large pool in which to bathe.

At the campsite an obvious game trail came down from the cliff towards the water. It signaled a possible threat from animals like buffalo so we placed our tent with one of its sides by the cliff drop-off. The other side bordered on a large tree that would block any intrusion. A good fire covered us on the third side and protected our last remaining flank. We cooked as the Africans do, balancing our kettles on three large rocks.

During the night I had real trouble in my attempt to get to sleep. I felt a presence of danger I had never before felt in previous camps. It gave me a strange disquiet.

Finally, after tossing and turning, I asked urgently, "Father, do you have something you want to say to me, because I feel so troubled in my spirit?"

The answer came back at once in a mocking way, "I am not your Father who is giving you this disquiet!"

I considered this to be a direct message that we were urgently needed to be used of the Lord to bring His message of deliverance and salvation to people in this area. It would involve us in a spiritual battle. Having gotten it clear who was attempting to trouble my spirit, I again committed our safety and future work in covenant to the Lord and then slept soundly for the rest of the night.

We spent several more days exploring, and then returned by the way we came to reach our car at its location. One time we got off the trail, and I decided to take a short cut to get back to it. We got into some very thick brush, and Jeanne accidentally was hit in the face on her lip by a thorn branch. A thorn pierced her lip, and the blood spurted out from the wound. That was enough to try her patience to the limit. I tried to make certain that we kept to the trail from then on.

When I was a child back in the '30s, a couple whose names were Martin and Osa Johnson, thrilled the American public writing books about their exploits in northern Kenya. They flew into that area using an amphibian airplane. They wrote in one of the books about the **HIDDEN VALLEY.** I believe the area we were now in was the location of that valley. In the upper end of the valley, the African Inland Mission had built a station which they called Ngurunit. The station was vacant at this time. As we drove out of the area, we stopped at the vacant station and looked it over, making a mental note to inquire about its use when we got back to Nairobi.

We drove non-stop back to Nairobi, arriving there after midnight. We were so tired that we didn't unload the car. That was a grave error, because during the remainder of the night while we slept, thieves broke into the car and stole our cameras and a lot of our safari equipment. Once again I was reminded at the close of this trip how fortunate I was to have Jeanne as my wife. Not one wife in millions would have agreed to undergo a safari like the one we had just completed. They would have stayed at home, or broken the safari halfway through its difficulties. But Jeanne was my special gift from God, who made my continuing service to Him possible.

The Samburu

CHAPTER 28

"After this I looked, and behold, a great
multitude which no man could number, from
every nation, from all tribes and peoples
and tongues, standing before the throne..."
                                                    Rev. 7:9

At the last count, the Samburu people numbered 70,000. For the census takers however, counting the Samburu has always been a formidable job. The reason for their fear is that the Samburu are very reluctant to give their names to anyone. When you ask someone to tell you their name, it's the usual custom for that person to give the name of his uncle or his grandfather. Better yet, they just hide, especially when they know a census taker is coming around.

The meaning of the name Samburu is not clear. Some say it has its origin in the meaning of "those who carry the sampur (handbag). Another source might be: "those who went to war with a basket for provisions." I have heard that it comes from the word "butterfly," and to support this idea people say that the life of the Samburu resembles that of butterflies (i.e. they are effeminate, stylishly elegant, etc). If this is true, it is true only of the Morans who will spend hours a day under select trees doing up each other's hair. The women and elders of the tribe certainly would not qualify for such a description.

The old name by which the Samburu were known long ago is Burkineji (a corruption of Loibor Kineji -- those of the white goats). The people themselves like to call themselves Eloikop, "those who have the land."

Their territory covers the so-called Samburu District, plus some border zones of the Marsabit District, a total area of about 11,000 square miles.

I am indebted to a Samburu pamphlet published by the Consolata Fathers in Nairobi for some resource material I have used together with my own observations in the account that follows.

"The Samburu are the most northerly group of those speaking a form of the Maasai language (of the Maa language group.) Where they came from and how they separated themselves from their brother nomads, the Maasai, is still a mystery. It seems to be accepted, however, that they originated from what is now called the Sudan and that they branched off from the Maasai many years ago, though remaining homogeneous. The old Samburu assert that they came from a place called Pagaa following a severe drought and famine. The kinship with the Maasai is confirmed by the close similarity of language and customs."

In the migration south, the Maasai were reported to be almost as hard on themselves with their intertribal warfare as they were on the people they pushed out of the way in their southern migrations. They succeeded in completely eliminating one whole Maasai clan. The Samburu are reported to have tired of this constant battle. For this reason they remained in the north, while the rest of the Maasai clans moved on to the south.

"Samburu society is governed by a gerontocratic (rule by elders) system. Women have no particular value in the society, as they are not destined to remain in the clan. A woman is a valued one who provides her husband with sons to establish his name, and with daughters who will eventually fetch bride prices when they are around fourteen years old.

"As it happens in practically all tribes -- whether Bantu, Nilotic or Cushitic -- the social setup is made up of age grades corresponding to the stages of growth of the individual and his related social responsibilities. After the grade of Nkerai (child) comes that of Layeni (young boy, shepherd) a period extending from the age of around twelve to the age of eighteen or nineteen years.

Then comes the grade of Lmurran (circumcised warrior). The length of time spent in this grade is determined by the Elders of the tribe. When they decide after anywhere from six to fifteen years, that the Morans currently in that status may now become elders, this 'rites de passage' will take place.

The final grade is Lpayan, married man, and responsible citizen of his tribe. It is the desire of every Lpayan, (mzee - head of the manyatta) to generate a large herd of cows, sheep and goats and now camels as well. As he succeeds in managing his own manyatta with order, he is respected by the whole tribe and his counsel is sought everywhere.

The life style of the community is very dependent upon the weather. The yearly rains, or their absence, are a matter of life and death. The cycle is usually to utilize the grass in the valleys during and after the rains stop falling in May. Then the herds must forage farther and farther up into the hills and the mountains when the valley's grass supply is exhausted. Often, herds will be taken in migration to places far away as the dry season progresses in order for them to survive. When this happens, the wives, young children and old people are left behind. They barely make it through this season by eating the meager supply of milk from a goat herd that has also been left behind with them.

The tribe has developed a current taste and desire to eat Ughali (the standard food of the East African farmer who tills the soil). It is simply ground white maize flour cooked into a dough like consistancy. Since the Samburu do not till he soil, they must buy all the flour they consume. Money to purchase this food, and even access to a supply of flour can often pose real problems.

The Samburu in times past looked down upon their neighbors, the Rendille, because they herded camels and not cows. Paul Spencer wrote a book entitled, "Nomads in Alliance" which was published in 1973. Its title points up the fact that the Samburu and the Rendille could co-exist in the same area because the two tribes herded different animals: the Samburu--cows, the Rendille--camels. These animals eat different foods.

In the last few years from 1985 on, a change has been taking place among the Samburu. Forced by a dearth of good pasture and a depleted ecology, they have seen the need to rely more on goats and sheep. These animals further devastate

PLATE   V

UHURU HIGHWAY LUTHERAN CHURCH
THE OLD BEING REPLACED BY THE NEW

UHURU HIGHWAY LUTHERAN CHURCH
THE NEW BUILDING

HELIMISSION & ITS CREW

LAND ROVER & NATIVE HELP TO RAISE
AN ANTENNA

the ecology.

Now as they have been encouraged by an emphasis on camels from a group called Farm Africa, the Samburu are seeing the wisdom of herding camels. A camel will give much more milk than a cow. A camel will also tolerate famine conditions to a much greater degree than a cow is able to do. It will be interesting to see what affect this change among the Samburu will have on the former 'alliance' they had with the Rendille.

I was often troubled by thoughts about the future of the Samburu whom I served during the ten years we lived there. Life in the Northern Frontier District is very trying at best. Cattle raiders, famine years and disease all take a heavy toll on people living in this area. Nor are there other places for the people to migrate so that they can escape this harsh life.

We learned in talking with the Samburu in our area that the whole tribe was divided up into three classifications: White Cows, Black Cows and Blacksmiths. These designations were used by all the tribal people in determining who they would be allowed to marry.

Your designation also had a voice in what you could do with your life. For example I couldn't get a White Cow or a Black Cow to make charcoal which we used for cooking. Only the people in the Blacksmith section of the tribe would do that kind of work. I learned that if you were a Blacksmith, you would normally find it impossible to marry a White or Black Cow girl.

The Samburu have some customs that caused me, as a pastor, a lot of trouble and heartache. When a man marries a woman, she becomes his property for life. It may be that she will desert him, or that he will desert or drive her out, but she still remains 'his' property. Later if she marries someone else and they have a child, the first husband often will appear, and demand the child - it's his by "right" of blood.

Probably the greatest problem I had as a pastor, however, was in trying to minister in the situation of the Levirate. This is an old Jewish custom. In Samburu it is a custom obliging a man to marry the widow of his brother who died without leaving children as his heirs. The tribal elders decide who will become her surrogate husband. This choice of the elders will see to it that the widow becomes pregnant each year but his responsibility ends there. The widow and her family will get no help to feed the new mouths that appear. At first, among our Christian women we tried to give food and clothing relief. When it became apparent that the church was encouraging this custom by our gifts, we had to stop being helpful. We insisted that the widow refuse to participate in this old custom. This brought us into direct confrontation with the elders. Of course, when the widows were forced to choose between the decision of the elders and the ruling of the church it put them in an almost impossible position. In the short time I was there, we had just begun to make some headway toward resolving this matter.

The Samburu prefer polygamy as a value out of their past

culture.

It takes a lot of illumination from the Holy Spirit to convince the elders and the tribe as a whole that God desires a man and a woman to become one throughout their lives. Just as we left our work upon retirement, requests were starting to come in for the enactment before the congregation of the blessing of a marriage. This signified that the couple now is committed to a monogamous marriage for the rest of their lives. Many who have two wives now agree that it is not the way to live.

The Samburu have a number of ideas concerning God -- Nkai. They believe that He is a deity that is present yet not always listening to you or seeing to your needs.

Originally, God and man were in good, direct fellowship because there was a rope extending from heaven to earth. This made it possible to always be in touch with God and to get His benefits. Then one day man became angry with God and cut the rope. From then until now, God is not all that available. He is manifested in holy things like: the rain, holy mountains, eggs, special trees, streams, water etc.

But since He is not a merciless and vindictive deity, He will pay attention to your requests more often than not.

Samburu prayer is carried on by the men -- elders -- as they squat in a circle. The leader will present petition after petition. Following each one, the members of the group will say together in unison, "Nkai". which means "God hear us as we agree together." When the prayer time has been finished, each member of the group stands and spits in both hands. Water is very holy for the Samburu.

Individuals also pray. It is the task of the elder of a manyatta to stand beside the entrance of his manyatta each morning and 'pray out his herds' as they go forth at daybreak to graze under the care of their herders. Then at dusk when the herds return, the elder is again in the same position praying his flocks safely home again.

When a young man is ready to become a Moran, he will go through a Lmugit ceremony. At the time of his circumcision he will sit on the ground. Positions of honor will have been given to three people, one who holds his right knee, one who holds his left knee, and the most honored position of all is that of the surrogate father who sits behind him and embraces him from behind. I was given this honor by Thomas, a lad who assisted me with a lot of translation work. I will be his 'second' father for as long as he lives. I cut out a pair of sandals from cow hide for him to wear in the days that followed the ceremony.

After the actual circumcision, two or three of us carried Thomas into his mother's hut where a special bed had been prepared for him. A day later, he and his age grade companions who numbered a dozen or so youths, all received a bow and arrows with sticky ends and were sent out to hunt. They were not to appear at any manyatta for a month. They hunted birds, shooting and retrieving them with their sticky arrow tips. This was their only food during that time. They were garbed with a sheep skin that had been made sticky with fat and covered with powdered charcoal. We saw the group periodically during the month. The boys had quite a collection of birds woven as a garland around their heads and necks.

At the close of this hunt, another Lmugit was held. This was one in which each youth was to take a knotted club and break the thigh bone of an oxen. There was great feasting by the whole community as the meat of the slaughtered animals was roasted over a number of fires which had been started by the firestick elders. Jeanne, who was Thomas' surrogate mother wore a garland around her head of the birds that Thomas had hunted.

Thomas now entered into the status of being a Moran. During this period, he was to spend his time away from the manyattas living with his companions in remote locations. The distance of these Moran camps was decided by the elders who used many ways to taunt and haze the Morans.

In the evening each day about nine o'clock, the Morans would come as a group singing an invitation to the local young girls of the community to join them for a dance. The girls would be prepared to reply by their own song of response. Then the two groups would meet and dance for several hours before everyone returned to their homes - the Morans to their camp.

We had high hopes for Thomas' future. He seemed to be very good at translation work. So we sponsored him to go to Secondary School at Maralal. He spent his first year there fighting allergies so that he missed most of his classroom work. He tried for a second year with the same result. Then we decided that he should move to Baragoi Secondary school, where he might benefit from a much higher land elevation. He did very poorly, although he did manage to graduate. Then it occurred to me that he was not able to study well because of his diet in early life. This matter of going without adequate food when you are a child has very serious consequences for some people later in life. All we can do now is pray that the Lord will direct Thomas in the future.

Ngurunit ~ Our First Samburu Home

CHAPTER 29

"I promise you," returned Jesus, "Nobody leaves
home or brothers or sisters or mother or father
or children or property for my sake and the gos-
pel's without getting back a hundred times over,
now in this present life, homes and brothers and
sisters, mothers and children and land -- though
not without persecution -- and in the next world
eternal life."   Mk. 10:29-30   Phillips

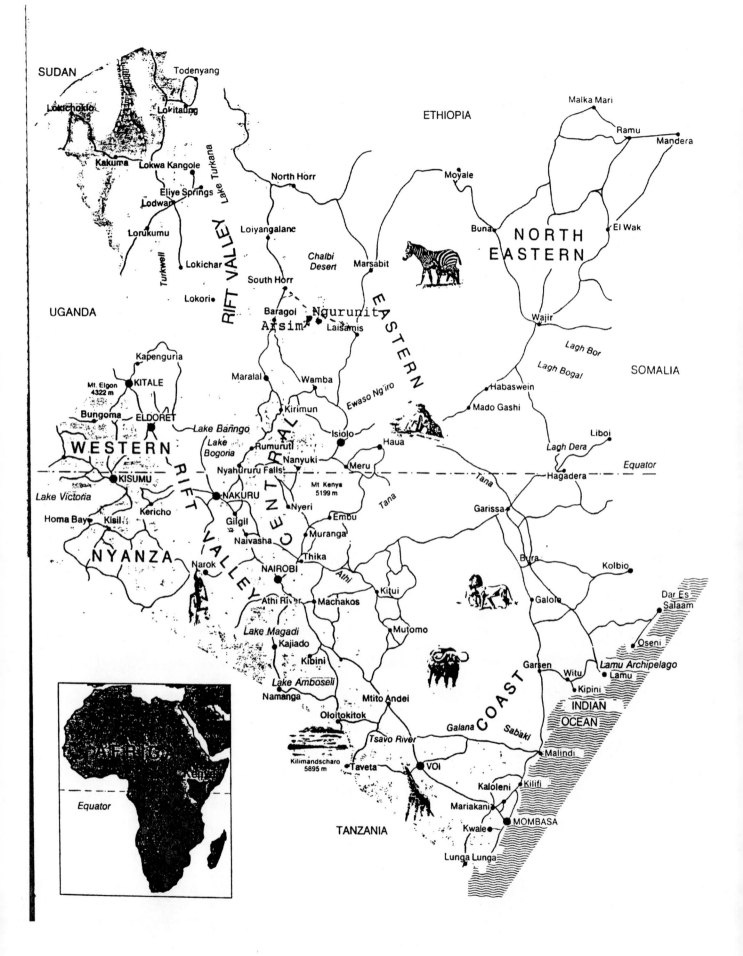

We had passed through Ngurunit on our survey foot safari in August of 1981. We saw the empty A.I.M. station. When we returned to Nairobi we began to make inquiries about our living there, even purchasing it from the Mission. The kind reply we received was "that we could rent the facility for a time, but the A.I.C. would probably never agree to sell the station."

We left Nairobi and moved up to Ngurunit on February 5th, 1982. We didn't really have a vehicle suited to that country. Our Nissan E-20 Van which had served us very well in Nairobi was not the car for the Northern Frontier District. Its first fault was the lack of four wheel drive. Even so it was all we had, so we loaded it to the ceiling and somehow included

our big black Doberman dog. He kept trying to climb into the
front seat with us <u>all</u> the time. It took us 11 ½ hours to
reach Ngurunit over some of the worst corrugated roads in Kenya.
Very large and overloaded trucks running between Nairobi and
Marsabit pounded the gravel roadbed to conform to their huge
tires. The trucks packed this gravel into unforgiving
corrugations which smaller cars bounced over in travel. It
was pure torture to try and adjust one's speed to 'the best'
accommodation for the road. Nothing one could do would stop
the abusive pounding a smaller car had to take. We had about
one hundred miles of this kind of road to face on our trip
up after we left the paved roads. When we finally reached
the little village of Laisamis, our turn off from the main
road to go west, it was well into the night. We gratefully
started traveling on a rather smooth and distinct track. We
came to junctions with tracks turning off from the road we
were on. There were no signposts to direct us in the dark.
We knew that several tracks led off to the north to go to a
small village called Korr. So we tried to keep bearing to
the left whenever we were forced to choose.

After what seemed like hours of traveling in the dark,
we saw a turn leading off to the left. Could that be the way
we should go, or would it simply lead us off the way we were
following and in a short distance abruptly end at a pile of
rock? We had already made that mistake once.

We took the turn and it kept stretching out in front of
us. Tire marks showed that someone had recently traveled this

way. It was nearing the fifty mile mark on our speedometer from the turn off we had made at Laisamis. This should have meant that we had reached the Ngurunit Dukas(stores) by now. And then, there they were coming up to meet us out of the dark.

We followed the road several more miles into Ngurunit station.

We were exhausted.

We opened the door of the Ngurunit house.

We made a quick cup of coffee, ate a biscuit and gave some water to the dog. We lay down on an unmade bed and prayerfully thanked God for a safe safari. We had hardly finished praying when we were fast asleep. It was after two A. M. in the morning.

*   *   *   *   *

Ngurunit is a place of many birds. We were awakened the next morning at 6 A. M. by their singing. It was a completely different experience from that of being in Nairobi. We felt enfolded into the countryside and of being a part of it. There was no noise, only the musical calls of the birds which greeted our ears.

Several days later the lorry carrying all our furniture and belongings arrived from Nairobi. Ngurunit is located about 330 miles northwest of Nairobi and 55 miles southeast of Lake Turkana.

The African Inland Mission chose the Ngurunit site because it was close to that most precious thing of all in the N.F.D. -- water. A stream flowed in front of the house during the rains and well into the dry season. But the station's water supply came from up the mountain because the Mission and the Government in cooperation had laid a pipeline over a mile in length to the station. This pipeline provided the whole community with water. Farther down the valley, the taps were never closed and because of this the water was free flowing 24 hours a day until in short supply it ran out much to the chagrin of the missionaries.

Ngurunit was in a bowl. I called it a cauldron. It was in a valley surrounded by high rocks and on one side by the Ndoto Mountain range. This limited the amount of wind that blew, and made the place unbearably hot during certain seasons of the year. Then the air became stagnant.

April is the month when the rains begin to fall, and immediately prior to that time it becomes more and more difficult to find a cool breeze. We were in that time shortly after we arrived. We were set up to begin language study with all our energy. However, two things defeated our good intentions.

The first was the heat. Charles Barnett the A.I.M. missionary who had built this house had given a priority to ventilation in its design in an attempt to keep cool. But the house hardly cooled off at all at night during this time of the year.

The second was that we needed the help of a good teacher. We thought when we got Job's help -- a first rate informant -- that we would progress very quickly. But able people have a lot of things to do with their time. Job who was a teacher was often called away for several weeks.

We used the L.A.M.P. method of study. Our book said 'motivation' was what counted. But it was just too hot following our arrival -- over 100° every day, and for several weeks in a row we recorded 108° in the shade. Those temperatures ruined our motivation. However, we still worked at studying even while we were covered with sweat.

The time quickly came when we began to see the tree covered hillsides start to turn a buff white. The trees were blossoming out in anticipation of the coming rains. The local people took a long look at these blossoms and said: "This will be a good year for honey."

April 1st the rains started early in the morning, and oh how wonderfully refreshing and cooling they were. It was a beautiful April Fool's Day treat. Jeanne and I tried hard to 'pull' some good April Fool's Day jokes on each other. But that rain was no joke. It was real. The dry river bed outside our house came alive with water and everything the water had picked up on its way down to the valley: branches, snakes, and lots of mud.

The Ngurunit house was only available for us to use until August of that year, 1982.

We redoubled our search for a place to locate our new outreach center.

Keno~
A Possible Location?

CHAPTER   30

"And I say unto you, Ask, and
it shall be given you; seek,
and ye shall find; knock and
it shall be opened unto you."
Lk. 11:9   K.J.V.

On March 13th I took several Samburu men with me to have
another look at the Milgis River valley. Local people had
suggested that a location called KENO would be the ideal
solution to our quest.

It was visible.

It also had an artesian spring providing permanent water.

On the morning of the 13th, we got an early start from
the Ngurunit airstrip -- our jumping off place. Jeanne drove
us there the three miles from the station.

Lukupa Lasadala, the man who had encountered Jeanne with
his mules when we made our last Milgis safari, was one of our
party now. The other member of the safari was a young moran
whose name was Longero Ilibosoli.
We had shared in packing our loads of supplies for this foot
safari that we expected would last three days.

It was 7:15 in the morning when we said good-bye to Jeanne
and left the car to set off. I learned very soon that the
Samburu are like elephants. They give the impression of just

slowly walking along, but if you follow them you find out in a hurry that they are covering a lot of ground.

We walked non-stop until 1:15 P.M. Then we stopped for lunch of a sandwich and a banana. This was for my benefit. Samburu do not normally eat lunch. We tried to rest about an hour but the infernal sweat bees, about the size of a gnat, made being stationary almost unbearable. They tortured you by crawling into your eyes, ears, and giving your skin small bites as they scraped off the salt your sweat had left deposited there.

We set off again and now it was the hottest part of the day. This is the time when sensible animals and humans seek out a shady tree in order to escape the sun. It was hard going for me because the bottom of my feet were feeling the rapid pace we had kept up till this time, and the heat being reflected to them from the sun-burned trail. It was so hot!

It took two more hours of fast walking for us to reach KENO. Lukupa, who was now in his home area directed us to the nearest water. We were all very hot and very thirsty. The Samburu make it a cultural value to deny thirst to prove they can go without water.

We reached a stream having water in its sand. We arrived there about 5:15 P. M. While I got a pot of tea brewed the other two men enjoyed a quick bath in the abundant water of one of the pools in the stream. After tea, while my companions washed the cups and pot, I had a chance to bathe. What a refreshment that was, especially for my feet.

I was truly ready to call it 'quits' for the day. My companions insisted that we could not stay close to this water at night. They said there were too many buffalo and lion around. If we stayed in this area these animals would give us trouble. Later I learned that the men's real fear was that of the Shifta(Somali bandits) who were roaming the area.

So we set off again, following up along the course of the riverbed. We were traveling in the lower reaches of the Ndoto Mountain range.

An hour later we reached a site chosen by Lukupa. It was just turning dark.

We spread out our tarp on the sand next to the river's bank. There was a little water flowing from pool to pool on the opposite side of the river.

I was told to "relax", that Longero the youngest member of the party would prepare supper. I gave him the sack of maize meal so that he could cook the ughali for our evening meal. When I saw the large amount of water he had in the cooking pot on the fire, I told him to pour some of it out. By then it had grown completely dark and I couldn't see what he was doing. He put in more than 2/3s of the sack of flour into the pot -- enough to feed an army. I chided him because we were on limited supplies.

"Oh well," he replied, "We'll eat it for breakfast."

We were in an area that didn't have people around at this time. There were manyattas visible but they were all deserted. Longero stoked up a big fire. He was stung by a scorpion as he collected dry dead wood for the fire. I used a "home" remedy, a powder of cream of Tartar and epsom salts, on him which took away his pain. As we prepared to go to sleep Longero informed us that he, the Moran, would sleep in the center of the tarp between the two wazee(elders) because there was real danger of a lion attack. We who were older, said he, had already lived our lives and had our children. He had not had the chance to become an elder. So we 'elders' apparently should be the first to go in the event of an attack and give him a chance to get away. Longero arose often during the night and restoked the fire which was kept burning brightly.

We had evening prayers and I lay for a little while identifying a satellite that was passing overhead from north to south in the night sky. Then I fell into an exhausted sleep. My leg muscles unused to hitting the trail so hard were very tired and sore. It was a beautiful balmy night. I was awakened several times when Longero had trouble with his nightmares and awoke to stoke the fire again. No lions attacked us.

We awoke early the next morning. It was decided after a quick breakfast of cold ughali and tea, to leave Longero in camp. Lukupa would show me Keno and point out where the road and forest camp from Colonial days had been located.

We had devotions and then set off traveling higher up into the mountain range. After a short hike we came upon the site of the deserted forest camp and saw the trace of what had been its supply road coming up from the valley below. It was simply a site now, but you could see the places that the foundations of the buildings had occupied. This was the location that Lukupa suggested we use for building our outreach center. He said it would be possible to repair the road for service again. The stream which had water flowing in it the year around ran adjacent to this site. The amount of water in the stream increased the farther up we followed it above the proposed site. The scenery of the surrounding country-side was very beautiful even though this was the very apex of the dry season. Lukupa knew the topography of this whole area by heart. As a child he must have been raised here. Small waterfall after small waterfall came into view the farther up-stream we traveled. We saw nothing in the way of wildlife, but there were recent droppings made by buffalo. The area also showed signs of heavy over-grazing. One manyatta appeared to have been deserted just a few days before our arrival. Going farther up, we attained a position to get a good view of the two valleys into which the upper section of the area was divided. Both valleys were small and filled with dense thorn vegetation. I imagined many buffalo were probably there sleeping during the daytime heat.

We continued to climb out of the water-course up onto a plateau area. Here we got a birds-eye view of the whole countryside. It was very majestic and beautiful, but quite empty of people. Cattle and goats were visible far out on the plains of the Milgis valley to the south.

After having a good look around, we began our descent of probably 1500 to 2000 feet to reach the level of our campsite. When we passed the site of the old forest camp, Lukupa found a tree filled with berries and vowed that he would return later in the day to pick a sack full of its fruit. It was 1:30 P.M. at the time we reached our camp again. We moved our loads into the shade - - it was another scorching day of heat. Everyone rested after a cup of tea. Then the two men bathed down stream. After bathing they went to the forest campsite to pick berries. I stayed in camp and read, listening to a tape for devotions. I treated my sore feet with a bath and some rest.

Lukupa and Longero returned at 4:30 P. M. For supper we cooked a large pot of rice and prepared cans of corned beef and tomato soup to make a sauce for the rice. It tasted very good and was the first substantial meal we had eaten all day. We washed down cookies with quantities of tea mixed with milk powder and plenty of sugar. I had to dole out the sugar to make certain our supply wouldn't be used like Longero had used our maize meal. Following supper, we had a time of devotions around the fire. Neither of the two men were Christians. I explained the meaning of Sunday and about the person of Christ and His salvation to them. They asked many questions about the Christian faith.

Then a satellite passed overhead in the night sky. There was a discussion about this modern mystery. From there the discussion turned to our plan for returning the next day. Lukupa suggested that if I could make it over the mountains by a different trail from the one on which we had come, it

would be a much quicker way to return. It all hinged, they
said, on whether I could climb. I said I thought we ought
to try and return this shorter way.

This was a great tactical error on my part!

Lukupa continued trying very hard to 'sell' Keno as a
very good site for the base of our new work. Later I was able
to understand why he worked so hard at trying to persuade me
of this.

After I committed us all to God's gracious care, we fell
asleep only to be awakened about midnight by another of
Longero's nightmares.

I was up and dressed well before dawn. My thought was
to get as much of our traveling done as possible before the
sun reached its zenith. Lukupa cautioned that travel before
full light was very dangerous because of the thick thorn brush.
So we took time to make a substantial breakfast of what was
left of our supply of maize meal made into uji -- a cornmeal
gruel. Then we got our packs ready for travel.

Lukupa complained of some real soreness because of the
load he was carrying. I treated him with an aspirin which
quickly took away his pain.

We started across the valley and then began an ascent
which was steep and hard work to climb. Crossing the valley
we literally had to chop our way through thorn forests using
the Samburu Lalem's(machetes) each of us carried. Sometimes
I fancied that Lukupa was really happiest in the middle of
a thorn thicket squatting and crawling -- a very hard place

to get a backpack through. It took us about an hour and a half to climb several thousand feet out of the valley. When we reached that point we were treated to a panoramic view of the whole countryside: the valley, the Milgis River, traces of the old road, and views far into the distance to the south, the west and the east. The air was more cool at this higher elevation so we quickly pushed on following around the crests of hills. Strangely enough we came on artesian outcroppings of water quite often on these hilltops, so we were never very thirsty.

The trail went up and down and passed through a lot of thorn forests which made it a lot more difficult to travel than it had been when we came in on the lower trail the first day. Again and again, we enjoyed views of the surrounding countryside from various vantage points. Our progress was slower than the men had expected because of the difficulties of getting our packs through the thorn forests. In spite of that, we made good time and at 1:30 P. M. we stopped at a water outcropping where I brewed a big pot of tea. I also warmed two cans of beans over our fire and these were served on buttered slices of bread. Powdered milk mixed with the tea together with an ample supply of cookies made us quite a meal. While we ate, several baboons scolded us soundly and frequently during our short stay there. They sat in some trees off to the side of where we sat, apparently thinking we wanted to take over their domain.

I was told that we had just <u>one more</u> crest to climb and

then I was given the glad news that we could see Ngurunit
from there. This information was just a bit premature.

As we finally got to the top of the crest I found to
my disappointment that Ngurunit was still a long way off. The
scorching heat of the noonday sun didn't help improve my
chagrin about the overly optimistic report my friends had given
me.

After cresting that hill, we began the descent into a
broad valley. While we were still high up, we stopped at a
cattle manyatta -- the owner was a close relative of Longero.
Immediately the owner produced a gourd of soured milk for us
to drink which was very refreshing. The elder of the manyatta,
a very old man, asked me for a box of matches. Matches were
apparently highly prized by the old one. When I gave him his
request, he was overjoyed.

After a short rest, we continued our safari down the
hillside into the valley below. I wasn't too happy about this
long descent because I could see the trail going up the other
side of the valley and knew the price coming up that we would
have to pay for our descent. The men encouraged me by telling
me about the very wonderful water supply in the valley, and
the rest and bath they were both looking forward to enjoying.
It was 3:30 P. M. when we reached this waterhole. Longero
immediately striped off his clothes for a cool bath. Lukupa
followed his example. I was content simply to sit by and rest
and drink the cool water. Lukupa suggested that we spend the
night at this site.

I made my second great tactical error in assuming that Ngurunit was not too far away.

I suggested that we carry on and reach home. That was a gross error on my part. I was assured by both men that this was possible without too much effort. We then began a very difficult ascent along the face of a huge rock. Both men lost the trail at one point in some very thick brush. At one time in this passage we came to an artesian outcropping noted for the fact that when you drink its water it makes you cold all the way down to your stomach. This report proved to be correct. We filled our canteen with this water for later use and that was really appreciated. Close to this outcropping, it was reported that some Shifta had grabbed some Samburu children recently. Many of these events are never reported to the authorities.

The trail was very very steep and continued to be so as we ascended during the hottest part of the afternoon. We finally cleared the crest of the hill and came out several thousand feet above Ngurunit station. Because of an intervening hill we were not able to see the station proper, although the dispensary and airstrip were visible to us. To reach the station we had a short descent to negotiate, then a very steep ascent of about 500 feet and finally a descent to reach the valley floor. The first descent was through some dangerous snake country. The men warned me repeatedly to be careful as I walked and where I placed my hands to support myself.

We reached the ascent and it was through heavy thorn bushes

-- literally straight up! I pulled myself and my pack up by the help of some saplings which grew along the path fearing with each clutch that I would grab a snake rather than a branch.

At last we began our last descent. It was 5:30 P. M. and now the men cautioned haste because at the base of the valley was a section we had to pass having heavy scrub thorn without a defined trail. They wanted to clear it before it got dark or we could be in great trouble.

We descended for a full hour -- at times the trail was very steep.

Almost up until the last 20 minutes of our travel the trail was choked with thick thorn brush. We now had reached a clearing just before we were to enter the beginning of the heavy scrub thorn forest. We rested just a few minutes and then pressed on hoping to get past it before dark. It was just 6:45 P. M. now and the light was fading quickly. As we set off, any number of times one or the other of the men who was leading at the time would stop, indicating that he had reached an impasse -- skirt to the right or to the left a few yards and try to pass forward again.

It was a horrendous forest.

It was totally dark when we broke out of the thorn forest on to a cattle trail. The men had eyes well able to see in the darkness. Unfortunately the moon would not rise for several hours.

I asked that we stop now and rest a bit since we had cleared the forest. I was exhausted. The men refused. They

had heard a lion roaring a short distance off. Now they wanted
to get to the outskirts of the settled manyatta area as quickly
as possible. So we walked on and on into the darkness. It
was almost pitch black.

The batteries of the flashlight I had were almost dead
so the light was of little help. I lost my footing twice
and fell in a heap. Then I quickly picked myself up,
embarrassed that my exhaustion was beginning to show. Finally
my guides, as a concession to me, stopped at the bank of a
dry river to rest a few moments. We then carried on until
the huts and manyattas started to come into view. Their hearth
fires were a welcome sight. We passed them silently and I
was warned not to use my flashlight or to let them know we
were passing.

I later learned that Longero who was a Moran was not
supposed to be carrying a pack, or any load, according to
Samburu tradition. Therefore he didn't want anyone close to
his home seeing him do it even in the darkness.

We reached Ngurunit at 8:15 P. M. and I was totally bushed.
Jeanne was in Nairobi. Our house helper, Lopejekwe was at
his manyatta. I called him by starting the station light plant.
He made up a big pot of tea for the weary travelers. So ended
the Keno investigation safari. We closed the trip off with
a prayer of thanksgiving for God's care and protection for
us on the steep trails and the other dangers from which he
had protected us.

During the next several days I tried to carefully assess

Keno as an option for establishing our outreach center. It had a very good water supply. However the danger from the Shifta in this area was considerable.

We later learned that the Kenya Government would not have allowed us into this location because of a long history of Shifta trouble. We also learned from the Samburu that they would like to see us at Keno because they believed our presence there would protect them from Shifta attack. Lukupa had tried to sell Keno to us because he wanted to live there in safety.

The conclusion we were forced to accept was that we must carry on looking elsewhere for a site to build our outreach center.

*   *   *   *   *   *

Just a short way down river from the Ngurunit station U.N.E.S.C.O. had put up a semi-permanent camp. They were doing all kinds of investigations. Scientists used the camp as their base while they were in Kenya. We became close friends with the director of the camp, Dr. Chris Fields. We were invited to attend meetings at the camp. At one of their meetings, the Chief of this whole area of Samburu was present. His name was John Bosco Lempei. He had been baptized a Roman Catholic taking the middle name of Bosco, an important personage from that church in Italy.

Chief John spoke to me at the U.N.E.S.C.O. meeting, and said that he had heard about our search for a site to begin work in Samburu. He made the suggestion that we look at a place called Arsim. He also said there was no competing mission work being done in the Arsim area. He volunteered that whenever we might care to see Arsim, he would be willing to go with us on that safari.

Chief Lempei's court was located 12 miles north and west from Ngurunit and Arsim's location was another 8 1/2 miles from there. We were overjoyed by the Chief's disclosure and his willingness to show us this new area.

Arsim-At The Road's End

CHAPTER 31

"For these are our instructions
from the Lord: 'I have appointed you
to be a light for the Gentiles, and
a means of salvation to the earth's
farthest bounds.'" Acts 13:47 N.E.B.

We sent word to Chief John Lempei at Ilaut a week before our first trip to Arsim took place. On March 27th, 1982 we drove to Ilaut and reached there at 11 A.M. Chief John was waiting for us to arrive. He said he would be happy to accompany us.

Our safari party from Ngurunit was made up of Jeanne and myself, Kompani (brother to the sub-chief at the Arsim location,) and Lopejekwe our worker. At Ilaut we were joined by Chief John and Lamantoi Lekuye, who was the Subchief at Arsim.

We continued on our way to Arsim. Several miles after leaving Ilaut following the road which leads west to South Horr, we left this road turning left. We now were traveling on a well developed track leading south which the Chief told us had been made by the local people.

We had heard that the Chief himself had a permanent manyatta located at Arsim. His original home however had been Baragoi.

The track we were now on passed over an almost table top flat plane. It gently rose in elevation the farther south we went as it skirted the base of the Ndoto Range of mountains. We crossed several sand rivers and at one time had to negotiate one made up of stones instead of sand in its bed. It was like a road under construction in the U.S.

The track ended at a forest camp 8.5 miles from the main road. The camp had two roundel type huts which the Forest Service had built to house its personnel. Sometime after these huts had been built the shifta had driven out the forest guards. Now with security restored, the guards were back in residence.

In the distance up the side of the mountain a rather large forest fire was roaring as it burned following up the slope. This slope was on the base of the tallest peak in the area. It is called Mt. Alimission. Its elevation is over 8,000 feet above sea level. The elevation where we stopped the car was close to 3,000 feet according to my altimeter.

It was already well after lunch time and we were all hungry. We shared some sandwiches, cakes and tea that Jeanne had brought along. Then we took a look around the immediate area. We found ourselves in a heavily wooded area surrounded by hills and mountains. A small river ran out of the mouth of a canyon.

I said I would like to follow up the water course to check it out. Jeanne did not have good hiking shoes along so she decided to stay with the car. The Chief, Lekuye, Kompani and I set off. Lekuye and I set the pace with Lekuye acting as guide.

It took us about 45 minutes to reach the crest of the

hill in the canyon and to get a good look at the water's flow at that point. I was told that its true source was a huge artesian pool on top of the mountain. I estimated that the water flowing past the place where we were standing would fill a 2 inch pipe with a good speed of flow.

We rested in the shade here. The Chief continued to speak of the cooperation we could expect from him if we would establish our Outreach Center at Arsim. He said there would be no difficulty in acquiring a plot of land stating: "My brother is chairman of the District Council at Maralal." Maralal was the headquarters for the whole of the Samburu District.

The Chief had heard about our survey trip to Keno and said Keno was just on the other side of the line from his jurisdiction. He said that the road from Arsim to Baragoi was always open and passable, but that wasn't true of the road from Ngurunit to Laisamas. This news certainly surprised me. I hadn't thought either road would be passable during the heavy rains.

We then began our return trip to the forest camp where we had left Jeanne and the car. Lekuye and I set off at a good pace and left the other two men far behind. When we reached the forest camp we rested in the shade. The Chief and Kompani caught up with us sometime later.

Chief Lempei asked us to delay our return to Ilaut until he could write a letter for someone in the valley who was illiterate. We agreed to this and when the letter was written it was given to the Sub-chief Lamantoi. He set off on foot at once to take the letter to Baragoi a distance of 50 miles away.

Then we began our return trip to Ilaut. There was one sand river that gave us a problem on its far side as we crossed it. It had a steep incline on that side. We resolved the difficulty by choosing a spot which wasn't so steep farther down on the river's bank to make our exit.

The Chief left us at Ilaut. We gave him our sincere thanks for accompanying us. We promised to return soon to look over possible sites. We then carried on with our return to Ngurunit.

We made good time on our return until we came to a wide sand river. We all got out of the car which didn't have four wheel drive. With Jeanne as the driver, and the rest of us pushing hard in the soft sand we crossed the river without our back wheels digging in. We had almost reached Ngurunit when we came to a second dry sand river which had a bed of very soft sand. A steep bank on the opposite side promised trouble. First we bogged down badly in the sand half way across the river. We jacked up the car and moved forward slowly, but without a little speed there was no way we could climb out of the river bed on the other side. Without four wheel drive our back wheels just cut into the river bank of soft sand and dirt.

Finally, I used a long rope and a hand winch which I was carrying in the car for just a time like this. I winched us up the incline, short step by short step. The winch, a boat winch, had only a short operational length and had to be retied on our rope very often. Jeanne drove and all the rest of the passengers pushed. We got up the bank and on to the level road bed just before dark. We finally reached Ngurunit station just after dark. We had learned well the lesson that it was folly to try to use a two wheel drive vehicle in this country, even during the dry season.

Once again the time had come for us to seek the Lord's guidance in prayer to lead us in our choice of a place to establish our Outreach Center. Should it be Arsim, or should we look for yet another site? As we laid this matter before the Lord in prayer, we started considering the desirable points that Arsim had to offer. Arsim had probably 2/3's of the volume of water offered at Keno. However it had people in almost permanent residence in the valley. We had the report that 13 families had been living and moving around from location to location in the Arsim area for a number of years. We also had the report that the people in this area were probably the most traditional biased in the whole of Samburuland. They might very well be absolutely set in their refusal to receive a new message like the Gospel of Jesus Christ and His salvation. "Well," we said, "let's see what the power of the Lord can do!"

On the other hand, Chief Lempei had been very positive in his invitation for us to come in. No doubt he would be thinking of some extra favors from us that might be his if we lived at Arsim, such as a school or a dispensary. The

District Commissioner at Maralal had been putting pressure on Chief Lempei to move his court location to Arsim.

We decided we needed to make another trip to Arsim from Ngurunit before we made a final decision.

On this trip Jeanne and I managed the obstacles like sand rivers by ourselves. Maybe we succeeded this time because we knew what to expect and prepared ourselves by spurts of speed when we came to the bad crossings. Possibly the reduced weight load in the car made the difference.

We returned to look over a site that the Chief had said would be ours if we wanted it. It was a place where he had a shamba (garden) located. The only evidences I saw of his planting were a few dried cornstalks in one corner of a patch of land bordering the river. But this was a beautiful site. There were a number of large trees all around the area. Most of the plot itself was just a weed patch at that viewing. On the river's bank a huge boulder invited Jeanne and me to rest and pray. We crawled up on its flat top. Then together we once again asked God to guide us in our choice. "Is this the place, Oh Lord, or should we continue on in our search?"

We both felt that the Lord indicated -- this was the place! When we climbed down from the rock I felt a great sense of relief. Now we could begin again the wonder filled experience of opening up a new area and work for Him -- one of the greatest thrills a missionary can have. "And the Gospel must first be published among all nations." Mk. 13:10

Meeting The Deadlines

CHAPTER 32

"**Make Haste,** O God, to deliver
  me;
  Make haste to help me O Jehovah."
                        Ps. 70:1

Now that the decision had been made to choose Arsim for the location of our Outreach Center we had our work cut out for us.

A number of concerns all demanded our attention at the same time.

First, we had to apply for property rights at the new location. Because of some difficulties in other parts of Kenya, the President had declared that no new plots would be granted for a period of time. When we made up our request to the District Commissioner in Maralal, we found him very sympathetic but presumably his hands were tied. He couldn't change the orders coming out from Central Government. He said he would try.

But we needed to get started with our move out of Ngurunit which had to be completed by August.

It was now the beginning of May, and we were scheduled to take a month's leave from our work. The rains had begun in April, and the roads in our area now were 'difficult'. We set off from Ngurunit with real apprehension about making it out to the main road at Laisamis. We almost made it. When

we came to the last river before reaching the village we got
stuck. Dr. Chris Fields came along with his Landrover just
in time. With the help of a long line he pulled us through
the mud and across the river enabling us to continue our trip

After making a month's trip to the U. S. using an air
line pass from our daughter Kris we returned to Kenya. Those
passes were particularly precious to us those years because
my mother was in a care center with very fragile health.

Upon our return our next safari was to Mombasa to clear
a vehicle which we had so longed to receive. Mr. Dieter Opitz,
who was a deacon in the Lutheran Church of Wurttemberg as well
as being the Africa Director of Christoffel Blinden Mission
had arranged for the Wurttemberg church to fund a Toyota
Landcruiser for Samburu work. We gladly bade farewell to our
faithful Nissan E-20, and were the overjoyed possessors of
this new four wheel drive vehicle. Again and again as we drove
up to Ngurunit on that first trip north we rejoiced in the
provision which God had made for us through the Lutheran Church
of Wurttemburg.

We had just arrived in Ngurunit when a radio message came
that made it necessary for us to turn right around and head
back to Nairobi. Mr. & Mrs. Chet Strohmeyer from Juneau Alaska
had come to visit us. Their visit was not just one for sight
seeing in Africa. They had come to help us build at Arsim.
Chet was a craftsman in working with wood.

We arrived at Ngurunit again. Our visitors hardly had
time to get their breath before they were plunged into 'Africa'.

We were sitting around the supper table when a Samburu friend came to the door. He told us that a Shifta raiding party was reported to be coming to Ngurunit. The U.N.E.S.C.O. camp people had all fled. The Europeans were hiding in the river in a hastily constructed sand bunker.

What to do?

Our friends fresh out from America could only look at us in unbelief.

We had a time of prayer, and I felt that we should stay in the rather secure house we now occupied.

Then a second messenger came. He reported that the Shifta now said they were going to raid the town first, then they were coming to the Mission.

It was around 9 P.M. when the second message arrived. I then felt that if we stayed in the house, we might come under siege. I had no desire to battle it out with a band of outlaws. Someone could get hurt.

I got on the radio with a Mayday call for help to the police in Nairobi. The evening hours gave us very poor reception so I wasn't sure the Nairobi Post Office Radio Call service had received me.

We four left the house. We turned off all the lights by shutting down the light plant. We locked the place up as well as we could. Led by a Samburu we went off into the bushes across the river. The bushes were the size of small trees.

The two women got under the bushes overhanging branches and we men sat on either side of them. It was pitch dark.

Our Samburu helper came again.

"No, No -- this will never do," he said.

The ladies white legs showing below their skirts were like beacons even in the darkness.

The Samburu took us to a different location where we were completely concealed. I had no idea who our benefactor was. It was pitch dark, and our man had stripped his body of clothing. His black skin was absolutely invisible in the darkness.

The emergency lasted for about two more hours. At midnight, the messenger came once again and gave the all clear. The Shifta had made their raid, and had carried off bags of flour and sugar from the Ngurunit Duka(store). Now they were heading away from of our location.

We returned to the station house, grateful to escape the mosquitoes that had become more and more troublesome the longer we had stayed outside.

The folks from U.N.E.S.C.O. spent the entire night in the river sand bunker and were covered with bites by the time dawn came the next day.

I took Chet to see Arsim. Halfway there he scratched his head and asked: "Bob, how did you choose this location?"

I replied truthfully, "We didn't choose it, the Lord made it available to us."

Our next task was to set up a tent city at the Arsim location. We found a large tree in a grove of three or four different trees that we thought would be ideal. We were later

to learn that this big tree was a haven for snakes that liked
to lie concealed in its branches and hunt for birds.

*   *   *   *   *   *

We were delayed in our return to Ngurunit that day. Jeanne
and Mary Strohmeyer became very concerned. They thought we
might have been intercepted by the Shifta who were reported
by the nervous Samburu to be just about everywhere. Then to
their relief a truckload of police arrived going to the
U.N.E.S.C.O. camp and to Ngurunit town. The emergency was
now over for the time being.

Trips back and forth between Ngurunit and Arsim became
the routine of our days. I hired Samburu workers to help me
sink a well on our plot. We also chose and measured out the
location of the foundation of our house. A firm in Nairobi,
Aisthorpe Timber Engineers, manufactured prefab houses. We
had contracted with them for a house. Now all that remained
to be done was to get the pieces transported up to our location.
Mike Koski, one of our W.M.P.L. missionaries in Nairobi was
my contact person. He was trying to get a trucker to bring
us our supplies. No firm wanted to be of service to us because
of the lack of roads into Arsim. It took over a month of
waiting before we succeeded in getting delivery of what we
needed to begin building. Several large lorries(trucks) came
bringing the materials and prefab sections to us. We had
dismantled "Heidi's Room" at Cedar Road and that was brought
up to us as well. That room was assembled first and became
our kitchen and store.

By the time our prefab materials arrived, we had made the move from Ngurunit to Arsim. We got our water from the river at Arsim. But it wasn't long before the well we were digging produced water also. We cemented and sealed the sides of the shaft that was only 14 feet in depth.

Then we put a $1\frac{1}{4}$" semi-rotary pump into operation to draw water out of the well. A short distance away from the well, we built a shower stall. While one person pumped the well, another stood in the stall and got that day's dust and sweat washed off. This was usually a moonlight operation. We had been warned that the Samburu who had no background in a hard day's work would be useless in our construction work. However we found the men anxious to work with us. The only trouble we had was the language barrier. Very frequently a worker would acknowledge an order as understood, which had not been truly understood. Fortunately we finished our work without any serious accidents.

The river adjacent to the plot was filled with ideal 'hard core' building stone for our foundations. It was simply a matter of collecting the stones and packing them to the footing trenches we had dug to receive them. We also got all our building water and sand from the river.

Our work went ahead at good speed. Very soon our foundations were laid and capped with cement. Then the outside walls of the house were put into place following the manufacturer's plan. The rains had about stopped falling, but it was now the time of year when the wind can blow with almost gale force. Putting up the wall panels meant being careful that they were secured by supporting poles. We had one entire wall blow over before we learned the proper technique of stablizing a wall against the wind's force.

One evening just at sunset I was checking out the wall supports because a heavy wind was blowing. A lion walked around the far corner of the house and disappeared back into the uncleared forest area.

The trees that provided the cover for our tent city were a haven for snakes. The birds sometimes would congregate over one part of the upper branches of the tree and scold and scold. Whenever this happened I knew a snake was lurking up there, even if I couldn't see it. My shotgun became very useful in snake control. I became proficient enough in its use so that I could separate a snake's head from its body with one shot. Snakes have been known to bite people by a reflex action in Samburu even after they have died.

I had been told that we should not pour the cement floor for our house until we roofed it. The heat of the sun would dry out the cement so fast that it would dry and crack.

About this time in the building process, we were blessed by the presence and help of a young man from Kisii, whose name was Michael Kiriama. Michael had been a member of Uhuru Highway in Nairobi. Among his other abilities and gifts was that of writing songs. He came to help us build and was invaluable. Lining up the roof joists was his specialty and he was 'up and over' the beams as if he were walking on ground level.

We roofed the house using 8' aluminum sheeting. Then we began the job of laying the floor inside. We had a motor driven cement mixer that worked well in producing the large quantities of cement we required. Each evening, after that day's work was done, a finishing mixture was poured and smoothed on to the fresh cement. Then several hours later this had to be given its final 'finish surface' with a trowel. This made for long days and hours of labor.

The Strohmeyers continued helping us until September. Then we drove them back to Nairobi to conclude their visit to Africa. We finished construction by the middle of November. It was good that we did, because the early rains were very heavy that year.

The District Commissioner in Maralal had said that we could get on with our building, even though the ban was still current from Central Government. It wasn't until January 3rd, 1983 that we got the document from the County Council of Samburu authorizing us to build on and utilize the plot at Arsim. Even this notification was long overdue because the document stated that this permission and authorization had been granted on September 24th, 1982 by the Council. We wondered, "Why this delay?"

By the beginning of 1983 we had become well established on our plot. Our well supplied all the soft pure water we needed. It was pumped up to a tank in a large tree 20 feet above the well site. This 330 gallon tank, a heavy aluminum tank had originally been used in a Nairobi Airport firetruck.

Now by a system of pipes it provided our house with a gravity flow water system. I had installed plumbing throughout the house. I had installed several solar hot water panels on our back porch roof. These gave enough hot water for dishes and for several hot baths each day.

On that same porch roof lay five solar electric panels. I wired the house so that in each room fluorescent light was available whenever it was needed.

The room arrangement of the house was: two bedrooms, a bath/toilet, a storage room, a kitchen, a large living room, a dining room, and a study/office. We made extra additions to the original house by building a large screened in front porch and a back porch which was also screened. We also constructed an outside kitchen/store made from mud bricks which had an aluminum roof.

We had our first meal in our new house on November 27th, Thanksgiving day together with Betty and Harry Christensen -- visitors from Minneapolis, and their son Mike who was one of our W.M.P.L. co-workers serving in Kenya.

We didn't claim to be settled then, but at least we were in the house. Our visitors helped us move in our stove and kerosene refrigerator. They were helpful in so many ways. The past month had been filled with painting windows and doors, and assembling solar panels.

Our work of evangelism had continued on in spite of our preoccupation with building. We continued to worship under the trees. It was Christmas time just after we completed our

building project. Here are some excerpts from a letter that
Jeanne wrote at that time.

"--The day after Christmas, and what a different Christmas
this has been for us, all alone this year, and to those around
Arsim who experienced their first Christmas celebration.

Bob and I were up before dawn Christmas day and went around
with our flashlights caroling at all the manyattas. This really
brought the folks out of their huts wondering what was going
on. (I think they thought it quite nice!). Next year we told
them, they would all have to join us in the singing.

We had a service under the trees in an area cleared by
the people themselves in which Bob presented the Christmas
story using a flannelgraph. We played Christmas carols on
a tape recorder and Bob and I sang the words of the songs in
Swahili.

After the service we served tea and banana cakes to
everyone. There were about 50 who attended the service, but
over 80 turned up following the service for the treats which
included a gift of a piece of soap.

Bob explained our reason for giving gifts at Christmas
time. A short time later the Subchief stood up and handed
me some money saying it was for "mama" to show our
appreciation.

The women present at the service sang some of their tribal
songs of thanksgiving and joy. We pray that soon they will
be singing unto the Lord 'a new song' having Christian meaning.

For two days before Christmas and on the 27th as well, Bob showed films here at Arsim and at another village called Ilaut. They were very well received.

On Christmas day there was a wedding here at Arsim. It was not a church wedding. All the people who attended church, however, went to the wedding celebration and the dancing that followed. After the ceremony was over about half the folks who attended the ceremony flocked to our house to get medicine and treatment. I spent several hours with them. Many who came for the ceremony from far away slept in the Arsim area and attended our church service the day after Christmas which was a Sunday. We had about 50 adults at that service. At the close of the service Bob asked those who wanted to receive Christ -- God's Son -- His Gift to us at Christmas -- to hold up their hands. Just about everyone there responded.

Then Bob asked the people to take part in prayer. A group of men squatted in a circle Samburu style. A leader called out petitions as the rest of the group answered in unison with: "N'gai". N'gai meant: "Oh God, hear us." This was quite a thrilling experience for Bob and me.

We had another thrill this Christmas time. It happened on last Thursday evening at 5:30 P.M. The African Inland Mission plane flew low over the station and dropped our post bag delivering it to us from Nairobi.

We had been to Ngurunit several days before this to pick it up there, but it hadn't been put on that plane. What a disappointment!

On this trip the plane flew over and didn't drop anything. My heart sank and I got all choked up (I guess I was sorta homesick.) However, then the plane circled and came back and made the drop. That really made our Christmas -- so many cards and letters and even one that had been mailed and dated in the States on December 13th, and we received it way up here at Arsim on December 23rd.

I still stand at or run back and forth between the dispensing cupboard located under a big tree and the house at least 3 hours each day. Bob calls after me saying: "Don't run, walk!" So many sick ones again lately -- and some not so sick, but others very ill, and all wanting attention. May Christs' love show through all my actions and 'reactions'."

Additional Outreach-- Additional Witness

CHAPTER 33

"on one of his teaching journeys
round the villages he summoned
the Twelve and sent them out in
pairs on a mission." Mk.6:7 N.E.B.

Mike and Gail Koski had been united with us in the desire to evangelize the Samburu. Now they were interested in finding a place where they might establish an Outreach Center. They had already served as missionaries in Zaire and in western Kenya.

On December 1st, 1982, Mike and co-worker Andy Wendler traveled to the northern Kenya town of Nanyuki. They met Jeanne and me there to go in search of another site in Samburu. We wanted to choose a second place for a W.M.P.L./E.L.C.K. Outreach Center.

I had done preparatory work in consultation with Chief John from our Arsim location and had gotten referrals to Chiefs in the areas we would visit.

We spent the night in Nanyuki. Then we set off on December 2nd on the first leg of a four day trip. Our plan was to enter Samburuland from the south at Archers Post, where we would be able to contact Chief James Lenarei. He was the chief of an area called the Ngilai location.

We had lunch on the road and then arrived at a town called Wamba. The airstrip outside this town had served as our base for the original helicopter survey we had made of all

Samburuland almost three years before.

We visited the District Office and got directions enabling us to reach the Ngilai location. It is approximately 30 Kilometers(18 miles) north of Wamba.

Our route of travel crossed eight dry rivers which showed signs of heavy rainfall within the last few days. We had almost canceled our safari because of this very heavy and unseasonable rainfall.

The nearer we got to our destination, the more difficult and slow it was for us to proceed because of the rocks and ruts of the track we followed. Finally, we reached a hilltop within the Ngilai location where Asst. Chief Samuel Lekesio lived. He received us very cordially. Samuel is an Anglican Christian. After learning who we were, and of our purpose for coming, he did everything he could to be helpful. He sent a runner to inform Chief James of our arrival.

We waited a short distance down the road from Samuel's house for Chief James to come from his home in the valley. He soon appeared and we explained to him in Swahili our desire to receive his direction about choosing a possible Outreach Center's location in his area. Both the Chief and the Asst. Chief had just walked in from Wamba that day but were very helpful. They showed us around the area in which a former Anglican school was located. The school was now supervised and administered by the Roman Catholic Church. They then showed us a spot in the valley quite close to where two of the seven rivers there meet. They suggested that we make camp there.

They promised the following morning that they would go over the area more thoroughly with us.

We set up our tents and Jeanne prepared a very tasty meal. There was threatening lightning in the eastern sky, but we were able to view a very beautiful full moonrise. The rain drenched the hills in the distance but we only got a few drops in our camp.

The next morning we all arose, had a good breakfast, and after morning devotions waited for the Chief and the Asst. Chief to appear. After some time Mike, Jeanne and I took a walk leaving Andy in camp in case the Chiefs arrived. We crossed one river that was flowing by using stones across its bed. We then went on some distance to a very beautiful area bordering on the river which Mike likened to a park. He said this area would be a wonderful place to build a Center.

We returned to our camp and then sometime later the Asst. Chief appeared. He was surprised to find that Chief James had not come as yet. He said we should come with him and he would show us the place he had in mind for us to locate.

Jeanne and Andy remained in camp. Mike and I followed Asst. Chief Samuel. The route he followed was about the same route we had taken by ourselves earlier on our walk that morning. We noticed that there was a large shallow excavation in the place he showed us. We asked what purpose it had served. He said the forest department used it to plant and store their tree seedlings.

We then crossed a river which the Asst. Chief called the

Nolgisin. We took off our shoes and waded across the broad river of shallow water on very soft sand. Crossing it we came to an alternative site which the Asst. Chief offered to us. This site was on much higher ground.

The first location gave promise of available water directly from the river, and seemed to give the promise of water from a well like the one we had dug at Arsim. Neither of these opportunities seemed to offer themselves at the second site. In this country, water is always a prime consideration.

We returned to our campsite and struck camp in the face of an impending rain storm.

Chief Lenarei had not come but we were assured by Asst. Chief Samuel that he had the authority to make an agreement with us in preparation for presenting a request to the Samburu Council.

We took time for a bite to eat since the threatening clouds had passed us by, and then we returned Asst. Chief Samuel to his home. He lived on the road we now used to return to Wamba. We parted leaving this gracious man with the promise that he would soon be hearing from us.

We went to the main road and journeyed northwest 32 Kilometers to a village called Lodungokwe. We called in at the Chief's office and were cordially received by Chief Lolojuu and his staff.

After describing the purpose for our visit, the Chief assured us that there were many people in his area -- one of his staff said they numbered over a million.

Our visit was short. We did no actual site survey in that area. We left feeling that we would receive a cordial reception if we might decide to return later.

We then continued our trip using the road we were on to reach Maralal, the District Headquarters. Here we camped on the Anglican Samburu Rural Development Center's campgrounds where we spent a restful night.

The next morning after making a visit into Maralal town from our camp, we drove north to reach the town of Baragoi a distance of 95 Kilometers.(59 miles)

We had previously arranged to meet Chief Thomas Lekesaat of this location. When we arrived we learned that he had just left Baragoi to travel to an area called Lesirikan. He must have gotten tired of waiting for us because of the three hours we spent driving up from Maralal.

We ate an early lunch and drove east out of Baragoi to reach Lesirikan a distance of 25 Kilometers. We met the Chief who was just going off to a Harambee(self help) dam building project. He kindly interrupted his trip to discuss site possibilities in his area. He mentioned two in particular: Lataquin and Sereret, both located on the southern slopes of the Ndoto Mountains some distance on from Lesirikan. The Chief said that he would be happy to accompany us anytime in the future to see these places. Right at this time he was committed to go to the dam site where a number of villagers were waiting for him to appear before they began their work of constructing the dam.

We thanked him. He immediately went on his way. We returned to Baragoi and our party split up there -- Jeanne and I went north to Arsim, Mike and Andy south to return to Nairobi.

The consensus of opinion was that the Ngilai site was the one most favored by us all.

Later the Koskis did build a Center with the help of Jeff Stoopes, a volunteer from America. The plot they chose to build on was the one Mike had said looked like a park on our survey safari to Ngilai. The actual name of that plot was Lesugamar.

A Time of Famine in Samburu

CHAPTER 34

"But if a man has enough to live on,
and yet when he sees his brother in
need shuts up his heart against him,
how can it be said that the love for
God dwells in him?" I Jn. 3:17 N.E.B.

The Lord was very kind to us.

Had we known what was so quickly to come to pass we would have been troubled by an almost overwhelming fear.

The year 1983 was a year of settling in for us at Arsim. But there is an all important time each year in Kenya -- the coming of the April rains. It came and went in 1983 without bringing those rains. Since there is a lag in time before the absence of rainfall is felt, we were still experiencing the results of the 1982 rainfall. There was plenty of water flowing in the stream by our center. The supply of grass was adequate enough for all the cattle in the area. However the specter of an approaching famine loomed on the horizon.

In spite of this great concern, the evangelistic work at Arsim went forward. Two baptisms took place -- for the wife and daughter of our household helper, Lopejekwe.

I had hired a helper, William G. Lekusuyan, who was working with me as my translator as well as teaching nursery school half days. He was also instructing Jeanne and me in the Samburu language.

I worked with him to translate the Lord's Prayer, an order of a worship service I had made, the Ten Commandments, a portion of Luther's small Catechism and individual verses from the Bible.

A number of people had been asking for baptism and we encouraged them all to attend the regular Saturday instruction classes leading to Church membership. It was also important that they regularly attended Sunday morning services to join the fellowship.

Before I started holding classes on Saturdays, I laid the floor in our new house. I had an accident. I drove a piece of rusty metal floor screen(expanded metal) into my leg. It put me down for several days with a serious infection. The Samburu elders, always gracious in visiting those who are sick, came to visit me as well. Prior to that time I had noticed that the attendance at the Sunday morning service under the trees was dropping off. So my illness gave me the opportunity to ask my visitors why attendance was falling. Their replies amazed me.

"Some of us have been missing Sunday morning services because we don't know it's Sunday. You hold a class on Saturday, then everyone will know the next day is Sunday."

The Samburu have a different reckoning method than we do with our seven day week.

So we began to hold a two or three hour Saturday afternoon class. During the class those who came learned the following in their own language: The Lord's Prayer, a Bible story which they had to remember, a Bible verse, a portion of Luther's Small Catechism, Christian songs (with native as well as traditional melodies). All these had to be learned by rote memory because almost all of our people were illiterate.

The Saturday class was a very enjoyable experience. The first promise asked for was that a new convert stand in front of the group and say: "I (name) now accept Christ Jesus as my Savior." I have mentioned that the Samburu had a lot of resistance in using their 'real' names when they identify themselves. Here they were required by their neighbors and friends to B E T R U T H F U L !

In spite of this problem for some, the class was a very enjoyable experience. Here is an example of what went on.

One class member would try reciting the Lord's Prayer sentence by sentence. As he or she gave a sentence, the whole group in chorus would repeat it back. This would continue until the one reciting would forget and get stuck. There was a pause and a giggle or two. Then someone else helped out by saying the forgotten portion. Now everyone laughed and then the chorus repeated the sentence just as if nothing had happened. Men as well as women worked at this new method of memorization. When it got a bit heavy, we would switch the instruction to the learning of songs. Many of these songs would sound strange to people who weren't Samburu. Most of the songs came from the Samburu culture and tradition and had now been given Christian content. These were completely learned by the group often the first time they were sung. The African

Inland Mission had prepared a hymnal of many of these songs. We were very grateful for this resource.

At this time we made trips out to visit manyattas in the local area. It was our opportunity to present Christ as the Saviour of all men. We used preaching, tapes, pictures and singing in our witness. We made an extended safari of 13 days, which covered quite a bit of the area in our part of the Ndoto Mountains. The reception to the "Good News" was all positive.

Jeanne worked tirelessly treating people, morning and afternoon -- seven days a week. They came from far and near suffering from all kinds of illness.

She delivered several babies. New mothers traditionally after delivering are not given water to drink for 3 days. They receive no milk for a whole month. Jeanne mixed up rehydration drinks and told everyone it was medicine(which it really was). The new mothers benefited a lot from drinking this 'medicine'. It caught on and because of this treatment, new mothers stopped fainting dead away as they had previously been prone to do after their deliveries, some of them two or three times.

Jeanne had the help of the medical staff from the A.I.M. station at Gatab located fifty miles north of Arsim.

Miss Louise Cameron, and the Gatab plane flown by John Wollman were a team that assisted Jeanne in holding an 'under five' children's clinic at Arsim every six weeks and at Ilaut as well. The A.I.M. Central office staff in Nairobi also assisted Jeanne in her attempt to become a registered nurse with the Kenya Government Nursing Council.

At this time I laid a cement slab 3 x 5 meters (9 x 15 Ft.) This was a floor that awaited the delivery of a prefab dispensary building from Nairobi.

We also started a small school built from mud bricks. In Tanzania it would have been called a 'bush school'. In Kenya they called it a 'nursery school'. The Local Government provided food for the lunch program and gave us maize, beans and cooking oil which were gifts from donors outside Kenya. Attendance at classes ran in the high forty's. For many of the kids, this was the only really substantial meal they got each day.

We chose a site for a landing strip, and employing local help it was cleared and smoothed. This meant that the plane from Gatab could fly in during the daylight hours. We had radio contact with them for medical emergencies.

The women brought the request first.

"Bwana, we want a church".

I explained to them that this was an Outreach Center. My colleagues and I had decided we would not build churches at our Outreach Centers. We would concentrate on having 'manyatta churches' in the villages. This was unacceptable to the women.

"We will build a church" they said.

"Will you help us bring in the branches and grass we need for its construction?" I was hard put to deny this kind of proposal.

They built a church in the form of a large Samburu home.

The women faithfully carried out the project with the help of a few other men and me and our truck. The lattice like walls made from the interwoven branches of their church provided an ideal resting place for passing snakes. I had the experience several times of having my sermon interrupted by these unwelcome visitors on Sunday mornings.

We were praying that the October rains would fall in 1983. Although this is the 'light rainy season' anything would have been of help that year. All the grass was now gone and the animals were starting to suffer. The calves born then were born to die very quickly.

The families living in the Arsim valley, about thirteen in number, came to us. They told us that they desperately needed our help. They were hungry. Their cows and goats were dry, producing no milk for them to eat. The people were starving, would we help them?

I pointed out that we were only a small faith Mission group. We didn't have large resources, but I would do my best as long as our resources lasted. We had some money in our work fund account. So we bought powdered milk and shipped it up from Nairobi.

Rev. Clifford Anderson had visited us some months before. At that time we knew the famine was soon upon us. He said he wanted to help. I knew that the greatest need would be to purchase a large truck. We had paid outrageous charges to have our prefab shipped north to Arsim. We could use a truck to transport famine relief food supplies and for all our other hauling needs. Cliff returned home to Minnesota and because of his intervention we were soon able to purchase a rebuilt Bedford lorry. These lorries were rebuilt castoffs from the British Army and Navy. A Bedford was reputed to be able to haul a load of seven to nine tons and it had four wheel drive.

We now were in the midst of a terrible famine. At the close of 1983 our thirteen families living in the Arsim area mushroomed into a famine village built around our center of over a thousand men, women and children. People continued to move in on us from the mountains and the surrounding areas. They built typical Samburu huts and completely encircled our center. More and more came until we reckoned that we were feeding 3000 men, women and children. We soon ran out of food. The Kenya Government started bringing in shipments of maize. An organization called Food For The Hungry helped us a lot. They gave us supplies of corn, milk powder, beans, vitamins, famine biscuits/crackers, soup powders, and soya bean powder. We continued to buy full cream powdered milk and maize from our work funds supplied by donors in the U.S.

At first we depended on the Government and Food for the Hungry to deliver our supplies. There was very poor coordination to our needs when we depended upon others. When our own rebuilt lorry became available in mid 1984, we were able to plan the supply for our needs. How thankful we were for our Samburu lorry. We gave thanks again and again for Cliff Anderson and all those who had contributed so that we could fund the purchase of the truck.

As I drove to Arsim I <u>overloaded</u> the truck on its first trip. Jeanne was driving behind me with our Toyota Landcruiser. We were just a few miles out of town when she saw the lorry begin to zig zag, and then it headed for the ditch. The left front wheel then fell off. The wheel's subhousing had snapped. I had just turned a corner, so the truck wasn't going very fast, otherwise who knows what might have happened. The firm who had sold the truck to us were out immediately and repaired it on the roadside.

On our return trip to Nairobi, after delivering our load to Arsim, the steering again felt so loose that I stopped. I discovered that all the studs on the steering shaft housing to the wheel were broken except one. We were in a range of foothills and the road was hazardous at best. There was nothing to do, since we were several hundred miles from Nairobi, except to tighten the one stud which was left and try to make it into the closest town which was Maralal. I literally crawled all the way up and down the Maralal escarpments. It took us until well after dark to reach our destination. Jeanne followed close behind me in the Landcruiser. Her eyes were glued on my lorry praying all the time that the Lord would keep me and the lorry on the road. HE DID!

Jeanne later told me that we were getting too old for this stuff!

Another organization which assisted us in helping with the famine was the Christoffel Blinden Mission. Mr. & Mrs.

Dieter Opitz had kept track of us after we left Uhuru Highway where they were members. They arranged for us to receive C.B.M.'s help. They personally gave us money to buy food. Their organization gave us supplies of milk powder and butter cooking oil. The Lutheran World Federation also helped us with famine food supplies. When our funds were used up for us to buy more food, the Lord just supplied them again and again.

The opportunity then came for us to loan our lorry to the Food For The Hungry organization. They were short of transport, and promised with their driver to keep us supplied with shipments of food for our needs. At that time I was very happy to give up my driver's job. I needed to use all my energy at Arsim administering the famine aid we were receiving.

I strongly felt that even in a famine situation, the people getting food from us should do something in return. It is demeaning to give anything to anyone without allowing them to give something of value in return. In this case, the women of our village carried water three days a week. The men produced sun dried mud bricks to be used in building a nurses' house at our center. The men also dug a number of pit latrines.

We finished our prefab dispensary with the help of a volunteer from America, Mr. Jeff Stoopes. It had water piped in from our well and even had solar lights for night emergencies.

The peak months of the famine were August and September of 1984. Famine rarely comes by itself. Someone, during the influx of the many people who moved into our village, brought measles, and we had a severe epidemic of over 120 cases. It was very bad -- nearly all the cases had serious complications. Jeanne worked <u>day and night</u>, going around the famine village with supplies of rehydration drink, waking up parents and children. It was critical that the kids kept drinking fluids or they would soon enter the phase of dehydration that could prove to be fatal. Jeanne almost lost her own health in spending all of her energy reserves working nonstop. She was so thankful that only seven lives were lost to the ravages of the disease. These children were victims of malnourishment to begin with and also suffered from severe enteritis. Our own Arsim children had been immunized. None of those children who had come in from far away had. A total of 78 measles shots were given, but they proved to be ineffective because the epidemic already had begun.

The gathering of all these people gave us a wonderful chance to share Christ and His message of salvation for them. The famine relief program was a big task that required all we could give night and day. But it was a very rewarding time. We received some criticism of our involvement in helping people in this way. However from this time forward, where ever we went in Samburuland we were known and respected for the aid we gave these needy folks.

Our prayers were answered with the coming of the rains in November of 1984. The hillsides were green again and there was grass for the few animals who had survived. Most of the people moved back to their home areas although they returned periodically to get food. It was quite sometime before they would have milk enough to feed themselves. Compared to the famine in Ethiopia, we had a manageable emergency, but nonetheless an emergency. It was another case where we were forced to rely on God's help alone. I heard the story of one Borana man (a tribe that borders Samburu on the north). He had lost all his stock shortly after the onset of the famine. He went to his home and killed his wives and his children and then took his own life. He left the word that in losing all his stock neither he nor his family had anything left to live for.

I wept for him, if only he could have heard about Jesus and could have come to know Him, all would have not been lost.

Christmas was a joyous experience for all that year at Arsim. Christmas Eve we had a candlelight service in our "Stick" Samburu hut Church and our first communion service with eight of us partaking.

About twenty people joined us for our 5:30 A.M. caroling on Christmas morning. We visited many manyattas and invited the people to the service at 10 A. M. Our church was filled to overflowing with as many people sitting outside as inside -- about 260 people in attendance. For some it was their first time to hear the joyful Christmas message of Christ, God's Son, being born in a manger.

Restocking & Rehabilitation

CHAPTER 35

"...but those who hope in the
Lord will renew their strength"
Isa. 40:31   N.I.V.

As we came out of the famine time at the close of 1984, we continued to be very busy. We had the pleasure of hosting a Cross Fire team, #7 from Lutheran Youth Encounter. They spent nine days with us at Arsim. Their Swahili choruses were a blessing to our people who quickly learned them. The Samburu also thoroughly enjoyed the rest of their program.

Anita Vedell and Janice Woodward, young people out from the States, also stayed with us for five weeks. Anita was the daughter of Pastor and Mrs. Emerson Vedell who had invited us to visit their church on each of our furloughs.

My program was one of getting things ready for our upcoming furlough. Bruce and Sue Kemp and their family were due to arrive in February 1985. Nurse Alpha Jaques had also responded to God's 'recall' and was due to come to Samburu in February. She had formerly served with us on the field in Tanzania. I was struggling to get a new house ready for her.

We were planning to leave Arsim for ten months of furlough in the United States the middle of April.

We were still supplying powdered milk to those who had lost everything in the famine. We took Bruce and his family up with us to Arsim on February 16. The task Bruce set himself to at once upon his arrival on the field was restocking. He made a careful survey of people in our area and found that there were sixteen families that were destitute. They were unable to rebound from the famine without some kind of outside assistance. Bruce then got into the goat buying business so that he could provide that assistance. The figures were available to guide us on how many animals were needed by a family to meet their food needs.

At the same time he arranged to purchase five mules in Ethiopia that would become very useful in the following years as pack animals for our safaris.

Alpha Jaques also arrived in February and began her service to the Samburu at this time, a faithful ministry of medicine that continued on for nine years until she reached retirement age and returned home.

Jeanne and I left for our furlough in April having given our work over to the Kemps and Alpha.

Arriving in the U. S. we were kept very busy traveling and speaking in Florida, Ohio, Tennessee, Minnesota, Washington, Oregon, California, Illinois, Alaska, Idaho, Montana and Colorado. We were grateful for the privilege to be able to thank those personally who had supported us through the famine with their prayers and gifts.

Those weeks and months we spent on furlough that remained in 1985 flew quickly by. On December 11th, we attended the commissioning of our son Daniel and his wife Kathi at Bethany Lutheran Church in Seattle. They joined God's overseas service going out under the Christoffel Blinden Mission. This was one of the missions which had provided us with aid during the famine. Dan was stationed by C. B. M. to serve working in Nairobi as his base Eventually he became a Regional Representative and would serve many other areas in Africa as well from Nairobi.

We returned to Kenya on March 4th. Since the Kemps next assignment was to occupy Ngilai when the Koski's took their furlough later in 1986, we remained in Nairobi and took some Samburu language study. During this time, we enjoyed the hospitality of Dan and Kathi who were now living in Nairobi. However we made three trips to Arsim. This began quite a unique experience for us of loading up our Landcruiser -- to the roof -- with supplies each time we journeyed upcountry. Dan had a particular ability of knowing just how to pack each load for getting the maximum use of space in the car. He regularly helped me with our packing, because he and Kathi graciously invited us to stay in their home whenever we traveled to Nairobi during the remaining years we served in Samburu.

On one of our trips we made a survey foot safari together with Bruce Kemp to site in a location for Samburu Outreach Center No. 3. It was the plan that when the Koskis returned to Ngilai in 1987, Bruce and Sue and their family would then begin work at this new location.

I was concerned about Bruce traveling at this time. He had just had a foot infection and there was the possibility of a blood clot having resulted from this infection. He was not supposed to travel, but he insisted that he would be all right. He would ride one of the mules. There were five of us -- Jeanne, Bruce, myself and two Samburu. The safari took seven days to complete. Originally we had planned to meet Mike Koski at the southern point of our travel, but this didn't work out.

Altogether we walked around 60 miles to make this journey. However the pedometer fell off my belt the second day out, so we weren't certain about our exact milage. Believe it or not, the pedometer was recovered on the trail when we made our return.

We experienced God's special care on this safari. On our second day out, Narok -- one of our mules -- just gave up! She wanted to lie down <u>all</u> the time. We were concerned that she was very sick. She was the animal carrying Bruce. After resting in the shade for a couple of hours, we coaxed her along and finally reached the water holes at Ngare Narok around 8:30 P.M. We had walked and stumbled along in the dark for the last hour and a half, not knowing exactly where we were going, nor did our Samburu guides. This caused us a lot of anxiety. On top of being lost, I had great concern about Bruce. He had to walk now since Narok wasn't able to carry him.

Our donkey traveling in front of Jeanne, deliberately kept shifting the load he carried and tried to throw it off. When Jeanne tried to help steady his load, he stomped on her foot twice.

It was a time of rejoicing for the Lord's protection when

we sat sipping milk tea around 10 P.M. We had safely reached our destination and made our camp. Now we could relax in our tents.

The day had not been without the opportunity to witness to our Lord. We had seen several folks along our way of travel -- down in the dry Milgis River bed. These folks told us they had never seen a white person before. They chuckled at us when they saw us coming. Neither had they ever heard of our Lord, and we told them about Him.

We celebrated our 37th wedding anniversary in the camp at Ngare Narok. There weren't many people in this area, but one manyatta produced a sheep that I could purchase. I had brought along a box of chocolates in my backpack. Fortunately they had survived the heat in tact. So we celebrated eating roasted mutton served with rice, tea and chocolates. From what we learned on this safari, Bruce now had three possibilities for locating Samburu III: Keno, Ngare Narok and Sererit. Unfortunately none of these were ever realized.

With the increased staff at Arsim, we urgently needed a second car. C. B. M. had an eight year old four wheel drive car they were willing to loan to our Mission. It was worth a great deal more than we could ever pay. We rejoiced once again in this provision from the Lord through them.

In July 1986, the Koskis went on furlough, the Kemps moved to Ngilai and we returned to live at Arsim.

The Storm & The Harvest

CHAPTER 36

"He that observeth the wind
shall not sow; and he that
regardeth the clouds shall
not reap."   Ecc. 11:4

After we took up residence at Arsim again in July our lives were full of the activity of getting settled back into our house (painting, etc,). I was also putting the finishing touches on Alpha's house. We cleaned our well, added an extension on the dispensary and built a car maintenance shop with a grease pit.

The second week in August we made a six-day foot safari visiting manyattas in the Arsim valley and into the surrounding Ndoto mountains. The people welcomed us warmly wherever we went and wanted us to come back every week.

We returned to Nairobi where we spent a week together with Dan and Kathi and Lincoln Howes who had been married to Kris, our oldest daughter. Linc was in remission from cancer but was preparing for an autologous bone marrow transplant (using his own bone marrow): he returned to the U. S. for the transplant but overwhelming sepsis set in and he had to give up the battle for his life. He awaits us in our heavenly home.

The April rains had been scanty and inadequate. We had expected the sixteen families who were restocked with goats to be independent by now, and even to begin returning the first born of their flocks to help us to assist others in need. Instead, by July everyone had a serious food problem. The herds didn't have enough grass to eat to produce milk. We started our 'Food for Work' program again, which had to provide now for thirty-two families and units, (some were blind people and widows). The rains delayed coming in October but by mid-November, the rainfall was promising.

At Arsim life went on following our usual routine. I had daily morning devotions with the workers, a midweek fellowship service on Wednesdays (because illiterate people who cannot feed themselves from the Scripture need midweek spiritual food), instruction classes on Saturdays, and regular services on Sundays. Jeanne met with the Arsim women once a week for a time of fun, fellowship and Bible Study. She also held a Sunday School for about thirty little ones on Sunday mornings. She helped Alpha with her mobile under-five clinics and her dispensary work.

In October we made a trip to Nairobi to await the arrival of our first grandchild. Dan and Kathi presented us with an adorable and beautiful baby boy - Zachary Jonathan born on October 17th. I had the privilege of baptizing little Zachary when he was just nine days old. Then Jeanne and I returned to our duties up country at Arsim.

We had continued to worship in our stick church. But we had had several visits from Kenya officials who mocked our little sanctuary. When one of them came and demanded to see our church, I showed him the little church of which I was rather proud. After all, it had been built part and parcel by indigenous hands.

He responded: "That's no church", and left in obvious

disgust.

While we were still in Nairobi to welcome Zachary, we received a communication. The police had visited Arsim demanding entry into our house. They were told we were not at home.

Then they set about breaking in. Our household helper produced a key, and they entered and snatched up my amateur radio equipment and searched the house thoroughly. They then left leaving word that I report to them at the District Police Headquarters in Maralal at once.

This happened on October 8th. It followed on the heels of an event that shook the missionary community.

A small independent mission group who had come from Medford Oregon in the U. S. were beginning a work in the Pokot area in northwestern Kenya. The group had come out primarily to preach Christ to the Pokot people. They also were greatly interested in helping the people dig a number of wells so that the Pokot would find it easier to water their herds. They also were building schools because the Pokot area had a real need for more educational facilities.

The missionaries imported a large shipment in a seacrate. These were supplies to aid them in their life and work. This seacrate was intercepted by the police who said it contained:

Illegal high-powered firearms

Bolts of cloth to manufacture uniforms for
an insurgent army in Kenya

>   Illegal radio equipment to aid in the
>   insurgency.

The Police went through the whole country of Kenya, seeking out missionaries, particularly Americans, whom they viewed as involved in a coordinated conspiracy against the Kenya government. Officers arrested the people at the Pokot mission and took them to Nairobi without making any charges against them. One of the missionaries had a very bad heart. Apparently he was not allowed time to get his supply of medicine before he was arrested and taken away. It was reported that the group of missionaries was taken to the Central Police headquarters in Nairobi. While they were standing there in the lobby someone came by with a newspaper. The headlines were glaring in their accusations about the Mission's attempt to subvert the Kenya government. It was simply too much for the haggard missionary who had a bad heart. Now he finally had learned from these headlines why his group was in custody. He said: "Oh my God", and fell dead on the lobby floor.

The government incriminated itself by the newspaper pictures that were taken.

The bolts of cloth were the raw materials to sew school uniforms for Pokot students.

The highpowered rifles were pellet guns to scare elephants away from watering tanks the missionaries were building.

The illegal radio equipment: "walkie-talkies" which the missionaries had already licensed with the Kenya government to use for interstation communication.

On October 29th, I arrived in Maralal and went to the police. I was questioned for a period of two hours. All my radio equipment was properly licensed, but they kept pushing me to admit that I was using it to communicate illegally or outside the mandate of strictly amateur hobby use. Of course this was an absurd accusation and I pointed this out to them again and again.

Interestingly enough, the police took this opportunity to tell me that if I didn't build a 'proper' church at Arsim, I obviously was not in the country to do mission work, but had some other agenda.

The police continued to make periodic visits to Arsim to interrogate me and insisted that I was doing something illegal. Having just come out of a famine situation, this was like returning a slap in the face for all our good efforts in the emergency just recently passed.

When I returned to Arsim I shared with the Christians in our congregation about the accusations made by the Government. I said that we would probably have to build a structure that had a 'metal roof' which was the minimum required by the Police to qualify it as a church. The Christians all agreed that this was necessary.

One Sunday as our congregation was discussing this I remarked that I would be asking for guidance as to where we should build our next church. I presumed that it would be on the site where we were presently worshiping.

NOT   SO!

One lady stood up and said: "Come and I will show you where we will build our new church."

The congregation stood together and followed her. She led us to a site on the brow of a small hill above where our houses and the dispensary were located.

"Here", she said, "is where we will build our new church!"

No one disagreed, and this is the site where the Arsim church stands today.

*   *   *   *   *   *

Up until this incident, the African Inland Mission had allowed us to be part of their extensive radio network. This helped us in so many ways but particularly because the A.I.M. aircraft made flights to deliver our mail and other supplies once a month. Now, because of these difficulties with the Government, the A.I.M. asked us to leave their radio net.

What hurt us most was the uncritical acceptance by some of the people in our community that we were really guilty of the Government's accusations. "It must be true", they said, "our government doesn't have any reason to lie."

*   *   *   *   *   *

At this time, we received a great encouragement from the Lord. We had been faithful in sowing the seed of the precious Gospel of Jesus Christ among the Samburu, a group of people unreached with the Gospel. Now the first harvest was to appear.

On Sunday, December 21, 1986 the Lord reaped what He had planted through our work. Twenty adults and thirty six children were brought into God's Kingdom by their confession of faith

and in Holy Baptism. For the adults it was the culmination
of months of preparation. Most of them were illiterate. In
order to proceed with their faith and understanding of Christ,
they spent many hours learning by memory: Bible verses, portions
of Luther's Small Catechism, the Ten Commandments, The Lord's
Prayer, the Confession of Sins and The Apostles Creed. All
of these we had translated into the Samburu language. The
people had also come to know many of the stories from the Old
and New Testament of the Bible. We had laid heavy emphasis
on both head as well as heart trust in Christ as their Lord,
Master and only Saviour. The doctrines of: "Faith Alone, Grace
Alone and the Word Alone" were the truths to which the people
were now committed to witness and live out in their lives.

We remembered one 'miracle' of the Lord in particular
as this group was baptized. It was against Samburu law and
custom for young morans to be in the area where married women
congregate. Sunday after Sunday one young Moran would 'sneak'
into the area and furtively listen while Jeanne held her Sunday
School class under the trees. Those stories became the basis
for his beginning walk with Jesus Christ. This Moran was in
the first baptism class and took the name: Francis, Francis
Lakadaa.

Jeanne used the children at Christmas time to interpret
the Christmas story in a pageant they presented in story and
song. All the mamas and papas were on the edge of their wooden
'board' pews taking it all in for the first time in their lives.

A short time after this first baptism we held the first

communion service for our new Christians. We closed 1986 with
joyful hearts.

PLATE VI

CAMELS DRINKING AT ARSIM'S
WATER HOLE

MOBILE MEDICAL CLINIC
(l-r) JEANNE & ALPHA

OUR PRE-FAB ARSIM HOUSE

THE ARSIM CHURCH

A Home For A King

CHAPTER 37

"Behold I lay in Zion, a
chief corner stone, elect
precious: And he that be-
lieveth on him shall not be
put to shame." I Pet. 2:6
                    Phillips

The site had already been chosen by a lady from our congregation. Now we needed to set about building a Church that would honor the Lord and be acceptable to the Kenya officials who were so critical of the home style church which our people had built.

We had credits and debits as we looked at the project ahead of us.

We had very little financial ability as a group of new Christians but we knew how to trust the Lord for our supply.

From the beginning of our worship services at Arsim, we had included an offering as a part of "Church". We usually took in 20 or 30 Kshs a Sunday. Now at the end of August 1987 we had built up a balance of money that came to Kshs 3,631.20 ($214) -- that was a huge sum for most of the people in our fellowship. I had assured the Christians that this money would never be used for anything without their approval. I had given them reports from time to time as the amount continued to grow. Now I proposed that we use the entire amount for building our

Church.

The congregation agreed. The people also agreed to provide labor for the construction of the church. We chose to use native stone for our construction material. The people -- men as well as women -- gathered it into piles called metres. We collected these in our lorry and brought them to the site. Everyone in the congregation took pleasure in their different contributions to build the church.

When the building was completed everyone was very satisfied. The church even had a bell tower. The bell was donated by a ranch in Montana. People all over the valley could hear it calling everyone to worship as it was rung early each Sunday.

The foundation of the Church was laid July 1st, 1987 and the building was used for worship in mid-November after a building time of three and a half months.

I was very fortunate in getting a national builder, a Kikuyu whose name was Robert Kagema. His home was in Nanyuki on the lower slope of Mt. Kenya. Robert was able to work with the Samburu people in a wonderful way. He was also a very talented builder and a deeply committed christian.

He used a technique of building the stone walls similar to that which I had used in Tanganyika to build schools. In Tanganyika we called the method: 'Rammed Earth' and used soil from the ground as our building material.

In building the Arsim church Robert bolted long planks together leaving an inside gap between the planks of over a foot. This gap was filled with large rocks and concrete to bind the rocks together to make the wall. Then the planks were unbolted and raised up to build the next higher section of the wall.

Robert placed the flat sides of the rocks so that they faced out against the planks. When the construction was finished, the rock facings gave a very desirable 'finished' look to the outside walls. The inside walls were plastered and painted. Church building took place under a scalding hot sun most days. Robert never complained about working conditions nor did the Samburu workers.

The church was able to accommodate over 120 worshipers. It had a cement floor and wooden pews. A traditional European style pulpit and a baptismal font were donated by women from a church in Pottstown Pennsylvania. These appointments were crafted in a woodshop in Nairobi. The roof of the church was made up of aluminum sheets, except the roofing over the altar and in one or two other locations. Here we used transparent plastic sheets believing that our need for light warranted this choice. Later we learned that anyone sitting in these parts of the church found the penetrating sunlight unbearably hot. We painted the plastic but that didn't reduce the heat penetration very much.

We unofficially dedicated this house of worship on November 15th, 1987. Later, the President of the E.L.C.K. Rev. John Momanyi came in February, 1988 and made the formal dedication on behalf of the E.L.C.K.

I often thought of the hymn: "Built on a rock, the Church shall stand" as I looked at our building. It was most certainly 'built of many rocks' from the surrounding countryside. Our Samburu Church is also being built of many spiritual rocks -- People from Samburu -- that are standing on the foundation of the <u>TRUE ROCK</u> Jesus Christ.

The Christians of this new church, also so new in their experience of the Lord, suffer growing pains, stumblings, struggles and many conflicts. They have to encounter and endure many social and cultural adjustments. But they have learned very often the meaning of God's mercy and love and grace which are ever present for them. They have seen that the Lord can and will change their lives. They are able now to understand the meaning of the words:

> "Wherefore if any man is in Christ, he
>
> is a new creature: the old things are
>
> passed away; behold they are become new."
>
> I Cor. 5:17

Up on The Mountain

CHAPTER 38

"Take heed that ye despise not one of these
little ones; for I say unto you, That in
heaven their angels do always behold the face
of my Father which is in heaven. For the Son
of man is come to (seek) save that which is
lost. How think ye? If a man have a hundred
sheep, and one of them be gone astray, doth he
not leave the ninety and nine, and goeth into
the mountains, and seeketh that which is gone
astray?"..Matt.18:10-12   K.J.V.

1988 was a year filled with meaningful activity and
events. We dedicated our church officially, and I was very
busy at and away from Arsim. For several years I had been
employing a man as an assistant. He was a good and faithful
worker. His name was Jackson L. Ntokodie. He shared in the
work of the outreach center and also spent time preaching at
other places. His mother was Samburu and his father was
Turkana. In spite of not being pure Samburu, the people seemed
to accept Jackson and his ministry among them quite well.

I was making evangelistic visits once a month to places
away from Arsim. Places with names like Ketowan, Parakorren,
Kaisipo, Ilaut, Selewan, Sereit, Keno, Ngari Narok and Marti
Dorrop. I used our five mules to make many of these safaris.
I didn't ride them but used them to carry loads including their
own food. Their names were: Narok(Black), Naibor(White), Seben,
Longero and Satani. Satani had come by his name well. He
had been mistreated in Ethiopia where he began life. Every
now and then in typical mule fashion, he would seem to go
wild and become a danger to anything in his path.

I preached at Ilaut one Sunday a month. Either Jackson
or I preached every Sunday at Arsim. Every Wednesday a service
for spiritual nurture was held also at Arsim. On Saturday

afternoons we held mafundisho (instruction classes) for people seeking church membership. We made tape recordings of our services and sent these out to the out district evangelistic points to be used by the Christian fellowship leaders who had manually operated tape playback machines.

I showed evangelistic films using our mobile facilities at least once a quarter, and they were always very well attended in the open air after darkness set in.

I was building a school at Ilaut and a worker's house at Arsim for Janice Larson who was soon to join our staff. The school at Ilaut was one that had long existed without proper facilities administered by the Catholics. They told me that if I built a new school they would give me the school's administration and registration. I built the school but they refused to keep their promise.

Ilaut was a key location where the Chief held his court. Deep water wells were located there. These wells were utilized in typical Samburu fashion by morani passing up buckets of water from the bottom of the well to the moran perched on the next level up. Several wells had workers located on eight or nine ascending levels before the buckets were finally poured into the trough on the surface where the animals were watering. All this work was done while the men involved sang a chant-like song.

People came in from very long distances to water their camels and other herds. Water was precious, even water like that available from those Ilaut wells that had a high mineral and salt content.

I had heard about the people living on top of Mt. Alimission. This was the mountain that rose above us. We lived on the mountain's lower slope at its three thousand foot level. The mountain's peak reached into the sky to a distance of eight thousand five hundred feet. Sometimes I would look up at night and see a fire burning up close to the top of the mountain. When I asked the people at Arsim about it, they would shrug and say:

"No one can live on top of the mountain for longer than three days without freezing to death."

One day a man named Leshompira came to Arsim. He told me he lived on top of the mountain in a village called Selewan. He was cultivating a garden and wanted to get some seed potatoes from me.

I was overjoyed to grant him his request. Part of my calling was to try and improve the diet of the local people. Here I had a man who already had been successful in raising food for himself and his family.

I invited myself up to visit his home. I had no idea what I was going to encounter on this safari, but I decided to use a band of porters to go up the mountain.

I learned later that it was a distance of around nine miles to reach Selewan. But miles in Africa, particularly mountain miles do not follow the usual rules for travel.

Climbing Mt. Alimission is very hard work. Stretches of the trail are pleasant. But the higher one climbs, the more difficult the trail.

Finally, after being roasted by the sun, and sustaining several falls on slippery gravel, the climber enters a different world. Turning around, one looks back over the landscape far below. There appears a dusty, dry panorama of land stretching out for miles in all directions.

Looking forward, you enter the beginnings of a cedar forest. The aroma of this forest is exotic to one coming from the plains below. The trees, often covered with moss, are a tonic of green for sunburned eyes. Often a small stream coming from above softly trickles its way down the slope to disappear into the green underbrush. Once or twice the trail has to detour around a large tree that has fallen blocking the way.

On top of the mountain are the results of a classic forest fire which has left the skeletons of very large old cedars, majestic even as they still stand in their death.

Leshompira welcomed me and my party of ten porters with true rural hospitality. Because of the incursion of all kinds of animals, he had 'fenced' in his home and garden. He used thorns and huge bushes, to keep predators out. He had over an acre under cultivation. The only tool he had to use for cultivating was a simple machete. In his garden he had potatoes growing in hills, tomatoes, onions, and a lettuce like plant called sukuma wiki, which we call collards. With this supplement to his diet and the regular milk and meat he got from his herd of cows and goats, his family was in robust health. He also highly prized ground maize flour to make Ughali whenever he could get it. This required him to make a long safari.

We spent several days visiting him and preaching in the area. At that time we came to know an old blind man whose name was Lotokokai. This old man was wealthy because he had a big herd, but his blindness took all the joy out of his life. We tried to encourage him to return with us to Arsim, promising to see to his treatment and the restoration of his sight. At first he agreed to attempt to make what would be for him a very dangerous journey back down the mountain trail to Arsim. But when the time came for our departure, he refused to go. He feared the steep and dangerous trail might injure him or even cause his death.

While we were visiting the area, a report came that a rampaging buffalo was about and causing great trouble. He had a bad history. He liked to hide close to the water holes on the mountain. When the Samburu herders brought their cows for watering, he would charge from his hiding place goring and killing some of them. He had killed over a dozen animals at this time. The people pleaded with me to come and shoot the animal. I was not able to help them. Hunting had long been banned in Kenya and I was not able to do any kind of control work without breaking the law. I had to counsel the people to call in a game scout.

The people replied that they had asked for help repeatedly, but the game scouts would not come to this 'hard to reach' location.

The time came for us to return down the mountain. My ten porters shouldered their loads and we got an early start. An hour or so into the trip when we were still in the cedar forest I saw my porters, who were walking ahead of me in single file, suddenly throw off their loads and run for cover. I was carrying my 375 Magnum rifle. There were herds of buffalo in this forest, so I thought our group had gotten into a browsing herd. As I went forward, my guide pointed out a loan shaggy buffalo standing with his head in a thicket. His hind quarters were plainly visible and had the long silvery hair which uniquely identified him. He was the buffalo who had been causing all the trouble in the area, killing cows and threatening people.

I stood the position of 'guard' while the rest of my porters retrieved their loads and passed around behind me to the trail ahead. I still had no right to kill the animal unless it threatened our lives. It did not choose to do that, so we went on our way. Eventually, the animal was killed by several morani but not without injuring some of them.

We continued to make periodic trips up the mountain. On these later safaris we used our mules. Even with their surefootedness this was a rough journey for them. One mule had a great fear of passing over a flowing stream. We tied a cloth over her eyes and then lead her over this obstacle.

Coming up or down the mountain on the way to Selewan meant usually a two day safari and a camp overnight. This was through lion country.

On one trip we discovered the next morning that two or three lions had kept our camp under surveillance throughout the night. It was our custom to tie lighted kerosene storm lanterns in the trees surrounding our camp area. This lighted the entrance into our camp from every direction. Old settler reports claimed this would keep lions from attacking. We proved this report to be true a number of times on our safaris.

I had been to Selewan on several trips when Jeanne decided she would attempt to walk up the mountain. I was very happy about this. On each trip I made, among other things, I had tried to give out medicines and treat the sick. Now Jeanne would do this job properly.

I had been working with Leshompira and he had become our fellowship person on top of the mountain. He had a tape playback machine and with that he was doing the job of an evangelist even though he wasn't yet baptized.

Leshompira was providing a home for a six year old lad. The lad's name was Lanturi. On the first trip Jeanne and I made together to Selewan we were sitting in Leshompira's darkened hut playing Samburu evangelistic tapes. While Lanturi listened to the tapes, he sat close to me. He ran his hand along my arm. It was so hairy and different from his own smooth skin. At this time, the famine was becoming felt even on the mountain top. Milk was in very short supply.

Even so, the next morning Lanturi asked Leshompira to take his breakfast milk and send it to my camp for our breakfast. This meant that Lanturi would go without a meal to provide this gift of love for his new found friend.

My heart was deeply moved by what Lanturi had done. I responded by sending some other food back to Leshompira's house.

That day, I had scheduled a visit to other areas on the mountain. They were places I had never before visited. As I made preparations to leave, Lanturi came to my camp and then set off with me, taking my hand. As we walked into these new areas, what the people saw was Lanturi walking hand in hand with me, almost as if he were leading me. It was as if he were silently saying:

"This man is my friend, I am walking with him to commend him to you. Receive him."

This was a wonderful introduction Lanturi provided for me as we walked up and down the hills and valleys of this new area. It made me ask myself as we walked along:

"Into whose hand have I placed mine today? Will it be evident to all who see me that my hand is in His? Will that hand be the nail scarred hand of my Lord?"

Lanturi preached a sermon to me that day that I will never forget.

The people gathered several times and in several locations to listen to the Samburu tapes I had brought and to hear me describe the evangelistic pictures I was carrying. It was a good day!

The safari up the mountain for Jeanne had not been pleasant going. It was always a steep climb. The first day at noon lunch break, she had grabbed on to a bush to pull herself up on a high rock where I was starting a fire. The bush pulled out of the rock and Jeanne fell backwards causing a badly sprained ankle and a bruised back. She kept going and was able to make it up to the mountain's top. She was grateful that no bones were broken in her fall. As she had fallen backwards, she fell out of my range of sight. I heard a loud "pop". I thought she had fallen on to a huge rock behind her and cracked her skull. I jumped up and ran down the rock I was on crying:

"Jeanne, Jeanne!"

I was overjoyed to then see her stand in a dazed way, but in one reassuring to me that she hadn't been more seriously injured.

As soon as we arrived and made camp at Selewan people who were sick began to visit Jeanne, seeking her help. The word of her arrival traveled fast. She treated many sick people while we were in camp. I held two hour sessions of instruction daily for the people the three days we stayed.

Lotokokai, whom we had tried to encourage to come down from the mountain before, finally decided that he would follow Jeanne down. His son and Jeanne and a guide went down one side of the mountain. They were to meet Alpha at a clinic she was holding in the Kaisipo valley. Alpha had a car to give Lotokokai a ride the rest of the way into the Outreach Center.

My son Joel, who was out from the States visiting us, myself and two other men leading our mules returned by another

route. Jeanne said   that the trail she followed down was
very treacherous. It was a good thing Lotokokai could not
see how dangerous it was. She was leading him by holding one
end of his staff in her hand as they slowly made their way
down. Lotokokai's son fell several times, once rather
seriously. The descent was a very steep and narrow trail which
went down four thousand feet often with sheer drop-offs on
one side. I had never used this trail or I would have refused
to let Jeanne and her party take it. The people had assured
me that it was -- the short way down.

We took Lotokokai into the Kikuyu hospital close to
Nairobi. His left eye was operated on with a successful
cataract surgery. Unfortunately his right eye was beyond repair
because of a previous injury.

Lotokokai became a very cheerful and happy old man. We
prayed that his joy and vision would become complete in
accepting Christ as his Saviour in those remaining years of
his life.

Enrolled in God's School to learn trust

CHAPTER 39

"Trust in him at all times ye people;
Pour out your heart before him:
God is a refuge for us. (Selah)
Psalm 62:8

On Saturday October 8th, I drove the Bedford lorry from Arsim to Ngilai. I had some extra church benches from the number we had just purchased for our Arsim church. I took them in the lorry to Ngilai. I then planned to preach at Ngilai on Sunday and leave in the afternoon to return to Arsim.

Bruce Kemp had stored a number of bags of cement at Ngilai which now would not be used to build Samburu III. So, to redeem their cost I loaded them on the lorry to take them to Arsim.

All went well and about 3 P.M. Sunday afternoon I set off for Arsim with the lorry heavily loaded with cement.

It is about 35 Kilometers from Ngilai to the Seya River crossing. This river has quite a history of destroying lorries. This happens when a lorry tries to cross the wide sand river channel and gets caught in a flash flood. Many knowledgeable lorry owners will never use the shortcut road out of Baragoi to Wamba during the rainy season fearing the Seya River crossing.

I had no hint of trouble when I had come to Ngilai the day before. Coming from the Arsim direction is much more difficult because of a steep bank which must be climbed on the Ngilai side of the Seya River.

Because of the steepness of this bank, on my return I eased the Lorry down slowly entering the river's dry sand channel. When I got down on the river bed and tried to go

forward my wheels were not able to begin any forward motion.
Although the river was not flowing, still there was water in
the sand at the spot where I entered the river. The lorry
was in four wheel drive but I still couldn't get it to move
forward even an inch.

Not to worry, I thought. The truck had a very good winch
with a very long cable. I simply had to release the cable
and get it tied to a tree to pull myself out. It took me some
time to do this. When I finally engaged the winch to the lorry
motor to my surprise and mounting fear I learned that water
in the sand of the river had gotten into my clutch and I
couldn't get any power transfer -- the clutch was slipping!

I saw that it was raining off in the distance and at this
time it was beginning to get dark as well. Then my deliverer
appeared. This road was used by tourist busses -- lorries that
offer very low fare trips for young low budget tourists. To
economize on their travel the busses are always willing to
try to get through using this shortcut road. One of these
"Turkana busses" now came across the river toward me. After
it climbed the bank on my side of the Seya it stopped to offer
help. The bus was pretty rickety and I didn't think it would
be able to pull me out, but it was worth a try.

All the young tourists stood in front of my lorry pushing
with all their might as the tourist bus pulled it from the
rear using my cable. It was all to no avail. I was anchored
by my large wheels down in the sand bed of the river and my
load of cement sealed my doom.

By this time it was dark. I had a good friend in Wamba, Mzee Salim who owned shops there and a good strong lorry as well. So I begged a ride on the Turkana bus which soon covered the 50 kilometers to get to Wamba.

The Mzee and I knew it would be fruitless to try to return to the Seya in the dark. He found me accommodations for the night in a place called the Saudi Rest House. It was a night of earnest prayer on my part -- that I wouldn't lose my lorry.

Early the next morning while it was still dark, there was a heavy rainfall and I had visions of our lorry being buried in the sand. Lorries had been carried down the Seya and buried in the sand so deeply that their locations have never been discovered.

Fortunately, the small town of Wamba had a post office radio-telephone service enabling me to call the Koskis in Nairobi and tell them of my plight. They then called Jeanne at Arsim by Nairobi Radiocall and told her what had happened.

After I made the call, Mzee Salim and I were immediately on our way to the Seya in his lorry.

When we arrived it was a great relief to see that a flash flood had not carried our lorry off during the night.

We set about transferring all the cement to Mzee Salim's lorry. Then we tried to use the Mzee's lorry to pull my lorry out of the river. His tires were pretty bare, and on the hillside pull he didn't succeed in anything he tried to do to help me.

So I set a guard on the lorry, and then I returned to

Wamba with him.

There was a large Catholic Mission Hospital located in the town. I had seen a Caterpillar tractor in its maintenance yard. I went to them for help. Their maintenance director soundly berated me for using the Seya road during the rainy season. He said that the 'cat' I had hoped to use was no longer in operation.

I had just loaned out my hand operated winch before I left on this trip. It had a lift of seven tons. If I could only get the help of that winch, I thought I might be able to escape from the hold of the Seya. I sent word via Nairobi for Jeanne to try and get the winch and bring it down to me. I had loaned it to my neighbors the Beverlys, the A.I.M. missionaries at Ngurunit. It took some time for Jeanne to get word to them.

In the meantime, there was a government department that had some heavy equipment located at Wamba. I went to them with my plea for help. After waiting a day and a half for their supervisor to arrive, they made a futile attempt to pull me out, but again the slant of the hillside was a great problem. It threatened to overturn their tractor when they pulled.

It was now Friday. I had no way of knowing that the Beverlys had returned my winch to Jeanne and that at 2 P.M. she had started to make the long five hour trip down to the Seya.

I had heard that Mr. Bhola who ran a garage in Maralal had a very large logging tractor which some folks in Wamba thought was my only hope of getting a release from the river. So I left Friday morning using a local bus to travel to Maralal, a distance of 95 miles.

When I arrived, Mr. Bhola in his usual helpful way agreed that we would set out at dawn the following day with the tractor. His son, Hanif and I drove in a pickup following the tractor on the journey.

It had rained from time to time during the course of the week, but God's hand of protection had been graciously keeping the water level to a measure that rose and fell but didn't sweep my truck away.

Jeanne had arrived the previous evening at 6:50 P.M. at the river and was shocked to learn that I wasn't there with the lorry -- finding only the two men I had left to guard the lorry. She just crawled into the back seat of our car to spend the night. The crossing was in a remote area and there were a number of lions living close by.

In Jeanne's own account she was very happy to have successfully made the trip down from Arsim. "I praise the Lord, and give thanks that I made it safely down because our car had a low back tire, the radiator had a leak and the car eats oil like mad. We ran into heavy rains along the way and I was so very concerned about Bob and the lorry. Many cars have been washed away in the Seya river."

On Saturday morning, Jeanne and the two man maintenance crew from the lorry pumped up the car's low tire and then drove back a couple of miles to the nearest manyatta to buy some milk to prepare a breakfast of milk tea.

It was well after lunch by the time we arrived at the crossing with the pickup and the tractor. I was very happy to see Jeanne had made it through. She said lions had roared very close to her car during the night. She had slipped out of the car during the night for a very quick potty break, trusting that lions wouldn't attack her.

Her trip had been blessed because the low tire had held up to get her there. The spare tire in the car didn't have a tube, although the tube was in the car. Jeanne had no knowledge of this.

We attached the logging tractor to the winch cable of the Bedford, and I pulled with my winch from another angle. After several tries, there was something like a loud 'bang' and the lorry started to move backwards out of the river and up onto the steep bank. We all gave "sobs of joy," and heartfelt shouts of "Praise the Lord". It was 6:45 p.m.

Hanif had brought all the necessary things to 'renew' the lorry. The oil had to be drained and replaced. All the differentials had to be drained, etc. By the time the maintenance was finished it was well after dark. Jeanne drove behind me and we proceeded into Maralal. I was very concerned about the lorry's clutch because shifting gears was very difficult.

We made it into Maralal arriving at 2:15 a.m. Sunday morning. I stopped the lorry in front of Bhola's garage to awaken him so that he could open the gate. However, the Bedford had run its course. When I tried to shift it again, shifting was impossible. So we left it where it was and went to the Maralal Safari Lodge in the car that Jeanne was driving. We were both totally physically and emotionally exhausted. How wonderful that hot bath and bed felt that night. We both were again gratefully reminded of God's direct providential care over us.

It took some time for Bhola's garage to get the lorry in working order again. The clutch cover had to be removed and Mr. Bhola showed me the incredible amount of sand that had been impacted inside. How we ever managed to drive the lorry from the Seya with frequent shifting through 100 miles of hills and an escarpment to Maralal was simply the result of God's graciousness and mercy to us- in the darkness of those early morning hours.

Springs in the Desert

CHAPTER 40

"...for in the wilderness shall waters
break out, and streams in the desert."
Isa. 35:6

Arsim was just fourteen kilometers south of the beginning of the Kaisuit desert. It had a very marginal rainfall -- some years very good, some years almost nil. But Arsim was called the Arsim Waterhole, because on top of the Ndoto mountains which rose just above its location, there was a wonderful artesian pool. This pool provided water on both sides of the mountain, to Ngurunit as well as to Arsim. However the water flowing to Ngurunit stopped flowing in a dry year. The water flowing down the Arsim side of the mountain never stopped. Its supply would diminish, but it never stopped flowing.

We probably would not have been able to acquire such a select spot for establishing our Outreach Center had Chief John Bosco Lempei not invited us to build there. We always felt it was the hand of God that prepared in these matters for us.

I have already given an account of the famine of 1983/4 which so devastated the whole northern area of Kenya as well as Ethiopia. All through this terrible time, we were still able to get water from the stream that flowed down the mountain from its source at the pool. We had to travel up the gorge following up the water source, but water was still available to us without actually having to climb the mountain.

I have related how the director of the Christoffel BlindenMission had given us aid during that time of famine. I felt that in 1989 it was time to try and establish a water system that would be as uncontaminated as possible. The farther up the gorge into the mountain we could go would provide the maximum protection against humans and animals contaminating our supply.

I began by making a request to the Christoffel BlindenMission for a grant of money for this project. During the peak of the 1983/4 famine this Mission had given us some of the aid we needed by providing powdered milk and cooking oil. They also gave us funds to meet the burden of buying local food supplies (corn, beans and other vegetables) from the Kenya Government.

Then the Christoffel BlindenMission became very closely involved with the ELCK's Samburu work at Arsim in 1987 when through its East Africa Regional Director, Mr. Daniel Ward, it began sponsorship of the Arsim Lutheran Dispensary. From that time onward, it became greatly involved by providing various operating grants for the dispensary and its Mobile Child Health Clinics which served six widely separated locations. In 1989 CBM provided the Arsim Dispensary with a new four wheel drive vehicle for its administration work.

In 1990, together with giving its recurrent funding, CBM made a capital grant available to the Arsim Dispensary for a water project.

At the beginning of 1990, the amount of DM 35,000 (approximately $ 22,000) was granted for this project. This was later followed by a supplementary grant of DM 10,000 ($ 6,560) because of cost overruns to enable us to complete this project.

The justification for CBM to make this investment was found in the fact that this organization had seen in its worldwide work a very significant truth. The availability of water has a great affect on eye health. There is a very great correlation between eye disease and places having inadequate water supplies.

Therefore when we went to them with our request that they fund our water project, we received a very sympathic hearing.

The first step following their agreement in principle to fund us was to make a feasibility study. We turned to a local mission service agency of the African Inland Mission which was called AIM-TECH. In their survey Jim and John Propst, the AIM TECH experts determined that we would need approximately 1.2 miles of pipe to reach from a site catchment location to the Outreach Center.

It was determined that a one and a half inch pipe would be large enough to provide 38,000 gallons of water every twenty four hours of flow. By using a larger diameter pipe we could have realized a much larger flow, but this would have taken all the water from the stream. We didn't want to appear that we had robbed the people of all their water. Many herdsmen came from miles away during the dry season to water their herds at a point just opposite from our center. By using the smaller pipe the decrease in the water available for them was hardly noticable.

Another reason for going 'higher up' to get our supply was the presence of a blood-sucking parasite like a leach which attaches itself to the lips and gets into the mouths of the livestock drinking water at our lower location. These parasites can cause serious and even fatal consequences if the animals are left untreated. They were not a problem higher up in the valley's supply. The water that would come through our pipe would be safe and free for everyone to drink.

We did the initial routing of the pipe and found there was a fall or difference of elevation of about 1000 feet from the catchment location to the Outreach Center site. This meant that we would not have to use any mechanical means like a pump to speed the water on its way. After the initial flow was started, syphon action would keep the flow moving. We built a 150,000 Gallon storage tank just above the Center and the pipe coming down the mountain was free flowing into this tank.

The 150,000 gallon tank was built of rock, cement and reinforcing steel bars. It had a roof made of wood and aluminum sheeting to keep the dust, monkeys and birds out.

I was indebted to my builder, Robert Kagema. He had a plan for building the storage tank. Experts came out from Germany and insisted that Robert's tank would not stand up to the water pressure and would leak as well. I ask Robert for reassurance. "Would this tank really do the job?"

Robert replied with just one word: "Yes".

Robert had very successfully built us a nice Church and a Primary School, so I had no cause to doubt his word and promise.

The Propst brothers took charge of getting our galvanized pipe supply, and they got it for a bargain price from one of their contacts in Nairobi.

It was a great day when the lorries arrived carrying the pipe which came in twenty foot lengths. It was my plan to design a system of pipes that had a "T" valve at each juncture of forty sections of pipe. This would allow us to locate any trouble in the system at 800 foot intervals.
It was an aid in 'bleeding' the system of air as well.

Now began the logistic problem of getting the pipe up the hill to the locations where it could be installed. I had been warned before about how 'useless' the Samburu men would be in working hard. The two main jobs now before us were the transporting of pipe along narrow trails, and the digging of a continuous trench to accommodate the pipe so it could be buried and out of danger from humans and animals.

The first task began rather slowly. Carrying two twenty foot sections of pipe by two men is heavy, hard work. At first the men tried to carry it up the hill on their bare shoulders. That ended quickly resulting in bruised and bleeding shoulders. The men then got the idea of putting branches into the ends of the pipe. This made it much easier to carry. I warned them to always remove the wood from the pipes at the end of their journey.

The second task was that of joining or fitting the pipes together in water tight connections. It wasn't long before I had trained six men who became excellent pipe fitters. They learned how to file damaged threads on pipe ends and to thread pipe ends without cross-threading them. Our pipe fitters became so fast and efficient that we often had to wait for the carrying crews to bring up more pipe stock for them. Much later one of my fitters told me we had used 494 sections of pipe for the project. He had counted every one of them. This meant that the system fell 680 feet short of being two miles long.

I set up a competition between the carrying crews. Samburu love milk tea with a lot of sugar. I put a large bag of sugar on display with the promise that at the end of the week, the crew which had carried up the most pipe would take the bag home to divide as their reward. Our rate of pipe delivery accelerated amazingly and now the carriers were working ahead of the pipe fitters.

We all worked very hard during the hot season to finish this project. This took us several months to accomplish. Finally the day came when we started the water flowing down the system. The flow disappointed us.

We decided there must be air leaking into some of the pipe joints. Our check points every eight hundred feet were now to save us a lot of trouble. We started from the output point and began working back up the system. About two thirds of the way up, we found the trouble spot.

Water was not passing one section of pipes, and above that section when the check valves were opened, water shot out in a geyser. One of the carriers had left his carrying stick in the pipe.

We had to cut into that section of the system and dismantle pipes until we found the pipe where the stick was lodged. This was done without too much trouble. We then reassembled the pipes using a fitting called a union, and we had the flow at the end of the system we had hoped to see. It produced a flow of water amounting to 38,000 gallons a day.

I enjoyed standing close to the 150,000 gallon receiving tank and listening to the water rushing into it. The tank had an overflow pipe which carried water to a trough to water livestock. It was free flowing as well, the overflow from the trough returned to the stream.

After reaching the large receiving tank the water was also dispersed in a pipe system for use by the Dispensary, the Primary School and the Outreach Center houses. We also set up a grid of pipes to a garden area. This made it possible for people to irrigate small garden plots. The whole Arsim community were given plots thirty feet wide by fifty feet long, and nearly 100 families intensively grew vegetables and fruit for their own use. The people accomplished this using a hose irrigation technique from the pipe grid. Although this was a new experience for the Samburu who are pastoralists in culture and practice, their participation in the scheme was very successful.

In this very marginal and famine-prone area on the southern border of the deserts of northern Kenya, any food supplement was very important and added significantly to the health of the children as well as bringing increased vitality for the adults.

We had a dedication for the project when officials from CBM as well as Kenya District officials were present. It was a time for congratulations to be freely given to the sponsoring agency as well as to the local people who had accomplished this project by their hard work, completing it in August 1991.

From this moderately small investment provided by the friends of CBM, the ELCK had been enabled to offer to a small community in northern Kenya a way to modify and upgrade their expectations for a more satisfactory and better way of life.

I wished that those donors who made this project possible might have seen the joy experienced by so many residents in the Arsim valley. They came to our door with baskets full of maize and other vegetables which they had grown. They proudly said with deep emotion: "Thank you, thank you so much for making the water project available and showing us how to use it to grow food for ourselves."

I remember one family in particular who came with a basket full of maize -- their first harvest. They insisted that Jeanne and I take it even though they had not eaten any of it. We finally agreed to take half of the corn in the basket under protest. We returned the rest of the maize to these grateful people. Their gratitude touched my heart.

"Come over & Help Us"

CHAPTER 41

"During the night a vision came to
Paul: a Macedonian stood there appeal-
ing to him and saying, 'Come across
to Macedonia and help us."
Acts 16:9   N.E.B.

Few words gladden a missionary's heart more than the request, "Come over and help us." These words were first uttered by the man in Macedonia in a vision to the Apostle Paul. (Acts 16:9)

We knew that in the Northern Frontier District where we were, hosts of people had not heard the Gospel. For people to recognize their need to hear about Christ showed that the Holy Spirit was already working to prepare people's hearts and to 'open doors'.

*   *   *   *   *   *

Assistant Chief Robat Ngirtia, from Lon-Niruk in Turkanaland, stopped me in early 1989. I was passing through the border town of Baragoi which is on the dividing line separating the Turkana from the Samburu areas.

The Assistant Chief told me he represented all the people in his area in requesting that the Lutheran Church begin work in Turkana.

I was overjoyed at receiving this news. I promised him that we would make a survey of his area as soon as we could make the arrangements.

A short time later, Assistant Chief Korie Epodo, who was

from a location adjacent to Chief Robat's, also contacted me. He had the same request which was, "Come over and help us." His area was called Kawap. Chief Korie told me that people in his area had heard of what the Lutherans had done during the famine in Samburu, and what they were now doing in providing mobile medical service particularly for children. It was his hope that we would institute something like this in his area. He said there was no other church or evangelistic work being done at Kawap.

We replied to Chief Korie that we would present all these requests for beginning new outreach to our Lutheran Church of Kenya's Samburu committee. They would have to approve them. In the meantime, we would survey these areas, as time permitted. Surveys would make it possible for us to bring more complete information to our church's committee.

Jeanne and I were busy preparing for a short furlough so time was a problem.

On the appointed day we proceeded to Baragoi and were met by our old friend Jackson Tokodie. His parentage was half Samburu, half Turkana. Chief Robat and an elder from the Lon-Niruk area, Mzee Lomilia Ebongon, were also waiting expectantly for us.

As we began our travel west from Baragoi Chief Robat told me the district commissioner from Maralal had recently traveled over this same road. Our destination was twenty-nine miles north and west of Baragoi. The Chief said that for half the distance of our travel the road had been in use for some time.

The last half was brand new.

We left Baragoi and were pleased to see a very passable road. It was a single lane track. All the holes were filled in and the approaches and exits to river beds (dry at this time of the year) were in good condition.

We were able to travel at speeds of 15 or 20 miles per hour.

We rounded a corner and started to climb a steep hill that required low gear. I thought we would have to shift down even farther into tractor gear because of the steepness of the road but we made it to the top. Chief Robat told us with obvious pride in his voice that this road had just been cut through by the people of his location. The people had been pleading for a road to be built since before independence. The answer kept coming back from the district commissioner's office that building a road here was impossible. Finally the people decided to take matters into their own hands and "cut" the road themselves. It had taken a group of twenty men months to finish the work. Several locations along the way bore mute witness that just ahead was an impassable section. Abrupt turns and a bypass for an alternate route was made. Large boulders sealed off the original first right of way attempt by the builders.

At times the road's course dropped abruptly into a ravine/stream bed and followed it along for a distance. Then the road mounted up a canyon wall to the summit and over the top. At one of these 'peaks' I was overly cautious because as we topped the rise I simply couldn't see anything but 'air' beyond. I killed the engine. Chief Robat shouted to me, "Don't stop, this is a good road."

I started the engine and crept over the top of the rise into a very steep descent. I marveled at the work that had gone into constructing a road in this mountainous, rocky terrain.

I was embarrassed that the road was getting me on edge with its blind rises and steep descents. Chief Robat smilingly related how the district commissioner's driver had been scared to death when he drove it. The commissioner himself had gotten out of his Land Rover and walked some sections preferring not to ride in his car.

We were about two-thirds of the way to our destination when, as we came around a corner, a group of people stopped us. They said that a short way up the valley a man was critically ill. He and some others had cooked and eaten the meat of a camel that had died of an undetermined sickness. The man and his wife had barely been able to reach their home. She had eaten some of the contaminated meat -- her husband had gorged himself on it.

We left the car and walked up to the recently built manyatta. Jeanne treated the man and I offered a prayer for his healing. Having done all we could for the sick fellow we left telling his family that we would return that way the next day. If the man's condition had not improved by that time we would take him to the health center at Baragoi.

We continued on our way and soon came out at the top of the escarpment -- a thousand feet above the valley. This valley ends becoming the shore of Lake Rudolph (Lake Turkana). The valley is called "Bonde la Ufa" --"Death Valley". At this point the road was very steep and seemed to disappear into a mass of volcanic rock. We very carefully made our way down. It was now late afternoon and very hot. I worried about whether our tires would be able to survive the heat and sharp volcanic rocks. Slowly we gingerly crept down. We reached the bottom. We now had two alternative routes to clear the masses of boulders and get out on the flat valley floor. Although the sun was setting the heat in the air seemed to increase.

We made the right choice. The road now led us along the valley floor skirting the lower reaches of the escarpment. Just as it was turning dark Chief Robat guided us back up towards the foot of the escarpment. There was no road. We followed a dry stream bed driving on hard packed sand.

In a short time we reached a village. Building material was in very short supply there even by African standards. The people used the branches of the mock palm trees for building their huts. The nuts of the palms provide food to eat. Later the dried nuts are used for fuel. Bonde La Ufa is a good place for herding camels, cows, sheep and goats. It could be that the intense lasting heat of the valley brought it the name -- Death Valley. The name might come from the many cattle raids the people here endure from raiders called "Orenocos." People often are killed during these frequent raids. The Orenoco mercilessly stalk and kill the local residents and then steal their livestock.

As we arrived in this village the people came out with shouts of joy to welcome us. I looked around for a suitable place to locate our camp tents among the rocks. I knew with this terrain and heat, scorpions and snakes would make their appearance as soon as it got dark. While I got the tents pegged down to withstand a strong breeze that was blowing Jeanne made a supper of ughali (corn mush), meat sauce and tea. She cooked in the back of our vehicle to avoid the strong wind. I gave thanks for the small bottled gas burners we routinely carried with us -- no firewood was available in Bonde La Ufa.

It was still very hot after we had our supper. I had taken off my glasses because I was sweating a lot. I was sitting on the ground. I didn't see what was scurrying toward me. Suddenly Jackson jumped up and over me and crushed a large scorpion with his foot.

To say we had a rest-filled night wouldn't be telling the truth. Even though we were exhausted after our trip, sleep didn't come easy. We had our tents zippered up so we didn't have to worry about scorpions or snakes gaining access. But the heat continued without relief and increased. The wind gained in intensity and threatened to overturn our tent with its forcefulness. It felt as if someone had left the door of a blast furnace open. Several times during the night I rose and whenever I moved the sweat on my chest and thighs ran off. It was as if some had doused me with a bucket of water.

Morning arrived and our work began. First Jeanne prepared breakfast for us. She made a porridge of whole grain wheat covered with gift milk the people had brought. She also made tea from the same gift milk supply. We then had morning devotions for our group and for anyone else we could find to invite.

After some time when the village group had assembled I made a presentation. I used the chart -- The Heart Of Man. It describes the condition of all human hearts before they accept the salvation Jesus offers. I then presented the offer of Christ's salvation to all who were listening and would accept it. There was no immediate response, but the seed had now been planted.

Jeanne then held a mobile clinic for everyone. She gave many treatments out to people using the dispensary supplies she had brought along.

Our visit concluded with speeches of gratitude and farewell delivered with great sincerity by the Chief and elders of the camp. There was a gentle demand for us to promise to return again.

The Turkana people are very different from the Samburu in customs and in language. They are nomadic herders of livestock like the Samburu. However they live in a much more desert like country than that inhabited by the Samburu. In Turkana life is hard and grim.

The Samburu ridicule the Turkana for eating their donkeys

-- a horrible and taboo custom as far as the Samburu are concerned. Most Turkana still dress exclusively in skins. The Samburu use skins but also dress using a lot of manufactured clothing.

As we prepared to ascend the escarpment for our return journey we heard of a Somali trader in trouble close to where we were camped. He had driven a Land Rover down into the valley bringing a load of food (ground corn, tea, oil, etc,) for a Turkana man who had a small store in his hut. The Somali had been stuck in the valley with a faulty car battery for over a week. Would we please come and help him get his car started. We broke camp and after bidding farewell to our new friends in the village, we made the short trip to find the Somali. He told us that he had tried several things to get his Land Rover started. He only had one jumper cable so we put our cars bumper to bumper hoping to make a good ground connection between them. It didn't work. Finally I removed his battery and substituted the one from our car. His engine started with no problem. We put his battery back into his car while he kept his engine running. He made a beeline for the escarpment. By agreement I followed him in case his car stalled. He almost failed to clear the steepest point of the climb but then he got over it.

On our way back we kept our eyes out for the sick man we had promised to help. He didn't appear. We learned, by stopping at the entrance to his valley, that he had recovered.

We developed engine trouble as we traveled to Baragoi. One of our diesel injectors malfunctioned so we lost power. Even so we were able to complete our trip.

When the Samburu committee met at Arsim, the report of the survey into Turkana was presented. It was favorably received by the committee.

The committee's concern was whether we had adequate staff to open work in Turkana with the personnel we had available.

Once again I was reminded of our Lord's words: "The harvest is plentiful, but the laborers are few. Pray ye therefore the Lord of the harvest, that He may send forth laborers into His harvest." Matt.9:37-38.

I was very happy when we received word from the Lutheran School of Theology in Chicago that we would receive an intern to serve with us in Samburu from January 1991 to March of 1992. Mr. Dean Apel was a welcome addition to our staff and after finishing Seminary, returned to serve the Lutheran Church of Kenya sent out by the World Mission Prayer League as a career missionary.

Goforth

CHAPTER 42

"Go ye therefore, and teach all nations,
baptizing them in the name of the Father,
and of the Son, and of the Holy Ghost:
teaching them to observe all things what-
soever I have commanded you: and, lo, I
am with you alway, even unto the end of
the world. Amen."
  Matt. 28:19-20   K.J.V.

I believe one of the very important tasks a missionary has is to involve all those who are in the church at home in the work overseas. This can be done during deputation (visiting churches on furlough). In this opportunity the missionaries describe what it is like to live and work in another country and culture. They also encourage some people to go abroad for short periods of service. When these 'short termers' return from their experience overseas, they are like lamps shining in their home communities and churches for the cause of Christ and for world evangelization.

Over the years of our service overseas, we have had a small number of people come out to visit us and our work. Groups like "Crossfire", young people who were sent out by Lutheran Youth Encounter. They brought a cross cultural witness in song.

Pacific Lutheran University sent out a group of 17 students under the direction of Mr. & Mrs. Dean Buchanan (former missionaries) who were helped in this venture by Mr. & Mrs. Dave Christian and Dr. Steward Govig. It was called an African Study Safari on these students' interim period in 1973. The students became involved in education, medicine and evangelism as they worked and witnessed in various mission activities on the Iramba/Turu field in central Tanzania. We were working among the Bushmen at that time and took a part of that group to the Bushman area for an evangelism outreach.

Another group came from First Lutheran Church in White Bear Lake Minnesota. The sponsoring group was called the Great Commission Network. The group of people who came out to the field were called the GOFORTH TEAM. The title GOFORTH is an acrostic which stands for:

G - Going

O - Out

F - For

O - Our

R - Redeemer

T   - To

H - Hemispheres

Under the direction of Mrs. Toni Freer we were blessed to have three teams come. The first group of ten arrived in March 1990. It was made up of an age range that was a balance between youth and elders. Miss Kim Eastland and Kevin Callaghan represented younger volunteers. John and Dodie Burgeson, Harold and Ruth Whitlock, Barbara and Dick Guenthner and Reynold Erickson were in the elder category The group leader, Mrs. Toni Freer was about in the middle of the two groups age wise.

Toni had done an excellent job of preparing these people

for this unique experience in their lives. She prepared a very thorough manual which the TEAM members studied and used as their guide. They came out ready to 'go to work', not to experience a special kind of vacation. They involved themselves in every phase of our Center's outreach: evangelistic, educational and medical. Language did not pose the problem it would have had we been in Tanzania. In Kenya English was taught in the public schools and interpreters were numerous. It was possible to assign a personal interpreter to each TEAM member while they were at Arsim. The TEAM functioned so well that the trip was repeated again in 1992 and in 1995. Two of the families from the original team, Barbara and Dick Guenthner and Ruth and Harold Whitlock repeated, making the trip with the second team which also included Rev. Ruben Pedersen and his wife Helen, and on the younger side: Mss. Carol Sandbakken, Kelly Asleson and Andrea Knobel.

Three of the members from the TEAM of 1992 have become long term missionaries. Carol and Kelly are now serving in Africa, Andrea in Europe.

Barbara Guenthner's husband Dick died from an aneurysm, prior to the third Team's trip out in 1995. Even so she came out for a third time with her daughter Mary, a school teacher, and Diane Johnson, a young nurse. Other members of the '95 TEAM were Mrs. Erma Conboy, who had promoted Missions for years in Spokane, Washington, and Bill and Donna Irgen. Pastor Duwayne Dalen completed the roster of trip three.

High on the priority of each group were the visits they

made in house to house (manyatta to manyatta) evangelism.
The local people were very impressed and happy to have TEAM
visitors make frequent calls on their homes. The TEAM'S focus
was to give of themselves in any way that would be helpful
and in keeping with their individual talents.

A great deal can be packed into three intense weeks of
service. Summarizing all the activities I would write this:

Possibly each team member given a chance would have a
different response to share in describing the highlights of
their stay in Africa.

Would it be the Vacation Bible School with over sixty
children from the community sharing in all its activities?

Or would it be the early morning prayer and intercession
meetings that were attended in the church by TEAM members as
well as Christians from the congregation which brought "special"
blessings and answers to our prayers?

Or would it be the two and a half day Spiritual Life
Conference held at a campsite located about a quarter of a
mile from the Outreach Center?

At these meetings the TEAM presented skits, sang together,
gave puppet shows, danced and preached.

A week prior to the beginning of the conference as many
as were able of the camp staff and speakers met at the Arsim
church. They gathered at six o'clock each morning for an hour
of urgent intercessory prayer. They prayed that the Holy Spirit
would touch and teach the hearts of all those who would attend.

The whole community in the Arsim area -- over four hundred

people -- did attend the program. People from neighboring missions also attended. The days, which began at 8 A.M., carried on until after the evening meal. All meals were eaten in common together. There were tea breaks between some of the hours. Choir music, lots of congregational singing, and the TEAM's guitars, skits and dances added to the preaching and lecture program.

On the final day of the conference twenty-three children and one adult were baptized into fellowship with Christ. Eighty-two Christians from the Arsim congregation were communed on their knees as they received the sacrament together with the TEAM. Two couples had their marriages blessed.

Truly, this was a high point in the TEAM'S experience.

On the last night before the TEAM left the field, a very intense debriefing session was held. It was also called re-entry. The purpose of this time was to focus in on what the group had experienced during their time abroad. It was also a bridge to keep this emphasis alive as they returned to their homes in another part of the world. Finally the re-entry time prepared the TEAM members to expect the possibility of a lack of interest to be shown by some people at home. This can be a cause of wonder and disappointment for those who have experienced so much overseas as TEAM members. Many were filled to overflowing from their great trip. Toni Freer was a gifted organizer and leader who kept the day to day operation of these TEAMS functioning well.

I was grateful and relieved that God kept the TEAM members

in such good health because Arsim was not the place to experience a medical emergency. TEAMS like GOFORTH are very useful in the life of our churches who often do not have regular visits from long term missionaries.

These ventures require a lot of planning and the stocking of food to accommodate TEAM members. My wife, Jeanne, did a marvelous job of anticipating food needs for the TEAMS' visits. TEAM members helped in food preparation, but because of Jeanne's careful planning there were always stores on hand to meet all our food needs.

TEAM members experienced the realization and joy of knowing with all the servants of our Lord of Mission that they had the privilege of being part of our Lord's plan to reach the nations with His message of love and salvation. Everything they did had only one end and purpose in His service, to honor and glorify Him. This is the wonderful opportunity He gives to each of us as we live our lives for Him.

Vignettes

CHAPTER 43

"I will open my mouth in parables,
I will utter hidden things, things from of old --
what we have heard and known, what our fathers have told us.
We will not hide them from their children;
we will tell the next generation the praiseworthy deeds of the
Lord, his power, and the wonders he has done."   Ps. 78:2-4
N.I.V.

WHAT ARE YOU WILLING TO DO WITHOUT?

> "And this the condemnation, that Light is come
> into the world, and men loved darkness rather
> than light, because their deeds were evil. For
> everyone that doeth evil hateth the light,
> neither cometh to the light, lest his deeds
> should be reproved." Jn. 3:19-20

I don't know his name, but I hope to meet him someday
- - that young man who tried to break into our house and rob
it. He was a young Samburu lad and he had his friend with
him. They got into our back porch by cutting into the screen
at night while we were away on safari. Then, surprised by
someone outside walking by in the darkness, they dropped every-
thing and fled the scene - - _everything_ including a Samburu
lad's most precious possession, his long knife called a "Lalem"
in their language. This knife is used for everything from
cutting meat to hacking down thorn branches that get in your
way. No young man in Samburu country is 'dressed' without
wearing his own knife, it's his identity.

I found the "Lalem" and its scabbard holder where they
had been hastily dropped. Picking them up, I returned the
long knife to its scabbard, and hung it on the wall in my
office, expecting the young errant to come and plead for his
property. **He never came!** After the attempted theft I was
told that the lads had run far away over the mountains.

Eventually Lapasori Kamara, the lad's father, did come.
He apologized for his son's behavior and offered to make

restitution for any damage or loss. Most of all, he wanted to recover his son's **Lalem**.

"No," I replied, "your son must come and ask for it himself."

The knife continued to hang on my office wall for nearly three years. Finally I gave it to the youth's father, knowing that the youth would **never** come to redeem it. His father himself had now moved far away from Arsim.

Too often we are just like that youth, aren't we? We sin! We know it! Our Lord certainly knows it! Our neighbors know it!

I John 1:9 makes it very clear what our next step should be: confession and restitution. Then there is the clear promise from God of cleansing and the chance to begin anew. But often, we won't submit to this - - God's plan. We don't want to come to the light. We would rather hide in the darkness or the shadows.

If that is our choice, we have allowed two very important things to be 'put on the wall', out of our reach. Without these things, no one can live as a healthy child of God. They are forgiveness and the cleansing from our sins. Unless we repent and come to the light, we will have to do without cleansing and forgiveness, no matter how much we want them or how much their absence hurts.

(LORD, may I be willing to have anything broken in my life except my fellowship with you. Amen)

*   *   *   *   *   *

PRAY AND SPEAK IN WITNESS

> "A bruised reed shall he not break,
> and the smoking flax shall he not
> quench. . . . . Isaiah 42:3a

Seseyon (pronounced say-say-on) was a little eleven year old Samburu girl living in the northern part of Kenya. In 1983/84, the rains failed to come to the lowlands of Kenya. Even on the mountain peaks in Samburu where it is normally wet and damp, it became very dry. It was as if the whole countryside were caught up in some terrible disease. The grass dried up, died and then disappeared. Without the grass the cows and goats that the Samburu herded each day found no food to eat. The animals began to die, and for a long period before had given no milk. Where before there had been food in abundance for the people to eat now there was none.

At Arsim, our remote outreach mission center in northern Kenya, Jeanne and I struggled to help the local people against over-whelming odds.

We tried to bring in food to our area from long distances away over a practically non-existant road. Soon, when people heard we had a small supply of food, they flooded into our location from long distances away. Before long, we had over 3000 mouths to feed; men, women and children. But the famine didn't come alone - - it rarely does! With the famine came an epidemic of measles, striking down famine weakened bodies.

Seseyon was one of those cases. She was with her parents

in the hastily constructed famine village. It was located just steps away across the road from our dispensary. Jeanne was working day and night to combat the disease and the dehydration which it causes in its victims.

Suddenly, a cry went up from the hut: "Seseyon is dead."

Seseyon's limp body was carried out of the hut to avoid the taboo caused when someone dies in a home. She was carried across the road and brought to the dispensary. She experienced two more convulsions before she arrived there.

Jeanne did all she could but was powerless to do anything more medically. Then she prayed a prayer in Swahili, asking her assistant to translate her prayer into the Samburu language. It was a simple request to our Lord, pleading with the Saviour:

"Lord Jesus, I've done all I can - - please, please don't let this little girl die. Amen"

Seseyon did survive the night. Once she awoke from the comatose state she was in and said in Samburu:

"Mama, Mama, pray to Jesus to make me well again."

As far as anyone knows she had never heard the name of Jesus until Jeanne prayed for her while she was in that coma.

Seseyon's survival was a miracle to us. During the days that followed she gained strength and soon was out of danger.

One day, some time later, Seseyon came to the dispensary and standing a short way off, stood for a long time watching Jeanne do her work.

Then, the famine passed, Seseyon returned with her family to her home area miles away from Arsim. We will never forget that little girl who, though "dead", heard the witness of the Name above all names, and became alive again. Many times our Lord waits for us to come to the end of our resources in order that He plainly shows us His power that He may be glorified.

It will always be so - - Our extremity is God's opportunity, because He will never desert nor forsake us.

*   *   *   *   *   *

Good-bye 'God be with ye'

CHAPTER 44

"He who goes out weeping
carrying seed to sow, will
return with songs of joy,
carrying sheaves with him."
Psalm 126:6 N.I.V.

Every avid gardener knows the experience -- seeing the coming of the end of the growing season. The harvest is there before their eyes and there is joy. We were now seeing the results of the work which the the Holy Spirit had empowered us to accomplish. We had been witnessing for the Lord in Samburu for ten years. Now the time had come for us to turn over that work to a younger missionary, Terry Pattison. How glad we were that we had a replacement to carry on discipling the Christians at Arsim and at Ngilai and to carry on in outreach.

I had reached the age of sixty-five, Jeanne was six months older than I. Sixty-five is that golden time when missionaries are told to retire and take the next step in their lives. For us, that meant returning to the Pacific Northwest in the U. S. It also meant leaving our home of Africa where we had now both spent more years living than we had in the land of our birth. We did this with very mixed emotions. I had been preparing the congregation at Arsim for our departure although they weren't aware of it. For a number of Sundays I had been teaching them to sing the words of a hymn in Swahili, "God be with you till we meet again." Each Sunday I did this the lump in my throat got a little bigger.

We had been packing down a few things to take home with us, pictures and some other articles that we thought we couldn't replace. Everything else was left for our replacements to enjoy. The Africa Inland Mission had an air freight service that was more reasonable to use than surface/sea transport. We took advantage of this and sent two foot lockers and a large basket on ahead to our friends, the Danielsons in Hillsboro Oregon.

But saying good-bye to all those people who had come to mean so much to us was a very hard thing for Jeanne and me to do. April 1st, 1992 was our last Sunday at Arsim. We had a good day of fellowship at the church. I was very touched in my heart, when five or six ladies of the congregation began weeping as we concluded the service. They had shown their love toward us in a project by making up a beautiful cane of beads. Now the outpouring of tears was from their hearts, and it continued on and on. How could we express the oneness we felt with them? We had come through famine, disease, hunger and threats of shifta attack together. We had experienced the goodness of the Lord as He called out His church.

We had visited them, worked and ministered to them in so many ways and agonized with some of them when they were caught in Satan's web. They were truly our brothers and sister and sons and daughters in Christ. Now it was time to say good-bye. But just for a time. At the date of this writing, 1998, we have returned four times during the years following our departure to visit our Arsim family. My listing of Arsim Christians has been updated as well, so that I can pray for five people in that church each day.

Monday morning early, following our Sunday farewell, we had the car packed and after a quick breakfast got into it and drove off. There was no sorrowing crowd to see us off. Almost as if by unspoken consent we knew each other's sadness at parting, and were confident that: **God would be with us all until we could meet again.**

During those years of service, two portions of scripture were written and underscored in our hearts. They were like our banners. The first was from Mark 13:10, "for before the end comes the gospel must be proclaimed to all nations." Phillips

The second portion no less important to us was from Psalm 32:7, "Thou art my hiding place; thou wilt preserve me from trouble; Thou wilt compass me about with songs of deliverance." And in Psalm 56:3, "What time I am afraid, I will put my trust in thee." KJV

Epilogue

I have tried to recount the experiences of our family in the service of the Lord Jesus Christ as we served overseas in Tanzania and Kenya for thirty eight years. Of course many of our experiences, even those which I would have liked to include, had to be omitted. Those which were included are probably the highlights of our lives as I think back over our time of service.

I have put the accent on how the Lord worked with and through our family. But you will draw the wrong conclusion if you believe I am not also acknowledging, **with deep gratitude,** all that fellow workers and colleagues (nationals as well as expatriates) have added to our witness as we have worked together with them.

Jesus Christ is Lord. He is the Lord of Missions. His Lordship is built on His love. Paul's letter to the Corinthians is probably the best human expression or picture of Christ's love. It also can be the measure of how well each of us succeeds in our work as **MESSENGERS OF LOVE.**

"If I speak with the tongues of men and of angels, but have not love, I am become sounding brass, or a clanging cymbal. And if I have the gift of prophecy, and know all mysteries and all knowledge; and if I have all faith, so as to remove mountains, but have not love, I am nothing. And if I bestow all my goods to feed the poor, and if I give my body to be burned, but have not love it profiteth me nothing. Love suffereth long, and is kind; love envieth not; love vaunteth not itself, is not puffed up, doth not behave itself unseemly, seeketh not its own, is not provoked, taketh not account of evil; rejoiceth not in unrighteousness, but rejoiceth with the truth; beareth all things, believeth all things, hopeth all things, endureth all things. Love never faileth; but whether there be prophecies, they shall be done away; whether there be tongues, they shall cease; whether there be knowledge, it shall be done away. For we know in part, and we prophesy in part; but when that which is perfect is come, that which is in part shall be done away. When I was a child, I spake as a child, I thought as a child, I felt as a child; now that I am become a man, I have put away childish things. For now we see in a mirror, darkly; but then face to face: now I know in part but then shall I know fully even as also I was fully known. But now abideth faith, hope, love, these three; and the greatest of these is love." I Cor. 13

Who can measure up to the standard of being Messengers of Love after reading Paul's inspired words? We acknowledge with heartfelt gratitude that the Lord allowed us to serve Him as His messengers over these years, in spite of our sins and our shortcomings and weaknesses.

But we rejoice in the fruit which He has used us to produce. That is the promise of grace which we want to pass on through this book to the next generation of Messengers who are to follow Him. **HE WILL DO IT!**

Rev. Robert E. Ward
October 14, 1998